D0548427

WITH A SMILE AND A WAVE

WITH A SMILE AND A WAVE

The life of Captain John Aidan Liddell VC MC
3rd Battalion Argyll and Sutherland Highlanders and
Royal Flying Corps

Peter Daybell

BOURNEMOUTH
2005
LIBRARIES

Pen & Sword
AVIATION

For Aidan Liddell, his family and friends, and for the soldiers and airmen that served with him in the Great War of 1914 to 1918

First published in Great Britain in 2005 by
PEN & SWORD AVIATION
an imprint of
Pen & Sword Books Limited
47 Church Street
Barnsley
South Yorkshire
S70 2AS

Copyright © Peter Daybell, 2005

ISBN: 1 84415 160 3

The right of Peter Daybell to be identified as
Author of this Work has been asserted by him in accordance
with the Copyright, Designs and Patents Act 1988.

A CIP catalogue record for this book
is available from the British Library

Typeset in 10pt Plantin by Pen & Sword Books Limited

Printed and bound in England by
CPI UK

For a complete list of Pen & Sword titles please contact:
PEN & SWORD BOOKS LIMITED
47 Church Street, Barnsley, South Yorkshire, S70 2AS, England
email: enquiries@pen-and-sword.co.uk
website: www.pen-and-sword.co.uk

CONTENTS

Acknowledgements

My interest in the First World War began in 1965 at Stonyhurst College when I read Robert Graves's *Goodbye to All That* and Siegfried Sassoon's *Memoirs of an Infantry Officer*. A seed was sown then which was reawakened in 1995 by Professor Brian Bond, when I studied the Great War with him at King's College London. Shortly afterwards I came across Aidan Liddell's papers in the Public Record Office, and was greatly moved by what I read. An interest grew into an idea for a book and my research began in earnest in 1998. Since then I have been assisted along the way by scores of organisations and individuals without whose generous cooperation and wholehearted support *With a Smile and a Wave* could not have been written.

First I must acknowledge the enthusiastic support and generous hospitality of two members of the Liddell family. Aidan's niece Gillian Clayton, and his great nephew Mark Liddell have together made available to me a wealth of unique family material, without which this book could certainly not have been written. They have followed my slow progress with undiminished enthusiasm, and a great deal of patience. I am particularly grateful to Gillian for her permission to quote from 'Uncle Aidan's' letters and diaries and to Mark for the extended loan of the wonderful family albums. I must also express my gratitude to my friend John Mulholland for his advice and encouragement throughout this project. John is the expert on the seven Stonyhurst VC's and the extended loan of his Liddle file, his dozen bound volumes of the *Stonyhurst Magazine*, and a large selection of other books has also been immensely helpful

I am grateful for the enthusiastic support of Fr Joe Marren, then the Parish Priest of Our Lady and St Cuthbert, Prudoe and for his help in putting me in touch with a number of local historians and researchers in Northumberland, including Mrs Anne Fettes and Alastair Fraser. At Stonyhurst College I wish to acknowledge the assistance of David Knight, the Archivist and Editor of the *Stonyhurst Magazine,* the late Fr Freddy Turner who was the previous Archivist, Tom Muir, and Major John Cobb. Balliol College has been equally supportive, and I am grateful for the support and assistance of Dr John Jones, the Vice-Master and Archivist, and of Alan Tadiello, the Assistant Librarian. Following on with the Oxford connection, I would like to thank Mr TC Hartley for permission to consult and quote from the papers of his grandfather Sir Harold Hartley, now lodged at Churchill College Cambridge. My thanks too to Alan Kucia, the Head Archivist at the Churchill Archives Centre.

I must also acknowledge the assistance of the Oxford Union and the Newman Society.

I have also contacted and visited a large number of libraries, museums and research organisations in various parts of the country, including the North East and Hampshire. Without exception, my queries have been dealt with speed, accuracy and courtesy. Help was given by the Hexham Library, the Newcastle City Library, the Tyne and Wear Archive Service, the Northumberland Record Service, the Northumberland and Durham Family History Society, the Willis Museum Basingstoke, the Winchester Museum Service and the Hampshire Record Office Winchester. The British Library, the Cambridge University Library, the Public Record Office/National Archive, the Imperial War Museum, the National Army Museum and the RAF Museum have also been of great assistance. A particular thank you must also go to RHQ of the Argyll and Sutherland Highlanders, and in Stirling Castle, and I am most grateful for the support and assistance of Mr Rod Mackenzie in the Regimental Museum.

Thanks must go too to Wing Commander Steve Falla, then commanding No. 7 Sqn Royal Air Force, to Flight Sergeant Bob Funnell the No. 7 Sqn Historian, to Seb Cox at the Air Historical Branch and to several fellow members of Cross and Cockade International, the First World War Aviation Historical Society. These include our President Air Commodore Peter Dye, Paul Leaman, Peter Cooksley, Kevin Kelly, Norman Franks, Mike Pierce and Chaz Bowyer. I must also thank Honest John of the *Daily Telegraph* who identified Aidan's Humber motor car, John Tarring of the Humber Register, and Annice Collette, the librarian of the Vintage Motor Cycle Club. My thanks too, to Pen and Sword for agreeing to publish *With a Smile and a Wave,* and to Ray Bollom who helped me with the preparation of many of the photographs.

The following publishers are thanked for allowing me to quote from published works: Macmillan, Albatros, Greenhill Books, Air Research, Sutton, Orion and Constable. Similarly I acknowlege the permission of AP Watt Ltd on behalf of Lord Tweedsmuir and Jean, Lady Tweedsmuir to quote from John Buchan's *Memory Hold the Door.* I am also gratefull to the Regimental Secretary of the Royal Welch Fusiliers for permission to quote from *The War the Infantry Knew.* Every efford has been made to trace copywrite holders and accurately attribute all source material, but I would be grateful for information that would enable me to correct any errors or omissions.

Finally I must thank by wife Mary and my daugthers Johanna and Nicolas for their extraordinary patience over the last six or so years. It was not their choice to share their husband and father with a long dead hero, but they have all assisted me greatly along the long road to publication.

Introduction

Requiescat in Pace

It was Friday 1 October 1915, and the Great War that so many had believed would be over by the end of 1914 was now approaching a second Christmas. In rural Lancashire, far away from the sound of guns, the day dawned bright and clear and the autumn sun lit up the grey stone walls and tall towers of Stonyhurst College and the adjacent Roman Catholic church of St Peter. Set in the Ribble valley between brooding Pendle Hill and Longridge Fell, the old school could be a wet, cold and unwelcoming place. But on this particular day, the weather was kind, and the sometimes austere buildings were softened by sunlight.

Despite the early hour, there was great activity in the church and school, for the Stonyhurst community was preparing to remember and celebrate a fallen son. Few now recognise the name of John Aidan Liddell, but for a brief period in the late summer of 1915, his name was on the lips of a nation hungry for news of the war. His face and story, and a series of remarkable photographs, filled many newspaper columns. Already decorated for bravery as an infantry officer, Aidan Liddell had transferred to the Royal Flying Corps (RFC), and it was as a pilot that his skill and fortitude was to attract national attention. Badly wounded in the thigh while flying deep over enemy-occupied Belgium, Aidan had lost consciousness as his two-seater RE5 aircraft was raked by enemy machine-gun fire. The aircraft turned over and plunged out of control towards the ground, and his subsequent actions were later described as 'one of the finest feats that has been done in the Corps since the beginning of the war'.[1] Despite terrible injuries, and the extensive damage to his machine, he recovered control of the aircraft and flew on for a further half an hour to the safety of the Allied Belgian airfield at La Panne, where a photographer captured the dramatic scenes for posterity.

For his courage and flying skill in saving the life of his observer, 2nd Lieutenant Roland Peck, and for bringing back a valuable aircraft to the safety of a friendly airfield, Captain John Aidan Liddell MC of the 3rd (Reserve) Battalion of the Argyll and Sutherland Highlanders and the Royal Flying Corps was awarded the Victoria Cross. Presented 'For Valour', the VC was the highest military award of the British Empire, and Aidan's Cross was only the fourth air VC. It was also the second of three crosses awarded to Stonyhurst men in the Great War. No doubt part of

9

the attraction for the British public was that Aidan had seemingly cheated almost certain death and had lived on to be proclaimed a hero lying on a stretcher, cigarette in hand, he had smiled and waved for the camera. However, the celebrations were short-lived, for despite rallying bravely, he died of his wounds a month after the action, and a week after the VC was gazetted. Now, a month on, the boys of his old school gathered to remember him, to pray for the repose of his immortal soul, and no doubt to recall the fifty other old boys who had already given their lives in their country's service over the preceding fourteen months.

The Liddell family had travelled north the previous day from the family home in Hampshire to attend the memorial service. Those present were Aidan's father John and mother Emily, his two elder sisters Dorothy and Monica, and his brother Cuthbert (known as Bertie), a Captain in the 15th Hussars. His youngest brother Lancelot, a Sub-Lieutenant on HMS *Monarch*, was at sea as he had been three weeks or so earlier for Aidan's funeral. Veronica, the youngest of the siblings and a particular favourite of Aidan's, was it seems too upset to attend.

The evening before the service the family dined in the parlour with the Rector, the Reverend Fr William Bodkin SJ*, who was both headmaster and leader of the Jesuit community. Aidan had liked and respected William Bodkin who had at one time been his form teacher, and it was Bodkin who had celebrated the Funeral Mass at the Jesuit church at Farm Street in London, as well as attending the funeral itself in Basingstoke. The meal cannot have been easy for any of them and must have been both a profoundly sad and yet an enormously proud occasion. The family, the school and the Society of Jesus were fully engaged in the defence of their country, and were making every effort to do their patriotic duty. All three Liddell boys saw active service in the Great War, the family home was given over as a convalescent home for wounded soldiers, and two of the three sisters served as volunteer military nurses ministering to wounded soldiers. The Jesuits of the English Province were also fully committed to the war. As well as continuing their important work in education, the Stonyhurst War Record shows that twenty-two Jesuit priests who had been old boys of the College were to serve as military chaplains. Three of these were to die in the service of their country, and many other British Jesuit Fathers would offer their time and their lives to the cause. We can only guess at the topics of conversation that evening, but it is safe to surmise that words like duty, service, courage and sacrifice were much in evidence, as Aidan and many other young men were discussed and remembered.

John Liddell and his family rose early the next morning for the Solemn Requiem Mass, an important part of the Roman Catholic liturgy. The Liddells were a devoutly religious family, and this was their opportunity

---

*SJ are the post nominal letters denoting the Society of Jesus, which was the formal title of the Jesuit religious order of teaching and missionary priests founded by St Ignatius Loyola.

to both honour the life of their son and brother, and to pray that he might rest in peace. The Stonyhurst community echoed these intentions. The boys began to arrive at 0710, and the Officers' Training Corps (OTC), to which Aidan and Bertie had both belonged, was drawn up in stiff khaki ranks on the playground adjacent to the church, before finally filing in to take their places in St Peter's. Many of those youngsters in their rough uniforms would soon be joining the colours. Of the 1,012 Stonyhurst boys who eventually went away to war, 207 did not return.

The ornate Jesuit church had been prepared for the Mass for the Dead, which was celebrated by the Rector, dressed in the customary black vestments. A catafalque had been set up in front of the altar, covered with the Union flag, and on it rested Aidan's claymore and the dramatic black feathered bonnet of the Argyll and Sutherland Highlanders. Throughout the solemn sung Gregorian Mass, prayers were offered for the repose of his soul, and almost all the congregation took Holy Communion for that same intention. The music was described as 'suitably mournful and plaintive'.

The *Stonyhurst Magazine*[2] recorded the events of the day, noting that after Mass the OTC formed up in squares outside the church. As the 'beautiful bright sunshine' of the autumn morning shone down upon the spectacle, the drums rolled and the bugles rang out the last post, while all heads were 'reverently uncovered and lowered'. We can only hope that the family, no strangers to Stonyhurst, and in particular father John who had been a frequent attendee at Easter retreats at the College, and brother Cuthbert, himself an old boy, drew some comfort from that last salute. And with that, the band struck up again with 'cheerful music', and the boys marched off across the playground to their lessons, arms straight and chins held high, to whatever else a most uncertain future held.

Another three years of conflict and the horrors of the Somme, Passchendaele, and countless other battles still lay in the future. At the final count the war was to cost some 743,000 British lives and shape the history of the twentieth century. But this book records the life of John Aidan Liddell, who appeared a thoughtful, self-effacing, immensely likeable and modest young man. Scholar, scientist, naturalist, astronomer, musician, aviator, photographer and diarist, Aidan embraced the challenges of the new century and the Edwardian era with enthusiasm and no small degree of talent. He had a promising future, but perhaps the most remarkable thing about him, and about so many other similar young men, was that for most of the time they were not really remarkable at all. The war was the catalyst. In changing a generation of peaceful young men into soldiers, it provided trials and challenges previously unimaginable to any of them.

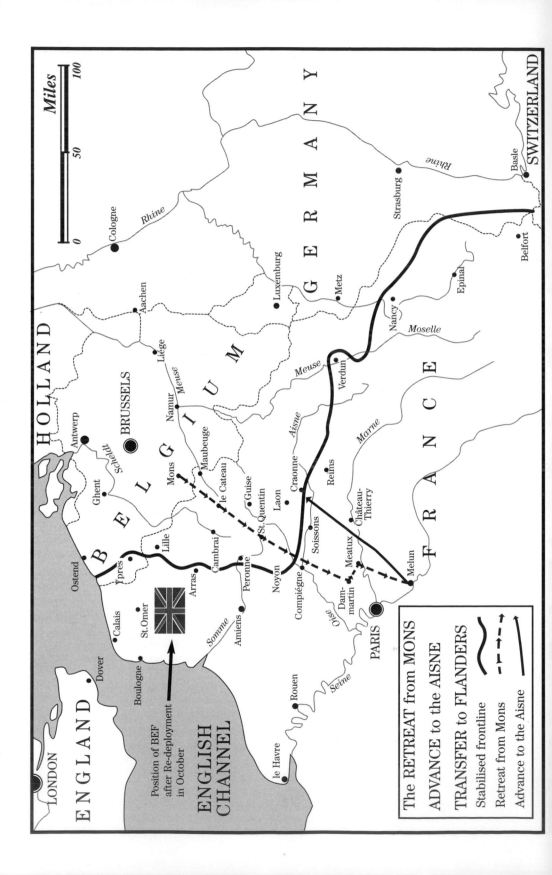

Miles

100

50

0

COLOGNE

SWITZERLAND

Basle

Rhine

Strasburg

Belfort

G E R M A N Y

Epinal

Metz

Nancy

Moselle

Aachen

Luxemburg

Liége

Verdun

HOLLAND

Namur

Meuse

Meuse

Aisne

Marne

Antwerp

Scheldt

BRUSSELS

B E L G I U M

Maubeuge

Craonne

Reims

Château-
Thierry

F R A N C E

Ghent

Mons

le Cateau

Guise

Laon

Soissons

Melun

Lille

St.Quentin

Cambrai

Meaux

Ypres

Ostend

Arras

Peronne

Noyon

Compiégne

Dam-
martin

Calais

St. Omer

Somme

Amiens

Oise

PARIS

Dover

Boulogne

Position of BEF
after Re-deployment
in October

Rouen

Seine

ENGLAND

LONDON

ENGLISH
CHANNEL

le Havre

The RETREAT from MONS
ADVANCE to the AISNE
TRANSFER to FLANDERS
Stabilised frontline
Retreat from Mons
Advance to the Aisne

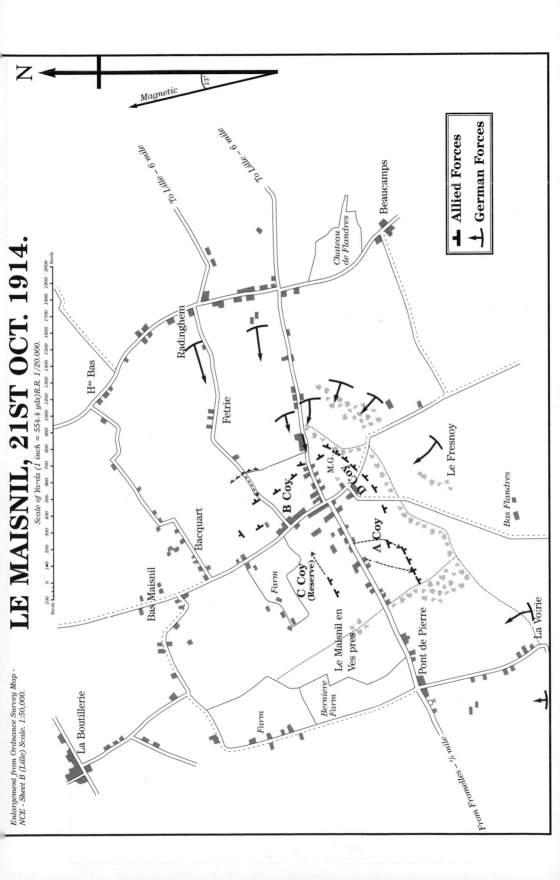

LE MAISNIL, 21ST OCT. 1914.

Enlargement from Ordnance Survey Map -
NCE - Sheet B (Lille) Scale. 1:50,000.

Scale of Yards (1 inch = 554.4 yds.)R.R. 1/20,000.

N

Magnetic   13°

Allied Forces
German Forces

To Lille – 6 mile

To Lille – 6 mile

Beaucamps

Chateau
de Flandres

Radinghem

Fetrie

Le Fresnoy

H^au Bas

Bacquart

Bas Maisnil

M.G.

B Coy

D Coy

A Coy

Bas Flandres

C Coy
(Reserve)

Farm

Le Maisnil en
Ves pres.

Berniere
Farm

Farm

Pont de Pierre

La Voirie

La Boutillerie

From Fromelles – ¾ mile

THE ARMENTIÈRES AREA BETWEEN 20 OCT 1914 AND JAN 1915

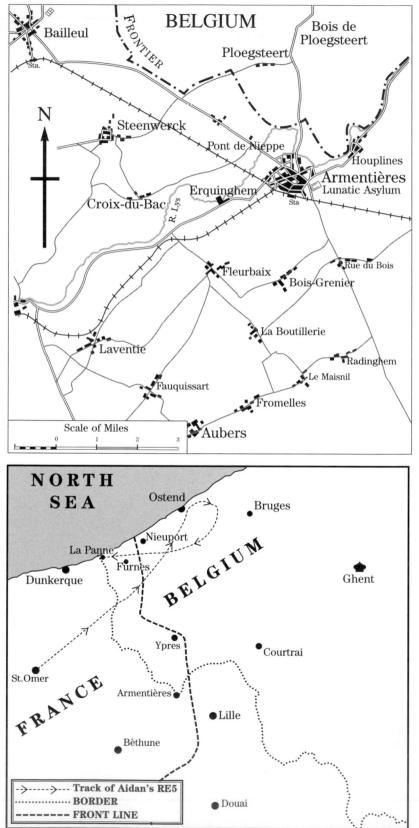

Chapter One

From Benwell to Basingstoke

John Aidan Liddell was born on 3 August 1888 in Benwell, and although he was to move to the south of England early in his life, his roots were firmly in the north east, and in particular in Newcastle upon Tyne. His family were prosperous land and coal owners whose determination and business acumen had advanced the family fortunes over successive generations. Indeed, they were typical of the successful nineteenth century north-eastern entrepreneurs whose industry and vision underpinned the development and growth of Tyneside after the industrial revolution. They were also devoutly Roman Catholic.

Aidan's great-great-grandfather Matthew Liddell was born in Jesmond in 1715, and was a gentleman farmer living at Boghouse in the Chapelry of Hewarth. He also rented an inn from the Dean and Chapter of Durham Cathedral, and his name appeared on a list of Roman Catholics sent to the House of Lords in 1767. This naming of the recusants was a final precaution against further Jacobite uprisings. His son Cuthbert Liddell, born in 1774, was Aidan's great-grandfather, and is described in the Newcastle Directory of 1826 as a tanner, but he was clearly a highly successful one. Growing in prosperity he obtained his own Grant of Arms, and died in 1853 a man of property, living in Benwell Hall. His son John, Aidan's grandfather, was born in 1811, and was admitted to be a Freeman of the City of Newcastle upon Tyne in 1831. He too was listed as a tanner, living first in Newgate Street in Newcastle and then from 1850 in Leazes Terrace. Latterly described as a coal owner, on the death of his father he finally moved to Benwell Hall, where he died in 1888.

John Liddell had four sons, Matthew, Henry, Charles and John who was the father of Aidan. All were men of local influence and all were to become Freemen of the City of Newcastle, an honour that was also to be bestowed on Aidan. When old John died he left a substantial legacy to be divided between the boys. This included a large interest in the Mickley Colliery at Prudhoe, which he in turn had inherited from his brother Matthew, a mining engineer who had developed collieries in the Prudhoe area in the 1860s. Young John Liddell had worked with his uncle at Mickley at that time, and Matthew's collieries included Prudhoe, West Wylam and Thirlwell, as well as Mickley and the Comb Coal Company near Hexham.   Matthew then exchanged land he owned at Sturton Grange near Warkworth with the Duke of Northumberland, for land at Dukeshagg Prudhoe, where he began to build a substantial mansion, Prudhoe Hall, in 1868.   He also owned farmland and woodlands together with sporting rights in the area.   So it was that young John and his brothers were to inherit not just from their father, but also a substantial share of their uncle's fortune too.   In John's case this included an interest in the collieries and Prudhoe Hall and its land, although his Aunt Susanna, Matthew's widow, was to continue to live in the Hall until her death in 1894.

Young John Liddell had lived with his father at Benwell after his siblings left home, and in 1887 he married Emily Catherine Berry.   Her father, Henry A Berry, had been a major in the Cameronians (Scottish Rifles), and her brother was a Catholic priest in Walker, a part of Newcastle.   John and Emily made their first home in Benwell Hall, sharing it briefly with his father, who died in 1888.   It was a substantial brick mansion, two storeys high and five bays wide, dating from the second half of the 18th century.   In those days Benwell was a rural area, much sought after by the gentry and emerging professions as an area to live, and noted for its open situation and commanding views.   It was here, in the year following their marriage, that John Aidan was born. His two brothers and three sisters were to arrive at approximately two-yearly intervals over the next ten years. Dorothy Mary was born in 1890, followed by Cuthbert Henry, Mary Monica, Lancelot Charles, and finally the baby of the family, Veronica Mildred.

The Liddells were a close-knit and happy family who enjoyed the trappings of their prosperity. John was to become a Director of the North British and Mercantile Insurance Company and a Justice of the Peace for Northumberland. Together with his brothers Matthew and Henry, all three heavily moustachioed, they enjoyed shooting and fishing; family photographs show them in their heavy tweeds and flat caps with expensive shotguns under their arms. At Benwell Hall there were horses and carriages, coachmen and gardeners, and the whole panoply of Victorian servants required to support a substantial country house. The census of 1891 records a gardener and his family of three living in the garden cottage and the coachman and his family of four living in the stables. The oldest son is listed as the groom. In the Hall itself are recorded the nurse and under nurse, the cook, a laundry maid and two chambermaids. No doubt other staff lived a little further afield. In addition, John Liddell is shown as 'living on his own means' with his wife Emily. Aidan, aged two, and Dorothy, one, are also recorded. There were in addition two house guests, Edward Russell, a barrister, and Thomas Bramwell, a solicitor. John Liddell was, after all, a man of business.

1. *Cuthbert Liddell, Henry Liddell and John Liddell circa 1897.* Photo Mark Liddell.

2. *John and Emily Liddell on box seat of family carriage at Benwell Hall circa 1891.*
    Photo Mark Liddell.

3. *Prudhoe Hall in the snow, with Monica, Veronica and Dorothy Liddell circa 1903, shortly before the house was sold to Colonel Swann in 1904.* Photo Mark Liddell.

The growing Liddell family was to move several times, and in 1898 moved to Prudhoe Hall following the death of John's Aunt Susanna. The Hall was a much larger, rather grim stone-built mansion, with a Jacobean -style oak staircase, panelled hall and stained glass windows decorated with the initials M and S and blue lovers' knots. The imposing front door was flanked by two stone griffins, and the family arms, again depicting griffins, was carved into the stone front. It was an altogether more impressive home than Benwell Hall, and it is not surprising that John decided to move into this grand house, which was so close to his important mining interests.

There had always been a Catholic chapel at Prudhoe Hall, and Matthew and Susanna had thrown it open to the local community, which had included many Irish immigrants who had come to work in the pits. Although a shrewd businessman, Matthew was also an enlightened and philanthropic Victorian gentleman who was keen to support the community in which he lived. In 1875 he had built St Matthew's Roman Catholic School in Prudhoe, complete with a house for the teacher; the establishment was actually attended by children of all religious denominations, so benefiting the whole community. After Matthew's death Susanna continued her charitable work, and in 1885 built St Matthew's Hall as a free reading room for the Prudhoe community. Once again the initials M and S were carved into the stone above the entrance. Both the school and hall survive to this day and are put to good use by the people of the town. But perhaps Susanna's greatest work was the building of a substantial Roman Catholic Church at Prudhoe Hall between 1889 and 1891, the family chapel having proved too small for the growing congregation.

When John Liddell moved to Prudhoe he maintained a keen interest in the philanthropic works of his uncle and aunt, and both John and Emily were frequent visitors to St Matthew's school. However, the most significant work undertaken by John Liddell was to move the Prudhoe Hall church, 'Our Lady and St Cuthbert's', from its site at the Hall to land in the town several miles away. This extraordinary feat took place in 1904, by which time the Liddells had plans to sell Prudhoe Hall and move south. John believed the church should belong to the community and so, stone by stone, it was dismantled and moved to the new site. It was reassembled in identical form, except that the east facing altar now faced west. In addition, John added a very substantial Presbytery with accommodation for a parish priest and two curates as well as a housekeeper. Matthew and Susanna are buried in the mortuary chapel adjacent to the main altar and the Liddell family is still remembered with gratitude by the Roman Catholic community in Prudhoe. John even made provision in his will for the work to be completed and 'Our Lady and St Cuthbert's' still benefits from his generosity.

1. The Roman Catholic Church at Prudhoe that was originally built as a chapel to the Hall. It was moved into the town by John Liddle.
Photo Mark Liddell.

In 1904, after ten years at Prudhoe Hall, John and Emily and their six children moved to southern England, living first at Sydmonton Court near Newbury, in what is the present home of Lord Lloyd Webber, the musical composer. There is no clear explanation for the family move, but Prudhoe Hall was sold to Colonel Henry Swann, a local industrialist, and the Liddells moved south taking many of their staff with them.

5. *The Liddell children circa 1906. Lancelot (aged 10), Veronica (8), Dorothy (16),*
Aidan (18), Cuthbert (14), Monica (12). Photo Mark Liddell.

Sydmonton Court was only a temporary residence, and it can be assumed that it was let to the family while suitable accommodation was found and acquired. In the event they remained at Sydmonton Court for only three or so years, and in 1908 moved to Sherfield Manor near Basingstoke, which was to be the family home until 1927.

Sherfield Manor was a substantial Queen Anne-style mansion built originally as Buckfield Park, but modernised by the architect Henry Wade in 1898. It stood in 840 acres of parkland a little over four miles from Basingstoke. The extensive grounds included tennis and croquet lawns, a swimming pool, an arboretum, rhododendron gardens and a series of lakes. An estate agent's brochure records 'two oak-panelled halls, billiard and five reception rooms, fourteen best bed and dressing rooms, nursery suite, seven bathrooms and ample servants' accommodation'. The reception rooms were nearly all panelled in beautiful carved walnut or oak. The house clearly made a lasting impression on Veronica Mildred Liddell, the baby of the family, when she first saw it. Then aged seven, she wrote in her nursery exercise book on 17 August 1907:

> Mr Liddell has bought a lovely new house called 'Sherfield Manor'. On Wednesday we went and spent the day there, it is a beautiful house. There is an aviary, and the end little house door is open and the little turtle doves fly in and out. The garden is full of these doves. I nearly caught one, they are so tame. The lake is also nice. One end is full of water lillys (sic), there are 6 duck on it, funny little things. We are going to live there in June 1908.[3]

John and Emily Liddell obviously shared the opinion of their youngest child and in 1911, having decorated and furnished the Manor to their full satisfaction, they engaged a professional photographer to take pictures of their 'beautiful house'. The resulting leather-bound and gold leafed album contains a series of magnificent photographs of the exterior of the house and grounds, and of most of the major rooms within. There are no people, but panelling and chandeliers abound, with intricately decorated ceilings, expensive carpets, enormous palms, ornate pictures, hunting trophies and ornaments. It was indeed a most suitable home for an Edwardian gentleman and his household, and for a keen sportsman like John Liddell it had the additional advantage of three miles of exclusive dry-fly fishing on the Loddon. It also included the Lordship of the Manor.

As at Prudhoe Hall the Liddells threw themselves into local life, with the added dimension that, as Lord of the Manor, John was now the squire – something that was still significant in 1908. He generously supported the local sports clubs and other institutions in the village. He was also President of both the soccer and cricket clubs, as well as a

6. *The front: Sherfield Manor 1911.* Photo Mark Liddell.

7. *The Hall: Sherfield Manor 1911. (opposite top)* Photo Mark Liddell.

8. *The Drawing Room: Sherfield Manor 1911. (Opposite bottom)* Photo Mark Liddell.

trustee of the club room, for which he purchased and maintained a full-size billiards table for use by members. Emily was similarly involved as president of the Nursing Association. She was also vice president of both the soccer and cricket clubs, as well as of the Basingstoke Boys Amateur Boxing Club. Sherfield Manor became an integral part of village life and the house and grounds were often used for local events and celebrations. On one occasion John presented a new post office account book to every child in the village, each with a shilling in it. On a personal level he remained a keen sportsman, enjoying both shooting and fishing, and he was particularly fond of croquet in the summer. He also regularly drove his own dog cart around the county.

John Liddell was also a staunch supporter of the Conservative Party, and for many years an active member of the North-west Hants Conservative Association. He and Emily remained devout Roman Catholics throughout their lives, and worshipped at the Church of the Holy Ghost in Basingstoke, although there was a chapel in the house at which mass was often celebrated. Indeed, on one occasion the King of

the Belgians worshipped there when staying close by. In 1908 John sponsored a fine bell weighing nearly three hundredweight for the tower of the Holy Ghost. It was named 'John' in honour of its patron and was inscribed 'Glory be to the Father and to the Son and to the Holy Ghost'. Perhaps not surprisingly confession, mass and visiting priests figure prominently in the young Monica's nursery notebook as religion was a significant factor in their family life. Notwithstanding his previous generosity to the church in Prudhoe and Basingstoke, John became a benefactor of Westminster Cathedral, then under construction, and was honoured by the Roman Catholic Church as a Knight Commander of St Gregory. In 1917 he was appointed to the bench as a Justice of the Peace, once again assuming the duties of a magistrate that he had previously carried out in Northumberland.

9. *The arms of John Liddell Esq.*
Mark Liddell.

Aidan Liddell's home environment was thus both wealthy and privileged, but his parents were also dedicated people determined to contribute positively to the community in which they lived and to the wider prosperity of Great Britain and the Empire. The ethos was very much one of duty, honour and service, and the family strove to live up to the ideal of the family motto, *Constans et Fidelis* – Constant and Faithful.

Of course, it is difficult to determine now exactly what it must have been like to grow up in this large and busy household, living in a succession of spacious country houses. Nevertheless, family records and albums do give a feel for this golden age before the Great War. Despite the fact that there were twelve years separating the Liddell children the family was remarkably close-knit, and the household was a genuinely happy and contented one. The numerous surviving photographs of John Liddell depict an apparently gaunt and humourless man with a dark moustache and sombre suit, or in later life a close-cropped grey beard. However, his popularity with his servants and the local community, and the warmth of the relationship that he so clearly enjoyed with his wife and children clearly give the lie to this impression. Indeed, he is still very fondly remembered by his single surviving grandchild who noted that 'his humour always shone through, even in adversity, also his patience with a, no doubt, irritating small girl'.[4] Emily was a dutiful wife and loving and supportive mother. She was also an efficient mistress of her large household, and took her duties seriously. None the less there was still time to travel, both around the country and to the continent. She even enjoyed one exotic trip up the Nile, travelling without John, and wrote home excitedly about the crocodiles and a hippopotamus!

The children all had nicknames that stuck. Aidan was often known as Peter, a name that he returned to at various times in his life (although to avoid confusion we will continue to refer to him as Aidan). A part of the grounds at Sherfield Manor was known as Peter's Garden for as long as the family occupied the house. No doubt the name marked a favourite spot, for Aidan became a keen and knowledgeable gardener. The eldest sister Dorothy was referred to as Doll or Dolly and as Tabby or Tabitha. Tabby dated from the Great War when Sherfield Manor was used as a convalescent hospital for wounded soldiers, and Dorothy, as the Commandant, starred in a comedy review. She played Tabitha, an automatic maid, or robot, as we would say today. Tabitha ran amok and smashed up the home. Her performance brought the house down, and so the name endured.

Aidan's brother Cuthbert was known as Bertie, Cuddie or sometimes Weary. He was to become a professional soldier. Mary Monica, the middle sister, was known as the Toad, the reason why now lost for ever. Lancelot was known as Lance or Pows and went on to join the Royal Navy. The youngest sister, Veronica, became knnown as Clara or Clam.

One other key member of the family unit was the governess, Miss Finnegan – Figs. She stayed on after the children had grown up and became a companion to Emily, staying with the family for nearly forty years. Indeed, many of the servants stayed with the family for many years, moving with them from house to house.

Animals played a major part in the lives of the young Liddells as the family albums testify. One of the earliest photographs of Aidan at Benwell Hall shows him, aged about three, resplendent in top coat, Eton collar and boater, holding the leashes of two large black Labradors, Sirien and Spring. A later picture taken at Prudhoe Hall shows him proudly

10. *Aidan with Sirien and Spring circa 1891.* Photo Mark Liddell.

11. Aidan with pony at Prudhoe Hall. Photo Anne Fettes/Prudhoe Historical Society.

standing, crop in hand, with his small pony. Horses were of course the principal form of transport in Victorian and Edwardian times, and the family maintained a number of both carriage horses and hunters, as well as a variety of horse-drawn vehicles, including John Liddell's favourite dog cart. At Sherfield Manor there was a little governess cart that the children could ride in, with seats sideways-on that faced each other, and a little door at the back. The family also had a two-horse brougham that was used to take the family to church on Sundays. Even the mowing machine for the lawns and tennis courts was horse-drawn, pulled by a little pony that wore special leather overshoes to avoid damaging the grass. However, although beautifully manicured, the lawns often had nasty yellow rings caused by the numerous family dogs, many of them French bulldogs and pugs, performing their business and damaging the grass.

The horses were also of course an important source of entertainment. All the children could ride but Dorothy and Bertie were particularly keen equestrians, and both hunted enthusiastically. On the other hand Aidan, and Lance, like their father, preferred shooting and fishing. Indeed, Lance positively hated riding, calling it 'bouncing on a hairy' and developed an early interest in the gun. As the nursery notebook reveals, an eleven-year-old Lance sharpened his shooting skills in the garden of Sydmonton Court with a bag of two thrushes and three blackbirds. It seems unlikely that his parents would have approved. Certainly Aidan, by now an enthusiastic ornithologist, would not have welcomed the culling of garden birds! Indeed, such was his interest that in due course he stocked his own private aviary, and eventually acquired a parrot that lived a long and comfortable life in his study.

The young children were instructed in the nursery by a governess, for most of the time the redoubtable Figs. The nursery also housed a large toy fort with lead model soldiers that each of the Liddell boys was to play with, and which were to survive to the next generation. Aidan's niece Gillian used to play with them in the 1920s with her cousin Peter and particularly recalled the lancers on their jet-black horses. She also played on Aidan's magnificent rocking horse, although her protective mother was always anxious about the animal's fiercely pricked and sharply pointed ears. In the end doting grandfather John had them filed off on the grounds of safety. Childhood in a large country house in late Victorian and Edwardian England was an idyllic time. There were friends to call, and parties and dancing, although this could be on a rather grander scale and somewhat more formal than those that would be encountered today. Little Veronica recorded in her notebook in 1907:

We had a party yesterday. It was very nice. There were about 47 kids. I was dressed in a white dress with pink roses in my hair and in my dress. It was fun. Dell ought to have come but she was not well. The Programme was Valse, Polka, Valse, Barn Dance, Swedish Dance, Valse, Highland Schottische, Valse, Polka, Barn Dance, Valse, Lancers, Highland Schottische, Valse, Polka, Barn Dance, Valse, Galop, Sir Roger De Coverly and Extras.[5]

They must have been very tired seven-year-olds at the end of that day!

At Christmas the mummers came to Sherfield Manor to entertain the family. At Easter the abiding memory was of dyeing Easter eggs by placing them in little bags full of flowers, leaves and onion skins. Once boiled, the now brightly coloured eggs would be rolled down a grassy bank. Those that survived the ordeal were eaten by the excited children. In the winter there was skating on the lake and in summer they could play in the boathouse or on the punt.

Music was also a popular pastime with several of the family playing an instrument, the piano being particularly popular. Aidan played the flute and piccolo as well as having a fine singing voice and Dolly played the violin. The house also boasted a billiard room, which was not just for the boys, as Dolly used to play too. Away from Sherfield Manor and its environs the family took a house in London each year for the season, close to Brompton Oratory. The girls became debutantes and were presented at Court.

Sherfield Manor had a large staff. There were fourteen gardeners led by Mr Pearman, a kindly man with a squashy felt hat and large moustache. He was fiercely protective of his greenhouses, where he grew an extraordinary array of flowers for the house. He alone was permitted to cut the blooms, after which he solemnly carried them to the house in a large flat wicker basket. There were also twenty-one indoor servants, led by Udall the butler, 'slight of figure and rather pink of nose'[6], but invariably immaculately turned out in a black jacket and striped trousers. He was supported by two footmen in yellow and black striped waistcoats,

12. Aidan in the family Humber. Photo Mark Liddell.

who reminded the smaller children of wasps. There was also Beckley as the Mistress called her, the Lady's Maid, a fierce woman of considerable status below stairs. She was 'Miss' Beckley to the other servants, and even enjoyed her own sitting room, to which the under footman brought her meals on a tray. One particular task of Beckley was to iron the Master's daily paper and then sew in the pages before it was delivered to him by Udall. Other memorable members of staff included Webb the chief groom, Alfred his assistant, Cyril the under footman, Mrs Whelan the cook who came up from the village, and Catchpole the chauffeur.

However, this was a thoroughly up-to-date household, which boasted every modern convenience. The phone number was Basingstoke 4, and motor cars soon made their sometimes noisy appearance at the Manor. The Liddells owned a 1908 15 hp Coventry Humber, and Aidan is pictured sitting proudly at the wheel. Later the family owned a large limousine, possibly an American Buick, with glass between the driver and passengers and a speaking tube. The chauffeur, Catchpole, wore a dark green uniform with a peaked cap, britches and leather gaiters. To the amusement of the children he used to rock backwards and forwards when going uphill as if to urge on the vehicle. Aidan, who was very interested in cars, engines and machinery, later had his own Sunbeam. He was also particularly keen on motorbikes. On one occasion, showing off with the Toad on the back, he crashed on the drive at Sherfield, leaving his sister bleeding and marked for life with a scarred hand.

For the Liddells, with six children born with more or less two years between each, bringing up the family and enjoying their childhood was a lengthy process. However, the gentle patterns of family life enjoyed by Aidan and his siblings were, for the boys, only a part of the process of growing up. While the girls stayed at home where they were taught by their governess and tutors, the boys were sent away to boarding school, and enjoyed a somewhat more austere and regimented lifestyle.

Chapter Two

Stonyhurst College

John Liddell and his brothers had been educated at Ushaw College, the large Roman Catholic school and seminary near Durham. Although this establishment had served them well and would have been very convenient while John and Emily lived in the North East, they looked further afield to educate their boys. It is not now clear when Aidan was first sent away to school, but he attended Mrs Ware's Academy, Frognall Hall in Hampstead, for his preparatory education, leaving there in the summer of 1900. A fellow student at Frognall Hall, or St Basil's as it was sometimes called, was an Irish boy from Westmeath called Maurice Dease, whose mother's sister was married to Aidan's Uncle Charles. Aidan and Maurice got on well together, and in 1899 slept in adjacent dormitories. Maurice was a year younger than Aidan and was to remain with Mrs Ware until 1901, but thereafter their lives would in some respects continue to run in parallel, as subsequent events will show.*

To complete his schooling Aidan headed north again. Having enjoyed his twelfth birthday the month before, on 20 September 1900 he arrived at Stonyhurst College in Lancashire at the beginning of the Christmas term. It must have been a long and tiring journey from Prudhoe by rail to Carlisle, and then on southwards, finally on the Blackburn and Hellifield branch of the Lancashire and Yorkshire Railway to Whalley near Clitheroe. The boys were met at the railway station by a fleet of horse-drawn carriages, and rattled the last few miles of their journey over the pitted Lancashire roads until they turned down the great drive of Stonyhurst College. The newcomers among them cannot help but have been

13. Stonyhurst College - The Old Front from the West. Photo Stonyhurst Magazine April 1906.

---

* Maurice Dease is included in Appendix Two: Notes on Persons Mentioned in the Text.

impressed by the imposing 'fronts' with the eagle towers, St Peter's church, and the long ponds on either side of the avenue. Aidan was always an enthusiastic photographer, and it seems likely that the picture of the luggage trap, with the large trunk generously daubed with the initials JAL, was snapped by the trunk's owner. But whoever the photographer was, the picture marks the beginning of what was to be for Aidan Liddell a very happy association with Stonyhurst College.

14. Boys and baggage arrive at Stonyhurst by carriage 1900. Aidan's trunk is marked JAL. Photo Mark Liddell.

The College was already a venerable institution, having been founded in 1593 by the Jesuit Fathers of the Society of Jesus. At first the school was of necessity located abroad, as Catholicism was proscribed during Queen Elizabeth I's reign and so the sons of some wealthy English Roman Catholics travelled abroad to St Omer in France to receive their clandestine education. They travelled to and fro with some secrecy, and faced hostility not just at home, but in France too, for the boys remained resolutely English. When a French army was defeated by the British the students joyfully threw their caps in the air and cheered wildly, which cannot have endeared them greatly to their neighbours! The school was thus both proudly English and defiantly Roman Catholic and a number of students were themselves to join the Society of Jesus. After rigorous training they returned to England as missionary priests. These men lived a secret life of danger and hardship, travelling in disguise, being hidden by supporters and sometimes facing betrayal, capture, torture and even death. Indeed, between 1608 and 1680 twenty-two old boys of the College were martyred for their Catholic faith, most facing public execution at Tyburn or in the northern centres of Chester, York and Lancaster.

However, even on the continent the school was not safe from periodic harassment and persecution and in 1762 it was forced to move to Bruges in the Austrian Netherlands. Eleven years later in 1773, when the Pope suppressed the Jesuit order, it moved again, this time to Liège where it remained until 1794. Then it was the threat of the rampaging armies of the French revolution that caused a final relocation, and this time the choice was to return from exile to England. This homecoming for the boys was made possible by legal changes that allowed Roman Catholic schools to operate in England, and by the great generosity of the Catholic Weld family, which made a substantial property and estates at Stonyhurst in Lancashire available to the Jesuits as a school.

These then were the unusual antecedents of the school that the twelve year-old Aidan Liddell joined in the autumn of 1900. The prospectus of the time records that:

> The School Course, which occupies seven or eight years, comprises the ordinary branches of a Classical Education, including preparation for the Lower Certificate of the Oxford and Cambridge School Examination Board, and for Matriculation in the University of London.[7]

'The latter examination' it went on to explain 'dispenses from the preliminary examinations for the Army and Civil Service and for the Legal and Medical Professions'. The terms, payable half yearly in advance were sixty guineas, and these did not include clothes, shoes, expenses incidental to illness, the weekly pocket money, the use of school books, and subscriptions for the library and for games. On the subject of clothes, while no specific uniform dress was prescribed, each boy was required to have 'two pairs of strong playground boots, two pairs of shoes for house wear, at least two suits of clothes, a great coat, two football jerseys, a cricket suit, and the usual quantity of

15. Crests of the College in exile and at Stonyhurst. Stonyhurst College.

underclothing'. Thus it was that Aidan arrived at Stonyhurst with a bulging trunk, a camera, and as the notes taken on his arrival record 'a little Latin' and a sufficient arithmetic to place him in the third set.

The College itself was based around Stonyhurst Hall, the sixteenth century home of the Shireburn family, but the original buildings bestowed to the Jesuits had been significantly added to by the beginning of the twentieth century. There were great courtyards, imposing gateways and towers, and a large church that some claim was inspired by King's College Chapel in Cambridge, as well as formal gardens, ponds and a bowling green. There was also a weather station, an observatory, a gas plant that was installed in 1811 to provide gas lighting, an indoor swimming pool and a huge indoor exercise area, the ambulacrum. Unusually for a public school the entire premises existed under one roof.

The number of boys at the College when Aidan arrived in 1900 was around 250 and most of the staff was made up of Jesuit priests and

16. *The Refectory at Stonyhurst College during Aidan's time, where his portrait was later to hang alongside the other six school VCs. Note the gas lighting. Photo Mark Liddell.*

scholastics, the younger members of the Society of Jesus who were studying for the priesthood and awaiting ordination. The school curriculum was a unified one with all boys studying the same broad syllabus, subject to specialisation at the top end of the school. However, while the basis of the education provided was classical with music and class drawing taught in the lower forms, there was increasing emphasis placed on science among the seniors, and it was in this area that Aidan was to excel. In contrast to some austere establishments of the time it was also seen as a civilised and civilising place. The Survey of the Higher Schools of England published in 1904 recorded that after visiting a named school of a particular type:

...where artistic influences are almost ostentatiously disregarded, the presence of such influences at Stonyhurst strikes very strong; the original Rembrandts and Dürers and Murillos on the walls, the care and taste with which the boys' playrooms are furnished, the fact that music is taught in school to a large proportion of the school, the point made of dramatic representations by the boys for one another's amusement, all speak of the continuous influence of a system that is not quite English, a system which knows and appreciates the importance of art in life and the importance of its careful if silent development by external surroundings.[8]

Nevertheless, in 1900 Stonyhurst must have been a strange, flickering, smoky place, lit by gaslight, heated by coal fires and patrolled by the black-gowned Jesuits, known by the boys as Crows. In the summer, with blue skies, shimmering ponds and sunshine it was a beautiful and inspirational place, but in the cold and wet of winter it could be cheerless, damp and drafty.* Situated some 400 feet above sea level in well wooded country Stonyhurst lies between the rising mass of Longridge Fell and the more distant Pendle Hill, the traditional home of the Lancashire

* Sir Arthur Conan Doyle, who attended the school between 1869 and 1875, based Baskerville Hall in his famous Sherlock Holmes novel *The Hound of the Baskerville* on Stonyhurst.

witches. Close by are two rivers, the Ribble, and its tributary the Hodder. It is beautiful country, but records from the school observatory show it to be one of the wettest areas in Britain.

17. *Stonyhurst College crest and motto. Stonyhurst College.*

Stonyhurst College was an establishment that aspired to greatness, and was seeking to confirm itself as the premier Roman Catholic school in the country. Founded out of adversity, subject to exile and persecution, by 1900 it was a community of boys, parents and the religious that was proud of its heroic past, and keen to play a full and active part in the life of Great Britain. Like other similar institutions, the ethos was of God, Queen and Empire. The school motto was *Quant Je Puis*, 'as much as I can'. The written work of the boys always began with the initials AMDG, *Ad Majorem Dei Gloriam*, 'For the Greater Glory of God'. Another brief prayer or motto LDS, *Laus Deo Semper*, 'Always Praise God', was appended at the end of each piece of completed school work.

A major difference between Stonyhurst and many other schools was that so many of the staff were Jesuits. Religion therefore played a particularly prominent part in the life of the boys, with the daily routine built around daily Mass, night prayers, and other frequent Roman Catholic devotions. The Jesuits wanted Stonyhurst to set the standard for Roman Catholic education in Britain, and this ambition chimed with John Liddell's own desire to provide the best possible Roman Catholic education for his sons.

Aidan flourished at Stonyhurst and soon showed himself to be a talented lad who was academically gifted. He did well in his studies and often finished at the top of his form, winning a variety of class prizes and medals. He was, however, much less comfortable on that other testing ground, the sports field. Soccer was then the main school sport, with fixtures against sides with such colourful names as Birkenhead Talbot, Blackburn Etrurians and Manchester Wanderers. There was even a game against Everton, and all those available would turn out to watch and cheer the school side on. But Aidan took little interest in soccer, or indeed in athletics and cricket, which were the school's summer sports. Although he was to grow into a tall, straight backed and broad

34

shouldered young man, he was never regarded as being robust physically and seems to have enjoyed indifferent health which might have accounted for his lack of sporting prowess.

Aidan's great interest was in science and modern technology held a particular fascination for him. It was therefore not surprising that when he passed his lower certificates in 1904, it was in chemistry and mechanics. This fitted in well with his burgeoning interest in astronomy, as Stonyhurst was at this time a centre of national excellence in this area of scientific endeavour. He was also an enthusiastic naturalist, taking a great interest in the local flora and fauna in the beautiful Hodder valley, and had a passion for country sports, particularly shooting and fishing. He also displayed a fondness for music, as demonstrated by his membership of the school choir. He also played the flute in the school orchestra. Although the nature of Aidan's youthful ailments are not recorded, it seems probable that he suffered from a weak chest. Then as now, youngsters were often encouraged to sing and play wind instruments to improve their breathing, but whether Aidan's flute playing was initially medicinal or cultural, music was to remain an enduring interest.

Stonyhurst was not organised into the traditional public school house system, which threw together boys of all ages, but rather operated in year groups known as playrooms. These were centred on a series of large common rooms, equipped with billiard and ping-pong tables, bound copies of improving magazines such as *Punch*, and back copies of the *Stonyhurst Magazine*. Chess and draughts, and for the smaller boys bagatelle, were popular pursuits, and there were frequent competitions and tournaments. There was of course a well-stocked library, and as well as many improving religious texts such as *Little Flowers of St Francis*, there were volumes of imperial adventure with such eye-catching titles as *Lumsden of the Guides, Ten Years' Captivity in the Mahdi's Camp* and *The Life of Gordon*. In library booklists of the time the names of Fenimore Cooper, Conan Doyle and Jack London appear alongside those of Lamb, Swift, Hilaire Belloc and Lewis Carroll.

Indeed, the British Empire figured large at Stonyhurst, not just in stories but also in the flesh. When Aidan arrived in 1900 two young Stonyhurst men had only recently been awarded the Victoria Cross. In July 1897 Lieutenant Edmund Costello of the 22nd Punjab Infantry received the award for his part in a stiff little action on the North-West Frontier at the Malakand Post. A 'Mad Fakir' preaching jehad led the tribes of the Swati Valley in mass revolt, and turned on the garrison at Malakand. The British compounds were assaulted by fanatical Swati swordsmen. After the initial attacks, Edmund Costello led two sepoys (Indian soldiers) to recover a badly wounded havildar* who was lying in

* A sepoy rank the equivalent of sergeant.

the open on a football pitch swept by enemy cross fire. The man was rescued at great personal risk by Costello and the sepoys, under the cover of darkness. But that was only the beginning, for the action continued over several days, and Costello was subsequently wounded, on 27 July, with a bullet in his right shoulder that passed through him and exited from his chest. Despite this obviously serious injury, he continued to lead his men and two days later on 29 July during another Swati attack was wounded again when a second round passed through part of his back and then broke his arm. Fortunately, the 'Mad Fakir' was wounded at about the same time, and the tribesmen lost heart and suddenly abandoned their attacks. Costello was awarded the Victoria Cross for his action to save the wounded havildar.

The second Stonyhurst VC was gazetted on 15 November 1898 and was awarded to Captain Paul Kenna of the 21st Lancers for his actions at the Battle of Omdurman, in the Sudan. The 21st Lancers were deployed to cut off the retreating dervishes and wheeled into line to charge a few hundred stragglers who seemed to offer a tempting target for a brisk light cavalry skirmish. But the dervishes had reinforced the position and it was only as the British cavalry closed on the enemy that it was revealed that the Khalifa's reserves of some 3000 tribesmen were drawn up twelve deep in the bed of a dried up river immediately to their front. The Lancers pressed home their attack regardless, and a bloody mêlée ensued, leaving several men unhorsed and vulnerable. Twice Captain Kenna returned to the midst of the fray to rescue stricken comrades, first carrying off Major Wyndham to safety astride his horse behind the saddle. Then he fought his way back to the unhorsed Lieutenant Montmorency and protected him until Corporal Swarbrick was able to catch a charger and bring it back, so that the Lieutenant could remount. The three gallant cavalrymen then fought their way to safety.

It was heady stuff for the youngsters at Stonyhurst, and accounts of both Costello and Kenna's gallant deeds were writ large in the *Stonyhurst Magazine*. Each received his Victoria Cross from the Queen, Kenna at Windsor and Costello at Osborne House, and each returned to their old school to be fêted as heroes and to tell their stories to crowds of spellbound boys. In the meantime, the Boer War was in full swing. Numerous old boys were serving with the colours in South Africa, and found the time to write back to Stonyhurst with accounts of their adventures. In December 1900 the *Stonyhurst Magazine* listed fifty-nine old boys who were serving in the war, of whom three had been killed, one had died, six were wounded and two were prisoners. The pages of the magazine were littered with references to Corps and Regiments and as well as the familiar British names there were now exotic new ones such as Paget's Horse, Thorneycroft's Mounted Infantry, Rimington's Guides and the Imperial Light Horse. Masses were said for those at the front, and victories were celebrated and lives remembered. Even the small boys attending the preparatory school at Hodder played wide games in Paradise, the glorious green valley beneath the little hillside school, between teams named Boers and British. When Ladysmith was liberated the flags were run up amidst general rejoicing, and 'On the Friday they had a football match and a concert in the evening, which was, of course, largely patriotic. Father Rector said a few words on the greatness of the occasion, and called attention to the prominent part taken in the war by specially Catholic regiments'.[9] The boys, large and small, listened spellbound. When, three months later Mafeking was relieved, lessons were cancelled and a whole day was given over to cricket in celebration.

The war had also served to focus minds on the creation of a cadet contingent at the College, something that had been under consideration for some time. The *Stonyhurst Magazine* recorded triumphantly:

> At last the Cadet Corps is an actuality. And, as usual, everyone is asking why there was not a Cadet Corps before? The answer might be difficult to find, but it is certain that the South African War has brought it home to us that a civilian soldier, with a good rifle, and a certain amount of drill and skill in firing is a very formidable foe: and our long casualty lists tell only too eloquently, what havoc a volunteer army can work when well handled and led.[10]

Thus on Tuesday 16 October 1900 the Cadet Corps paraded for the first time in the ambulacrum under the watchful eye of Sergeant-Major McHugh, late of the 4th King's Own Lancashire Regiment. The Corps was attached to the 1st Volunteer Battalion of the East Lancashire Regiment. Its new uniforms were of the same style and cut, and carried the same badges as the parent battalion. The Rector addressed the cadets, watched no doubt by a large audience including many of the smaller boys who were as yet too young to join. He congratulated them on their patriotic spirit, and wished them every success in their undertaking.

The School Diary recorded that:

> Some 60 from the Philosophers and Higher Line* have joined with their parents consent. A charge will be made to pay expenses. . . A military tailor has measured the members for a red Norfolk coat, dark blue trousers with a red stripe, leather belt and forage cap to cost about 25 shillings. Rifles will be lent by the Government. . . The use of the rifle for target practice will only be permitted to such as has qualified for drill. . . Ammunition will be supplied by the Government at cost price.[11]

The author was obviously a little nervous at the expense of this brave

---

* Philosophy was the collective name for the most senior classes at Stonyhurst and this is explained in more detail in Chapter four. The boys in it were Philosophers. Higher Line is a broader term used for the top segment of the school.

undertaking, but all was well and the Corps was to flourish with the foundation, in due course, of a junior branch for younger boys and the establishment of a military band.

When the Corps paraded for the first time in their new uniforms Brigadier General Brownrigg, commanding the Regimental District, came to inspect them as the other boys looked on. He delivered the following short address as recorded in the *Lancashire Evening Post*:

> My lads, I cannot imagine anything outside your religion which will be more useful to you in after life than the self-reliance, self-control, and submission to authority which even this elementary militarism ought to teach you. It is not expected that you are all to become soldiers, but self-reliance, control, and obedience is essential in every pursuit of your lives. Remember you have become volunteers at a time when volunteers are better thought of and more appreciated than they have ever been before and most deservedly so. Volunteers have been, and are now, serving the Queen in South Africa in the first line of the Army, and have proved for ever that they are no longer parade soldiers only. You are now associated with two regiments of the Army that have glorious traditions, the 30th and 59th, and you are also associated with a County which possesses a brilliant Roll of Honour of men who have distinguished themselves in every class of life. Let me ask you as volunteers always to remember this, and to have esprit de corps. It is that which has made England what she is as a nation. Have it in your religion. Have it in your college, and have it in this cadet corps.[12]

Those sentiments capture the spirit of the period. The Corps was to become an integral part of College life during Aidan's time at Stonyhurst. Records show that in 1904 Cadet JA Liddell was classified as a 'Very Good' shot with a score of 128 out of 168 in the annual musketry competition. In 1905 he raised his score to 131, which was well above the average of 114.5. That was also the year that Cuthbert joined Aidan

18. Cadet Corps Annual Review 1905. Photo Stonyhurst Magazine October 1905.

at Stonyhurst after he had completed his preparatory education at Hampstead with Mrs Ware. Bertie was also to serve in the ranks of the Corps during his three years at Stonyhurst, leaving in December 1908, only a few months after Aidan, to pursue a career in the Army. Lance, the youngest brother, was not educated at Stonyhurst, going instead to the Royal Naval College at Osborne, as a precursor to a career in the Royal Navy.

As the Boer War drew to its conclusion, Lord Kitchener issued a proclamation to the Boers. It was another former Stonyhurst boy, Lieutenant Henry de Pentheny O'Kelly of the 18th Hussars, who carried the missive under a white flag, alone on horseback, into the enemy camp. News of the eventual peace in South Africa reached Stonyhurst on Sunday 1 June 1901, and was met with much rejoicing. The School Diary recorded 'News has come that peace has been concluded in South Africa after a war that lasted 2 years and 8 months. *Deo Gratias*.'[13] The next day flags were flown over the College, a solemn Benediction was celebrated, and the *Te Deum* was sung in thanksgiving. Later in the week a catafalque was set up in the church. Father Rector sang a Requiem Mass for the fallen and absolution was given. There was also a free day with no school work for the boys in joyful celebration of the British victory. In due course, the Stonyhurst Association, the organisation of old boys, unanimously agreed that a war memorial should be erected at Stonyhurst to honour those of their number who had lost their lives in the war. John Liddell Esq. was pleased to donate the not inconsiderable sum of £5.

The Stonyhurst community thus felt themselves to be living the life of the nation as befitted an institution that would turn out young men of intellect and education who would make a mark on the world. When Queen Victoria died at the end of January 1901 the event was of course marked at Stonyhurst. The School Diary recorded:

Tuesday 22 Jan 1901. Her Majesty Queen Victoria died today at 7 pm having lived 81 years and 243 days; having reigned 63 years and 261 days. Longer in each case than any of her predecessors. The big bell was tolled.[14]

The news, as bad news always does, spread quickly through the school, and though it had been known that the Queen was failing fast, her end came as a dreadful shock. It was received at first in silence and then as the bell continued to toll little groups of boys and staff began to emerge and congregate to talk quietly of the sad news. The official announcement was made at night prayers, and the boys were asked to pray for the Queen. The next day the flags were floated at half mast, and dead marches were played after the various church services. The day of Her Majesty's funeral was also marked in a similar way. The boys wore black crepe armbands, and the great bell tolled between 1100 and 1130. The festivities that had been planned to celebrate the final vows of several priests were postponed until a more appropriate date.

Having mourned the passing of their Queen, the coronation of Edward VII was greatly looked forward to at Stonyhurst, and great celebrations were planned for 26 June. The ambulacrum was decorated with flags and bunting for a great banquet. Stands were erected in the playground with 1100 lanterns and a massive bonfire and fireworks were planned. Then two days before the much anticipated event came the awful news that the King had undergone an operation, and the coronation was indefinitely postponed. The news of His Majesty was not reassuring and at first it seemed that the celebrations would be cancelled altogether. But practical as ever, the Jesuits proceeded with the planned events, 'albeit somewhat curtailed'. The feeling was that it would be foolish to waste the expensive preparations, but on the other hand excessive revelry might be construed as inappropriate with the King so ill, and might prove positively embarrassing were his condition to decline further. In the event the solution of a rather more modest celebration worked well, for His Majesty recovered and was crowned in August. Having already celebrated once, albeit prematurely, the boys were not permitted a second party, although the flags were raised in His Majesty's honour.

It is well documented that Aidan was not strong physically, and serious illness in the first decade of the twentieth century was an ever-present threat to any community. Stonyhurst was no exception and the harsh Lancashire climate took its toll on the aged and infirm. The large Jesuit community inevitably included a number of older members, and prayers for the sick, masses for the dead and sung dirges at funerals were fairly frequent occurrences. Sickness in a school was a potentially disastrous occurrence, and there was the danger that some would not recover. This was brought home to the school when in February 1904 there were three deaths at Stonyhurst within a single month. The Fr Provincial of the Jesuits expired unexpectedly of pneumonia on 12 February. Two twelve year-old boys also died, one of complications after measles, and the other following a particularly vicious attack of what was described as 'the recent sickness' (probably influenza). The *Stonyhurst Magazine* mourned the deaths, and sought to offer some comfort, pointing out:

> . . .it is consoling that for sixteen years no boy has died here, and this lapse of time without such misfortunes leads us to hope that many future generations of boys may be spared the sad experience of losing any of their comrades.[15]

But in April 1907 another boy died of pneumonia, and the Rector and another master died suddenly in the same month. The grasp on life was much more precarious than it is today, and people generally were more accustomed to and perhaps more comfortable with death. At Stonyhurst, the prevailing presence of the Roman Catholic faith offered a meaning to the trials of sickness and bereavement.

Aside from work, sport and religious observance activities at Stonyhurst were necessarily of a communal nature. There were frequent plays and concerts and although Aidan never appeared in a school play, his singing and the ability to play the flute meant that he frequently participated in the various musical entertainments, which often had an imperial flavour, with marches and patriotic songs. A typical event might include 'Hearts of Oak', 'The British Grenadiers', and finish as always with the national anthem. There were also sketches and reviews, but a particularly popular form of entertainment, and one that appealed greatly to Aidan as he progressed up the school, was debating. This was carried out with great formality. The members were listed each year by constituency, and in 1904 the Board of Six that controlled the society met on Wednesday 30 November to consider new members, and admitted Aidan Liddell as the Member for Newbury. Subject for debate were typically historical, topical or political. Motions around this time included "This House disapproves of any attempt to limit by law the speed of road motors"[1] and "This House does not favour the construction of a Channel Tunnel."[2] Some, such as the motion that "Undesirable Aliens should not be permitted to enter England"[3] still have a resonance today.

In this way the boys sought to grasp the issues of the day, sharpen their intellectual skills and perhaps have a little fun too. Aidan's first recorded debate was against the motion that 'In the opinion of this house the adoption of conscription would be advantageous to the interests of England'[4], and it was following this performance that he was elected to the society.

[1] Stonyhurst Magazine, Vol 9 p.16.
[2] *ibid* Stonyhurst Magazine, Vol 10 p.189
[3] *ibid* p.479.
[4] *ibid* Vol 9 p.244.

Chapter Three

Science and Spain

Aidan came to Stonyhurst College already a countryman, but the rural Lancashire setting and the abundance of nature that surrounded the school reinforced his childhood interest, and his love of the countryside grew. Birds became a particular interest, and he was soon taking an active role in the management of the Stonyhurst aviary. This was an ambitious enterprise that had started in the early 1880s when Fr Eyre, the then Rector of the College, had purchased a number of canaries (it was said from a local lunatic asylum). He housed them in an old summer house, with a wire-netting flight outside. The early occupants were kept warm in winter by a small gas stove, the fumes of which had the unfortunate side effect of gradually poisoning the more sensitive birds. By 1900 the aviary had assumed the proportions of a veritable menagerie, occupied roomy new premises, and boasted an extensive collection of native and exotic birds and animals. Owls looked down from special cages on the walls. The window sills were wired to provide nesting areas for jackdaws, while hedgehogs, guinea pigs, gerbils, snakes and a great white rabbit roamed across the sanded floor of the enclosure. Great ingenuity was required to keep the charges safe from marauding rats, but despite buried wire netting, traps and vigorous rat hunts, the Aviary Boys were not always successful. Birds, even as large as jays or seagulls, were taken, or like a luckless pair of quails, found decapitated in the morning.

In Aidan's time the smaller inhabitants included a goldfinch, a white java sparrow, a pair of zebra finches, a cock twit, a pair of ribbon finches or 'cut-throats', and Patsy the three-year-old aviary-bred cockatiel. Birds of prey were difficult to keep, but the boys tried hard, and crows, jackdaws and ravens were particularly successful candidates for the aviary. Some birds were reared from eggs or from chicks taken in the wild, while others were the result of captive breeding pairs. More exotic species were often purchased and presented by boys, old boys or other benefactors. The aviary was a major and very demanding project, closer to a zoo than the modern school 'pet shed', and it helped to shape Aidan's interest in the biological sciences. His classmate Frank Ryan was the Head Aviary Boy in 1904, and Maurice Dease was also to become a keen member, first as clerk of works, and then as Head Aviary Boy. For a while he was also the prolific author of the Aviary Notes column in the *Stonyhurst Magazine*.

19. *The Stonyhurst Aviary circa 1904, when Aidan was an Aviary Boy. Photo Mark Liddell.*

Cuthbert Liddell shared his brother's enthusiasm and also became an Aviary Boy.

Aidan's burgeoning interest in nature and the scientific world was greatly aided by his association with Fr Aloysius Cortie, a science teacher at Stonyhurst, but also an astronomer of national standing. The Jesuits were then, and remain to this day, renowned for their study of the heavens. An observatory had been built at Stonyhurst in 1838 and under a succession of truly great Directors the Stonyhurst observatory won first a national and then an international reputation, for astronomy, meteorology and terrestrial magnetism. In 1866, with the help of a grant from the Royal Society, equipment was acquired that enabled Stonyhurst to become one of seven official meteorological weather stations in Britain, and this made it eligible for Board of Trade funding which helped defray the costs. The observatory also pioneered the art of stellar photography. Stonyhurst was thus firmly on the scientific map of Britain and in 1883 and again in 1887 the College hosted the annual gathering of the British Association for the Advancement of Science.

By the time Aidan arrived at Stonyhurst the Director was the accomplished Fr Walter Sidgreaves. In 1892 and 1901 new stars were identified, and in the latter case the exciting news was immediately flashed to all the principal observatories of the world by electric wire. Much work was undertaken on the new discovery at Stonyhurst, and Fr Sidgreaves won a Gold Medal in the St Louis exhibition of 1904 for his work on the Beta Lyrae star. Aidan's mentor though was Fr Cortie, the assistant to Fr

43

Sidgreaves, and in his own right Director of the Solar Section of the British Astronomical Society.

Fr Cortie travelled widely and was much in demand as a lecturer, addressing large audiences of many hundreds of people on such topics as the 'Solar Surface' and 'Spectrum Analysis'. But as a science teacher he also took the time and trouble to encourage boys who showed an interest in astronomy. Often his lectures were supported by photographs, and Aidan became increasingly involved in his spare time in the work of the observatory and developed a great enthusiasm for science. The mechanical systems associated with the observatory were of great interest to him, but he also learnt to manipulate the various instruments, and to understand the importance of precise scientific observation. He became an expert photographer, and his friends called him 'Oozy' Liddell, because he was always messing about with chemicals, engines and machinery.

The observatory was a wonderful place to learn and experiment. Aidan's enthusiasm was no doubt further fed by another visit by the British Association to the College in September 1903, when 150 distinguished visitors spent the day at Stonyhurst. They were given a most thorough understanding of the advanced research conducted there and the local ingenuity that supported it, as the *Stonyhurst Magazine* explained:

> A large party of astronomers, including Professor Simon Newcombe, whose recent book led Dr Russell Wallace to pen his new theory 'A Man's Place in the Universe', were shown over the observatory by Father Cortie, Father Sidgreaves and their astronomical assistants. The large telescope which commemorates the work of Father Perry (the first Director) was viewed with much interest, and the various photographic and other accessories with it showed much ingenuity in getting the best results with limited means. A snuff tin had been converted into a camera attachment, and portions of a superannuated lawn mower were used for rotating the telescope.[16]

Aidan's keen interest and practical expertise were such that he was invited to accompany Fr Cortie to Spain in August 1905 to observe and photograph a total eclipse of the sun. The eclipse was to sweep across Spain from the Atlantic in a south-easterly direction, the central line passing near Burgos, and leaving Spain near the town of Oropesa. The track was to pass over some fifteen houses of the Society of Jesus in Spain. Eminent Jesuit astronomers from around the world travelled to Spain to observe and record the phenomenon. Fr Cortie and Aidan were to travel to the small sea port of Vinaroz on the Mediterranean coast, very near to the central line of the eclipse.

This was by any standards a serious scientific endeavour, and the selection of the seventeen-year-old Aidan to assist is a clear indication of his enthusiasm and technical ability. Their equipment was large, complex and expensive. It consisted of four instruments for the photography of the solar corona, which surrounds the sun and is only visible during an eclipse when the sun is totally covered by the moon. Most important was the coelostat, a mirror mounted on a polar axis and driven by a clockwork mechanism, which would enable a beam of sunlight to be directed onto a photographic lens. This fitted into a camera box almost twenty feet long and so cast an image onto the ground glass of the camera and thence onto the photographic plate. The coelostat was borrowed for the occasion from the Royal Irish Academy, through the good offices of the Royal Astronomer of Ireland. The camera box would, they hoped, be built on site by a local carpenter.

The expedition was planned with military-style precision, with the heavier instruments being crated and sent on ahead from Liverpool by the steamer *Jacinta* of the Serra and Tontore Steamship Companies on 15 July, while the two travellers followed on the Bibby Company liner *Warwickshire* on 3 August. It was a great adventure for Aidan, and he was keen to share it with his family, writing home frequently and at some length.

On leaving the Mersey, the *Warwickshire* immediately encountered heavy seas, and Aidan reported water breaking over the side, as the vessel ploughed through the waves with an up and down motion. There was no rolling and very little vibration, which surprised him. Later that evening he visited the engine room, and judged the massive machinery to be "splendid". During the night the conditions worsened, and although Aidan gamely turned up for breakfast, he found he could not face food. He retreated to his cabin, where a steward brought him two apples. Fortunately by lunchtime the sea was a little calmer and he managed some soup and meat and then a turn around the deck. But the glass was falling. A gale was building in the Irish Sea and conditions worsened, as Aidan described in a letter home.

> On Saturday it was awful. We got part of a gale, and I stopped in bed. We got into the Bay of Biscay about midday and it was much calmer, but not half as rough as it was off Holyhead and the Lizard.[17]

Thereafter the weather eased, and Aidan and Fr Cortie were able to enjoy the pleasure of sea travel. There were twenty passengers on board, four of whom were women. To while away the time a sweepstake was organised in which each passenger contributed a shilling and had to guess the number of miles travelled during the day. Fr Cortie won and happily collected the £1 prize – a not inconsiderable sum, being worth more than £60 today.

Certainly the *Warwickshire* seems to have been very comfortable, and Aidan's cabin was the most forward one on the port side of the promenade deck, and boasted two port holes, a wash stand and a sofa as well as a berth. Most of the seamen were lascars, and he was fascinated to observe the caste system that operated, the frequent breaks for prayer 'on a little square of carpet', and the requirement of them to slaughter their own sheep. He quietly watched one man carefully washing himself all over and noted that he only used about three cups of water.

Food on board for the passengers was plentiful and rich, and he commented on the abundant supply of game, ptarmigan, grouse and pheasant that graced the dinner table. Despite its age it was, he reported, 'ripping' although ripe might have been a more appropriate description. But as the son of an accomplished sportsman, and already no mean shot himself, he had already acquired the taste for a well-hung bird. But he also began to enjoy the frequent and fiery curries that were served, no dought courtesy of the lascar sailors. The *Warwickshire* made good progress from Liverpool and on 8 August passed through the Straits of Gibraltar where Aidan was able to take some photographs of the Rock with a telephoto lens. That evening the passengers held a concert in which volunteers provided entertainment. Fr Cortie played and sang several items. They eventually docked in Marseille on 11 August and booked into the Grand Hotel de Russie et d'Angleterre. After dinner a jesuit Brother appeared to show them the sights, but was travelling incognito and without the usual clerical garb. The Society of Jesus had recently been expelled from France, and this clandestine arrival provided an odd echo of Stonyhurst's troubled 17th Century continental past.

Aidan the naturalist was particularly impressed by the zoo, and its magnificent entrance. He was also impressed by the electric train that ran along the harbour side pulling two open carriages. He noted with enthusiasm its speed! There was also a postscript in a letter home, courtesy of the expedition leader. 'Fr Cortie would like you to send one of the daily papers out to him at Vinaroz. The way to address the letter is not to Fr Cortie but Al Senor Don Aidan Liddell etc.'[18]

The next morning Aidan and Fr Cortie went to the church of Notre Dame de la Garde where the latter celebrated Mass, after which they 'fooled about' exploring the town. When Fr Cortie went to look up an old friend Aidan went in search of birds for the family aviary. Having found a suitable shop, he reported that 'The birds there are ever so much cheaper than in England. I sent four pair. Two "Cutthroats" (the ones with the red throats), two red birds, two birds that sing beautifully and two "workers". I think the "workers" build a nest (a hanging one) if you supply them with some nesting materials'.[19]

That night they boarded the Austrian ship *Lederer Sandor* bound for

Barcelona, arriving there at about 5 pm the following day. The ship was a good-sized vessel, but very crowded, and even the first class passengers were put four to a cabin. Aidan described 'a truly polyglot collection' of one German, two Austrians, two Spaniards, three Englishmen and a Frenchman among the first class passengers, and the captain was Hungarian with most of his crew Italian. During the voyage the 'three German speaking gents formed a community', while the Englishmen the Frenchman and the Spaniards spoke together in French. To his evident surprise Aidan noted in a letter home that he could 'understand every word that is said, and can talk fairly well now'.[20]

Arriving at Barcelona later than expected, the passengers were transferred to shore by boat. They were unable to clear their baggage through customs because the key official had left for the day. Despite the efforts of their Spanish friend from the voyage, 'the fool of an official' left in charge refused to release their hand luggage despite his 'gorgeous uniform and medal'. Aidan was clearly unimpressed, although they were swiftly taken to the Jesuit College in Barcelona, where he remarked upon the splendid laboratory. Reunited with their baggage and the heavy equipment sent on earlier from Liverpool, Aidan and Fr Cortie travelled by train to Tortosa, the headquarters of the Jesuit astronomers who were observing the eclipse. They were mightily impressed with the newly erected observatory for the study of cosmical physics. Aidan noted that 'on July 29th or thereabouts, there was a small earthquake in Scotland, and the seismograph which they have there registered it at exactly the time that it happened'.[21] Thereafter they travelled on to Vinaroz by rail, sharing their compartment with the Archbishop of Grenada.

They were greeted on arrival in Vinaroz by the mayor, and were accommodated in the curéê's house. However, it soon became clear that the local people had no real grasp of the complex requirements of the expedition, which were for a clear flat surface with an uninterrupted view of the heavens, capable of providing a stable platform for the erection of scientific instruments. An area behind an old flour mill, about a foot deep in dust and debris, had been set aside for them, but it was summarily dismissed by the expedition leader as being wholly unsuitable. Fr Cortie, who saw the expedition failing because of the lack of cooperation of the local people, was mightily displeased. He at once telegraphed Tortosa, explaining that local arrangements were totally inadequate and that he and Aidan would be returning on the midnight train. He was, in the event, persuaded to stay a little longer, until at least the following afternoon, and the locals did their very best to meet his demands. As Aidan explained:

> The mayor and corporation were very anxious to have us here so
> they did all they could. There was a very nice place in a garden

belonging to a gentleman, and the Doctor has a very nice house adjoining it but separated by a wall. So they knocked a hole in the wall and made a door there with steps up. That was done in about 7 hours. They then made a brick pillar about three feet high and with a foundation of about three feet in the ground. It has a wooden slab on top 3 inches thick, which is fastened securely down by two iron pieces which go right through the brickwork. They finished that in about 24 hours. So you can see they worked harder than the average British workman. When Fr Cortie finally decided that he would stay, the mayor and corporation invited us to the police station, and there we drank vermouth.[22]

It was now the 18 August, and the intrepid scientists had twelve days in which to prepare for the eclipse. The local people were amazingly kind. Dr Sebastian Roca gave up his whole house to their use, sending his family away to their country villa. The delicate coelostat was precisely positioned on the newly constructed masonry pier, and a local carpenter was found who was able to construct and position a pitch pine camera nearly 20 feet long.

The build-up to the day of the eclipse was marred by the weather. It was extremely hot and uncomfortable, and both Aidan and Fr Cortie suffered from the high temperatures. The latter recorded 'the first effect of the intense heat, helped by the mosquitoes, was to make our faces break out in large spots, and about a week before the eclipse the junior member of the expedition had collapsed temporarily while the senior member was somewhat out of sorts'.[23] Aidan wrote home to explain the circumstances. 'We used to go bathing in the sea, and one day I got stung by a jellyfish. It did not hurt much, but the heat brought on an awful itchy rash; all my wrists, ankles, hands and neck swelled up, and my face did a bit, and I was in bed for three days.'[24] He also thanked them for the copious supply of English newspapers that were apparently very much appreciated by Fr Cortie!

Despite the vicissitudes all was in place by Monday 28 August, and the instruments had been checked, assembled and put in place. Indeed, they were even afforded the added security of a twenty-four-hour guard by the local police. Additional volunteers also arrived in the form of two Spanish old Stonyhurst boys who having heard of the expedition were keen to offer their services. A Fr Morford of Saltash in Cornwall brought with him another camera, a refractor of four inches aperture, but he was somewhat less rigorous in his preparations and simply mounted it on an empty wine barrel on the day of the eclipse. The team were well drilled in the necessary techniques and on the evening before the great event they held one last rehearsal with everyone performing as if for the real event. Aidan controlled the big camera, while Fr Cortie and the two other Stonyhurst men each operated a spectroscopic camera. Fr Morford was appointed visual observer to call 'go' at the beginning and signal 'close' at the end of totality. All was set for the three and a half minutes of the eclipse.

The morning of 30 August dawned fine and clear. The astronomers made the final adjustments to their instruments and polished their lenses and mirrors. By 1030 the local people began to gather on flat roofs and vantage points and a festive carnival feeling was in the air, with much shouting, cheering and hooting of horns. Fr Cortie recorded that 'The first contact of the moon with the sun's western rim took place at 11 hours 56 minutes 3 seconds in a cloudless sky, and the moon began to advance rapidly over the sun's disk.'[25] As darkness began to fall and the birds fell silent, Fr Cortie determined that the assembled Spanish revellers should also mark the occasion with due solemnity. Raising his arm above his head he shouted in a loud voice '*Silencio*'. The courteous inhabitants of Vinaroz fell silent, so that the ticking of the clockwork mechanism of the metronome was clearly audible to the assembled scientists. 'Go' called Fr Morford as totality occurred, and the camera slides began to click as Fr Cortie called the seconds. He later wrote:

> After the first exposure had been made, we glanced up and saw the ball of the deeply black moon surrounded by an immensely brilliant uniform ring of light, the inner corona. Thence there proceeded three brilliant and long streamers tapering to fine points, placed roughly in the NW, NE and SW quadrants, while glowing red prominences of hydrogen gas clung apparently to the moon's limb, one set of five in the NE being particularly striking.[26]

As the seconds turned to minutes Aidan and the others continued to expose their plates, and all the while Fr Cortie called the time. 'Close' shouted Fr Morford, some eleven seconds too early. Then, with a cheer from the crowd, daylight returned, a cock crowed, and the eclipse of 30 August 1905 was over. The astronomers were clearly anxious to see the results of their handiwork, but despite the temptation to develop the plates in Tortosa or Barcelona they were packed up for the return trip to Stonyhurst. Aidan had already lost a number of his personal photographs of the trip when it became apparent that English film and Spanish developing techniques were not always compatible.

The mission accomplished, the expedition retraced its steps, stopping briefly in Barcelona for one last adventure. Aidan recorded that:

> . . .just after dinner, at about one o'clock, there was a big explosion just a little way up the street. It shook the whole place, and I was standing on the steps of the Hotel and saw a big cloud of smoke or dust rise. Everybody rushed up and we found that someone had let off a bomb. We saw them carrying away a little girl and a young woman, both very bloody. No one knows who threw the bomb, or

20. *Photos of the solar eclipse at Vinaroz 30 August 1905. Taken by Aidan and Fr Cortie. Photo Stonyhurst Magazine October 1905.*

how many have been injured, but one report says that three were killed and about twenty injured. We did not see any more but a huge crowd formed, and now 7.30 in the evening it is still there.[27]

The excitement of a terrorist attack was not enough though to deter the travellers from their planned visit to the bull ring. However, it turned out to be another harrowing experience, and Aidan's vivid description makes it clear that he did not enjoy the spectacle.

It was a sickening business altogether. They blow a bugle and open a door, and the bull trots out. He looks around and goes for the first thing which he sees which is generally a horse. It meets it with a thud and the man tries to keep it off with the lance. The bull generally succeeds after one or two tries to rip the horse up. It falls down and they draw the bull away with flags, and one of the attendants takes a kind of dagger and finishes the horse off. After the bull has charged about four or five horses and ripped up two or three of them the horses are taken out (and) the bull gets all his shoulders ripped up, and bleeds terribly. Next men come in with long darts. Each has two of different colours with paper wrapped around them. They go in front of the bull and when he charges, they step to one side and put them in his shoulders. After that the swell chap comes in with a flag and a sword; he messes around a lot and at last sticks the sword into the bull between the shoulders. If the bull bleeds from the mouth it is bad as he has hit the lungs. One of the bulls had the sword go right through him and it came out underneath. It did not kill him and they pulled it out again and he had another try. They killed six bulls but we only stayed for five of them.[28]

Passing judgement on the bullfight he finally recorded 'It was an experience, but I would not like to see one again'.

Bombs and bullfights aside, the expedition was a great adventure for Aidan, and a huge astronomical success. He had demonstrated a real flair for science. Fr Cortie wrote to congratulate him in the warmest terms.

My Dear Aidan,

Br William McKeon returned last night to College and this morning we developed the six plates you took with the long focus lens. As my telegram has already informed you they are perfectly beautiful, in fact perfect except for a slight fogging in three cases which is immaterial. Fr Sidgreaves is delighted with them, and I am deeply grateful for the efficient way in which you manipulated the camera and for all the other assistance that you rendered me during the expedition. I hope the Cortie and Liddell photos of the corona of 1905 will do much to increase the reputation of the College and assist us in our knowledge of the solar corona. As soon as the plates are dry Br William will start making prints and you may hope to receive copies in a few days. I am sure that your father and mother will be much pleased with your success. The clock behaved perfectly and the focus is perfect. *Deo Gratias*.

Kindest Regards to all,
Ever Yours gratefully
AL CORTIE SJ[29]

21. Fr Cortie SJ - Later in life. Stonyhurst College.

The eclipse expedition was a triumph for Aidan, and his enthusiasm for astronomy grew. The following year, because of his much mentioned but still unexplained ill health, it was decided that Aidan would take a long sea voyage in company with his parents. They departed in January, having been sufficiently concerned to delay Aidan returning to school after the Christmas holidays. The bracing sea air was expected to provide a tonic, and Aidan had enjoyed the voyages to and from Spain. The destination was Cape Town, and Fr Cortie provided a letter of introduction to Sir David Gill who was Astronomer Royal of the Royal Observatory at the Cape of Good Hope. In due course Sir David wrote back to Fr Cortie in a letter dated 23 March 1906:

I had the pleasure of receiving your letter of the 20th of January, introducing your pupil Mr Aidan Liddell. I made an appointment for last Tuesday, and he came to the Observatory, accompanied by his father and mother. I found him an exceedingly bright, intelligent young fellow, and quite 'ready at the uptake' as the Scotch have it. In fact I took quite a fancy to the lad and asked him to come back on the following morning to complete his survey of the observatory. His mother tells me he has been making numerous notes from which he can report back to you of what he has seen. . . .I think the lad might do far worse than to take to astronomy as a profession. No one will ever make money at astronomy, but no one will ever do any good at it unless he is born by nature that way. I do think this lad has both the taste and the brains for it from the little I could see of him.[30]

This was praise indeed and from a most distinguished source. Aidan continued to display a keen interest in astronomy. Almost a year later on 27 February 1907, on the nomination of Fr Cortie,* he was elected a member of the British Astronomical Association, his papers being endorsed by Mr Crommelin of the Greenwich Observatory and Mr Saunder, Secretary of the Royal Astronomical Society, both former Presidents of the Association.

---

* See Appendix Two: Notes on Persons Mentioned in the Text.

Chapter Four

A Gentleman Philosopher

After obtaining his School Certificate and gaining first class marks in advanced mathematics in 1905, Aidan moved on to the next stage of his education. He became a Gentleman Philosopher at Stonyhurst in the autumn of the following year, after an extended absence from school. Philosophy was a legacy of the days when Roman Catholics were not permitted to attend English universities, and so the College had of necessity provided its own form of tertiary education. Although by 1906 those days were long gone the Philosophic Body at Stonyhurst had endured, and now offered a preparation for university, rather than simply an alternative. Aidan joined to prepare himself for Oxford, and over the next two years continued to develop his interests in science and technology.

The Philosophic regime at Stonyhurst was very different from that of the school. No longer treated as boys, the students were known as 'Mister', afforded considerable freedom and independence and lived a life that was separate from the rest of the College. Indeed, contact with the boys was generally discouraged both by the Philosophers' own rules and by the prefects, the masters responsible for discipline lower down the school. Cuthbert had joined Aidan at Stonyhurst in 1905 from Mrs Ware's Academy, but Philosophers with siblings in school were only supposed to see them on Sundays, when he and Bertie were permitted to meet for 'Brothers' Walks'. Philosophers called the boys 'Natives' and the younger ones 'Brats'. It seems likely that many joining from other schools or overseas would rarely have spoken to the boys, and it would have been possible to go through the whole Philosophic process with no contact whatsoever. That said, the rest of the school were permitted to enjoy the Philosophers' annual play, and they sometimes also put on or paid for professional concerts for the general entertainment of the school community. There was sporting contact too, for the Philosophers played in school teams, and competed at cricket, soccer and golf against the senior boys. Another shared interest was the Cadet Corps, and, when first established in 1900, the Philosophers had provided the commanding officer and a fifth of the unit's strength. Although Aidan chose to abandon the Corps at this stage of his Stonyhurst career, several of his contemporaries soldiered on.

The regime set out to emphasise the different and separate status of the Philosophic Body. They had their own teachers, or 'Professors' as they were known, and although these had at first been exclusively Jesuit priests, changes to the curriculum made it essential to draw in expertise from outside. Great care was taken in selecting high quality lay teachers to prepare students for university entrance. Although their duties also included some teaching lower down the school, their status was that of Professor and most of their duties were associated with their senior charges. They shared much of the lifestyle of the Philosophers, living in adjacent study bedrooms, rather like staircases at Oxford or Cambridge, and dining in the Philosophers' Refectory. Professors and Philosophers worked and passed their leisure time together, enjoying tea and toast in each others' rooms around blazing fires. They whiled away the evenings with billiards or a hand or two of cards, and enjoyed tennis, golf and country pursuits together. But even such pleasant pursuits were not without their dangers, as the 1908 *Stonyhurst Magazine* recorded:

> Yet another escape from fire has been added to the list furnished by our chronicler in 'Glimpses of the Past'. On the 21st of February at about 7 o'clock, smoke was noticed to be issuing from a room in the Philosophers' quarters. Upon investigation it was found that a waste paper basket near the grate had caught fire and in turn had set fire to the flooring. Thanks principally to the prompt action of Mr Liddell and Mr Asphar the flames were speedily extinguished, little damage being sustained beyond that of the destruction of the paper-basket and a few boards in the immediate neighbourhood of the grate.[31]

Such accidents were not uncommon and explain the annual Mass against fire.

The Philosophers gathered on the first day of the autumn term each year. And after dinner, which included speeches and toasts, came the all important selection of rooms. Choices were made in order of seniority, and those returning late to Stonyhurst forfeited their position and went to the bottom of the list. Furnishing the rooms was down to personal taste, and some brought expensive items from home. However, it was the custom for those leaving to donate their furniture to the College servants, who supplemented their income by renting items to the new intake the following year. Roger Ormerod and Harry Hoden, known as Harry Doc, were the two principal Philosophers' servants, the former commencing his service in 1884 and the latter in 1887. Both continued until 1916. The Philosophers' log for 1905 noted that Harry and Roger were to be paid an extra 10 shillings a year each to clear up and wash the tea things from the Philosophers' rooms. The previous practice of tipping on every occasion had proved too expensive for the young gentlemen. Another important figure was the College butler, at this time the impressive Will Wilson, who had the vital function of serving wine at their meals and was a great supporter of the Philosophers.

Will inherited his office from his father Dick Wilson who died in 1885. However, his long reign reached an abrupt conclusion in 1907 owing to a public falling out with Fr Pedro Gordon the new Rector who filled the role of both headmaster and head of the Jesuit community. At an important dinner in the grand dining room reserved for special entertainment the Rector rebuked the butler publicly because the large joint of roasted meat was served on too small a plate. Will's peeved response was to return with the meat on an enormous dish, the largest plate that he could find. The austere Pedro Gordon, already in failing health, was not amused by what he regarded as dumb insolence, and Will Wilson's reign as College butler came to an abrupt end. Thereafter, Will was known as Napoleon, because he is said to have excused his behaviour with the comment 'Well even Napoleon had his Waterloo'.

At lunch on the second day of the academic year the Body of Philosophers would elect their Committee. The school would have already appointed the Senior Philosopher, and it was usual for him to be endorsed by the Philosophers and elected their President. They also elected a Vice President and Secretaries to look after the various important rooms and the sports and activities in which the Philosophers participated. The Committee usually held meetings monthly, and as well as ordering the lives and activities of the Body it had the important role of controlling the Philosophers' Fund, which covered the costs of communal living such as newspapers and periodicals, the cost of a groundsman for the tennis courts, and the provision of fish to stock the ponds. It was funded by subscription and fines, the latter being the Philosophers' method of punishment. Fines were posted daily on a notice board and were usually sixpence, a shilling, or two shillings.

In 1907, after a successful first year as a Philosopher, Aidan was elected Vice President and was Secretary of Fishing and Boating and of Shooting. Popular, academically gifted and scientifically inclined, he had grown into a tall and impressive-looking young man with broad shoulders, a wide forehead and a sharp and enquiring mind. The family measuring book indicates that he had now reached six feet and half an inch, which was a clear two inches more than either of his brothers were to attain. Certainly in terms of looks and physique there was no indication of the ill health that dogged him during his school and university days. Whether weak-chested or simply prone to infection, he certainly made little allowance for the lack of robust health and engaged in a wide range of activities with unflagging enthusiasm. His most notable quality, even at this stage in his development, was his ability to focus on a particular goal, and concentrate his mind and physical efforts until he had achieved his objective. This determination, coupled with his easy manner, slightly scholarly air and abundance of good humour clearly endeared him to his fellows. He made friends easily and inspired confidence. Although in both temperament and sporting prowess Aidan was a far cry from the usual public school 'blood', it was he who was chosen by the Philosophic Body to be their Vice President.

There were a number of comfortable rooms set aside for the use of the Philosophers, including their own refectory, drawing room, and billiard room. But the centrepiece of their existence was the smoking room, refurbished in 1906 from its previously rather austere appearance. It now enjoyed panelled walls and a carved oak Jacobean chimney piece. The clubby atmosphere was further enhanced by the presentation of a collection of big game heads by Lieutenant-Colonel Sir John Lane Harrington, himself a former Philosopher, and at this time British Minister in Abyssinia.

The Philosophers' Diary judged 1907 a good year, noting 'a great deal of esprit de corps among the phils this year'. One manifestation of this was the introduction of 'Top Hat Tea' on the green, which the Philosophers attended in top hats, opera hats, bowlers or any other sort of hat that seemed appropriate. As it was the winter term, they also wore overcoats and most tried to cut a dash by carrying canes or walking sticks. It was also the year of the replacement piano, an instrument that considerably brightened the Philosophers' lives, at times to the consternation of the Jesuits. The selection process was a most serious business and a committee was established consisting of the Senior Philosopher, the Smoking Room Secretary, who considered himself a player of note, and the Head Prefect. Catalogues were studied, salesmen summoned to explain the merits of their various models, and eventually visits were made to both Blackburn and Manchester to test the suitability of various items on offer. It was finally agreed that an auto piano was most suitable for their purposes, and the generous offer made for the old piano enabled them to purchase a very high quality Gors and Kallman piano listed at 115 guineas. It was noted that, 'Its tone was very sweet but very full: played as an ordinary piano by hand, it makes an excellent piano for accompaniments'.[32] The big advantage though was the automatic playing, and subscriptions to two libraries provided the Philosophers with thirty-five music rolls a month.

The Philosophers' Diary recorded the arrival of the new attraction:

Oct 25. Telegram arrives saying that the pianola will arrive at 2.0. However, it does not arrive until 6. After supper Mr Colona opened it with a key - there was a kind of a ceremony - phils gathering round with mouths open. Fr Gibbs stands by pianola holding keys in his hand - Mr Colona advanced and Fr Gibb presents him with the keys. The locks seem to stick and rather spoil the neatness of the ceremony, and take away from the solemnity of it. Mr Colonna then plays a piece of Wagner and the thing is open.[33]

It appears to have been a spectacular success, for a week later on 2 November the log recalls that the Philosophers were not freed for the customary afternoon's sport and recreation as a result of the riotous dancing that had taken place around the piano in the smoking room the previous evening. Although the Jesuits did not approve of this behaviour, the Philosophers clearly judged the piano a huge success. Restrictions were imposed from time to time. The Diary records various instances of excessive high spirits, as in July 1907 when they were 'Not freed' because they felt unable to deliver an undertaking that they would never again fool about during the Philosophy lecture. It was perhaps an ambitious request to have made of them, although their misdemeanours had been serious ones. The fooling appears to have revolved around throwing bullets and the importation of live ducks. Youthful high jinks were punished by denying the Philosophers their privileges and increasing the amount of study time.

Restrictions aside though, life was generally good. Indeed, so attractive was this comfortable existence that many among the previous generations of Philosophers spent three or even four years studying gently with pleasant companions, and enjoying the benefits of country living in what was after all a great house in a magnificent rural setting. It is clear that the atmosphere and character of the lifestyle that prevailed was very much that of the country gentleman. However, as well as British members there were many who came from abroad, and while titles were very rare amongst British Roman Catholics the same could not be said of the foreign students. Aidan's year group of Philosophers numbered twenty-four, of whom eight were English. Of the rest four were Belgian, three Irish, two Hungarian and single representatives came from Canada, Mexico, Germany, Brazil, Malta, Spain and Austria. It was a close-knit but cosmopolitan grouping bound together by a common religious faith, a desire to learn and succeed, and by wealth and privilege. Included among their number were the Hungarian Baron John Josika, who had been previously educated in Vienna, and the Austrian Count Otto Stolberg-Stolberg. Joseph Plunkett[34] an Irish boy, was the son of Count George Plunkett (a Papal Count) and Prince Adolf Schwartzenburg, the lord of vast estates in Bohemia, was to follow on a year behind Aidan. But the Philosophers did not stand on ceremony, titles were not used and double-barrelled names were cut off economically at the hyphen. When the grandson of the Austrian Emperor arrived in 1912, the servants were instructed to refer to the

---

* See Appendix Two, Notes on Persons Mentioned in the Text.

MESSRS. J. VILLAS BOAS, J. SABATES, J. DE WOELMONT, M. TIEFENBACHER, C. COULSTON.
MESSRS. J. KAVANAGH, O. RYAN, C. RYAN, A. DE LICHTERVELDE, R. DE BEAUDIGNIES, G. FOX, H. WIGZELL, O. STOLBERG, A. COOKE.
MESSRS. I. DE LA TORRE, A. ASPHAR, A. LIDDELL, B. SMITH, J. PLUNKETT, J. JOSIKA, J. DE TROOSTEMBERGH.
MESSRS. K. CALLAGHAN, J. EYRE, F. TROUP, F. WALDBOTT.

22. *Stonyhurst Philosophers 1908. They included two Hungarians, an Austrian and a German, as well as an Irishman executed for treason as a ring leader in the Easter Rising of 1916. Photo Stonyhurst Magazine July 1908.*

Archduke Franz Karl as 'Your Highness', but in notices etc. he was referred too simply as 'Archduke'.

The daily routine was, at least in theory, extremely demanding and was designed to give the students eight hours of work or study. They rose at 7 am with daily Mass at 7.30 and breakfast at 8. Then as now the Stonyhurst Jesuits were renowned for the speed at which some could deliver the Mass! For the hardy among them there was also the opportunity for a swift pre-Mass swim in the indoor swimming pool or plunge. The morning was spent in lectures, discussion with the Professors or private study in their rooms or the reference library. The formal published 'Order of the Day' indicates that after dinner at 1 pm the Philosophers were similarly employed for most of the afternoon and much of the evening, albeit with time allowed for the Rosary for ten minutes before supper, which was at 8.10 pm with Night Prayers at 9.45 pm. Sundays were less demanding academically, although there was the addition of two hours of religious instruction and Benediction in the early evening. If this sounds rather severe, to ease the burden Tuesdays were half-holidays and Thursdays whole holidays, which allowed for more extensive recreational pursuits. In reality, even during the working

A. M. D. G.

Stonyhurst Philosophers

Order of the Day.

Sunday.		Week-Days.	
7	Rise.	7	Rise.
7-30	Mass.	7-30	Mass.
8	Breakfast.	8	Breakfast.
	Recreation.		Recreation.
10	Studies.	8-45	Studies.
10-30	Religious Instruction.	12-30	Free Time.
12-30	Free Time.	1	Dinner.
1	Dinner.		Recreation.
	Recreation.	3	Studies.
5-30	Benediction.	5	Recreation.
	Studies.	5-45	Studies.
8-10	Supper.	8	Rosary.
10	Night Prayers.	8-10	Supper.
		9-45	Night Prayers.

On THURSDAY, Recreation before and after Dinner; Evening Studies at 6-30.

On TUESDAY, Recreation after Dinner; Studies at 6,—but after Easter at 6-30.

On SATURDAY, Benediction at 5-35; Studies at 6; Exhortation at 7-25; Supper at 8; Night Prayers at 9-35.

On the eve of a High Mass Day Recreation ends as on Saturday.

On a High Mass Day, Recreation before and after the Second Mass; Studies at 6-30.

Whenever there is Benediction at 9, Supper is at 8, and the end of Recreation at 10.

This order is to be faithfully observed by all.

week dispensations were often granted from the formal regime and many afternoons were spent in sport with soccer being the winter game and cricket played in the summer. But despite the services of a professional soccer coach being available at a guinea a term, Aidan was still not an enthusiastic games player. He enjoyed tennis, played at golf to be sociable and was a willing participant in the annual Philosophers' Handicap Golf Tournament.

Country pursuits were also popular, and Philosophers might arrange a riding party or join a meet of the Pendle Harriers. There was stabling for those that brought horses and mounts could be hired locally. As the Philosophers of 1908 photograph indicates, there was also kennelling for dogs. Aidan's particular interests, however, were shooting and fishing. The *Stonyhurst Magazine* recorded in 1906:

> The first covert shoot took place on Nov 8th and Hodder wood was shot through. There were 7 guns, Messrs Spranger Harrison, C. Trappes-Lomax and F. Berkeley, all past Philosophers with Messrs A. Liddell, B. Smith and R. de Trafford representing the present Philosophers. A very high wind and several cold showers of rain spoiled the sport; and although many birds were seen, most passed out of range. The bag consisted of 22 pheasants, 12 rabbits and 1 hare.[35]

It was a slow start, but when the shooting season came to an end in April the total bag was described as ' a very creditable one', comprising 135 pheasants, 2 partridges, 2 woodcocks, 14 wild ducks, 28 hares, 246 rabbits, 5 various, making a total of 432 heads. Perhaps surprising in view of the open waters adjacent to Stonyhurst was the small number of wild ducks, but the following season, with Aidan as the Shooting Secretary, things were rather different, as the guns applied themselves to the Stonyhurst ponds or canals on the avenue at the front of the College. The *Stonyhurst Magazine* takes up the story:

> There were 180 wild-duck on the Avenue ponds before the shooting began. It speaks much for the patience of the 'guns' that the numbers have been considerably thinned. The birds quickly rose to the fact that they would only be shot in the air, and they rose no more. All vulgar missiles failed to make them leave the water; and when they were literally swept with trailing rope and pendant branches to the very end of the pond, they sturdily waddled across the road, and all had to begin again on a new piece of water. Fortunately at intervals their fears flew away with some and they lost their heads. There survive about forty.[36]

Out of season there was the quaintly labelled Inanimate Bird Shooting Club, which has an altogether more gentlemanly ring to it than clay pigeon shooting. Fishing was Aidan's other great love and the Stonyhurst fisheries on the Hodder and Ribble enjoyed a fine reputation in those days. One of the largest salmon caught in the Hodder for over twenty years was caught by a Mr Harrison at Riley Pool near Whitewell in 1907. It weighed 32 lb, was 3 ft 7 in long with a girth of 2 ft 3 in, and took nearly two hours to land. Enthused by reports of this success Aidan accompanied a former Philosopher Mr Moylan, who was visiting from India, on two expeditions to the Ribble and Hodder. They even managed to entice old Will, the veteran Stonyhurst gamekeeper and fisherman, out of retirement to act as guide. He had become a legend to generations of Stonyhurst fishermen, and with the help of 'Owd Till's' craft and cunning, and his special knowledge of the waters, they hoped to emulate Mr Harrison. It was not to be, but 'Owd Till's' magic had not deserted him. While the Philosophers old and new returned empty-handed, the old man was rather more successful, bringing home 'two handsome salmon landed on a cast 20 years old'.[37] As well as being a keen country sportsman, Aidan was a naturalist and scientist. One of his long sighted actions as Fishing Secretary was to establish a small trout hatchery to keep up the stock of good trout in the ponds and to help replenish the Hodder.

Other activities were perhaps a little more cultural or cerebral. The Philosophers' annual play was a notable and much-anticipated event that provided entertainment for the entire school, but there were also regular Smoking Concerts held in the smoking room at which the Philosophers and their Professors provided musical and comical entertainment for their fellows. Sometimes professional musicians were engaged, but it was for the most part home-grown entertainment, at which whisky had become the customary beverage. Another much-anticipated event was the annual Philosopher's 'Good Day', the final treat of the academic year. Originally introduced as a day of country pursuits, it had by Aidan's time developed into a day out to Blackpool or Southport, usually by chauffeur-driven motor. It would be rounded off with a slap up feed at a suitably imposing establishment, such as Blackpool's Hotel Metropole. Perhaps this accounts for Aidan's uncanny ability to find a decent restaurant no matter how unlikely his location!

The Philosophers also continued the Stonyhurst tradition of debating and had their own society, designed to preserve their dignity from exposure to the younger boys. For Aidan his deep interest in astronomy doubtless endured and he continued his association with his friend Fr Cortie, not just through the observatory, but also with the orchestra, which the latter conducted while Aidan continued to play his flute and piccolo. He also retained his interest in the aviary, presenting a pair of nuthatches in his final year.

At the heart of Aidan Liddell's life as a Philosopher were his studies and his preparation for a scholarship to Balliol College Oxford with the emphasis on biology and zoology. The *Stonyhurst Magazine* recorded in Feb 1907 that:

> The Philosophy Academy was opened by an excellent essay on 'Theories of Colour Vision' in which Mr A Liddell brought out well the phenomena that have to be explained by any satisfactory theory of colour vision, showed how the two principal theories harmonised with the data and indicated the chief obstacles to further advance.[38]

At Easter 1908 John Liddell attended the annual Stonyhurst Visitors' Retreat, as did one FF Urquhart, a Fellow at Balliol College and an old friend of Fr Cortie. Francis Fortesque Urquhart was known universally as 'Sligger', meaning the sleek one. It was a name acquired in youth and it lasted him a life-time. It seems reasonable to suppose that Sligger was probably the reason that Aidan chose to apply for entrance to Balliol. A Roman Catholic, he had attended Hodder in 1879, and in 1881 went on to Beaumont College, another Jesuit Public School, in Old Windsor. Sligger returned to Stonyhurst College as a Philosopher in 1886, where he studied for an external London University degree in Latin and Greek, graduating with Honours in 1889. Thereafter, he started in residence at Balliol, reading Modern History. On graduation he was elected to a Fellowship, becoming the first Roman Catholic to become a Tutorial Fellow at Oxford since the Reformation.

Sligger would have met with Aidan that Easter and talked with John Liddell and Fr Cortie about the young man's future prospects at Oxford. In common with many other Balliol men it was to be for Aidan the start of a friendship that lasted a lifetime. But as well as prayer and talk of Balliol, there was also that Easter the excitement of the Cadet Corps' Annual Manoeuvres.

These were conducted on a grand scale, at least in the military terminology that was used. Four battalions of *Blue Force* were detailed to provide the military escort for an important convoy that was moving along the road from Whalley via Lower Hodder Bridge and Hurst Green to Preston. The convoy was, however, blocked by a similar number of *Red Force*, also organised in four battalions, but supported by pom-pom guns. The Boer War influence was not hard to discern.

Red Force, as it happened somewhat unwisely, determined on a bold and aggressive strategy, and marched forward to meet the convoy in total ignorance of the carefully sited screening forces that *Blue Force* had put in place. The attack commenced on Easter Monday at about 2.30 pm. The *Reds* swung round the south end of the Mill Wood and advanced in column straight up through the belt of trees and across the avenue where they met with very heavy fire from entrenched *Blue* troops in the Clump and Park Wood. The *Reds* then took cover in a belt of trees by the Hockey

Ground before advancing in open order up the slope, over the park wall and across the golf links. Believing from reports passed by scouts and signallers that the Clump was weakly held, the *Red* commander pushed a determined frontal assault right through Park Wood. It was a brave show, but the experienced Umpire ruled the virtual annihilation of *Red Force*, which he judged to have shown masses of offensive spirit but had advanced with little attention to cover, against an entrenched enemy armed with modern weapons. The lessons of the day were at the time very clear, and the Manoeuvres were watched with great interest by many boys, masters and visitors who had walked up the avenue to observe the spectacle. Sligger even managed to photograph the event, before the victors and vanquished, living and dead, marched home again for tea.

Aidan sat his scholarship papers for Balliol in July 1908 at the end of his time at Stonyhurst, and his examining Fellow was the brilliant and practically minded scientist and scholar Harold Hartley. It is difficult to

23. Aidan and Veronica in the grounds at Sherfield 1909. Photo Mark Liddell.

24. *The marquee on the terrace of Aidan's Coming of Age celebrations. 3 August 1909. Photo Mark Liddell.*

piece together exactly what happened that July from the fragmentary jottings in an old exercise book. However, it is clear that Harold Hartley warmed to Aidan, noting of his work 'thin, but inclined to be interesting and thoughtful'. This was rather more fulsome than the comments attributed to some of the other names in that book, which included 'poor stuff. . .not striking, several howlers', 'v scrappy and immature' and 'dull, very little promise'.[39]

Unfortunately, Aidan's efforts were not enough to win him the scholarship he desired, although he did secure a place as a commoner at Balliol, reading Natural Sciences. It was obviously a great disappointment for a young man already accustomed to achievement and success, but Stonyhurst was now behind him, his place at the Varsity secure, and the Liddell family had moved in June to their magnificent new home at Sherfield Manor near Basingstoke. What is more, in less than a month Aidan would be twenty-one.

25. *Family group for Aidan's Coming of Age celebrations. 3 August 1909. Photo Mark Liddell.*

With his coming of age on 3 August 1909, Aidan formally became the young squire, and the heir to the newly acquired estate at Sherfield and the Lordship of the Manor. It was a cause for considerable rejoicing, and gave the family the opportunity to celebrate Aidan's birthday and to stage a wonderful house-warming party for family and friends at Sherfield. It was a lavish affair, running over several days, and provided an ideal opportunity for John Liddell to introduce the family to their new community. A great marquee was erected on the terrace overlooking the formal gardens, for dining and dancing. Family and friends travelled from across the country to attend the festivities and visit the grand new house. Aidan's principal birthday present from his father was a pair of matching shotguns. It seems a safe assumption that these would have been pressed into service the following week and that the skills acquired as Shooting Secretary at Stonyhurst would have been put to good use on the grouse moor on the 'Glorious Twelfth'. For Aidan, with Oxford beckoning in the autumn and a long hot summer to while away, it must have seemed a wonderful world full of promise and opportunities.

Chapter Five

Peter at Balliol

Balliol was by all accounts a rather special place, although with drafty corridors, stone-flagged passages, smoky fires and youthful high spirits, there was much that would have seemed very familiar to Aidan. But an autumn in bustling Edwardian Oxford, beneath the dreaming spires, must have been an infinitely more appealing prospect than another wet and windy Lancastrian winter.

Balliol College had existed as an academic community since around 1263 when John de Balliol, the powerful Lord of Barnard Castle, endowed a home for scholars as a charitable act of atonement. On that basis it is the oldest college at either Oxford or Cambridge. When Aidan went there in 1908 numbers were still low by modern standards and in 1910 records show only 183 students in residence. Most were undergraduates, with a few graduates who stayed on for research or more advanced work. There were also about a dozen Fellows, again surprisingly few by comparison with contemporary Oxford, and most of these played an active role in the supervision of the undergraduates. Tutors worked very closely with their charges, teaching long hours, and like the Professors at Stonyhurst College enjoyed a close association that would be considered unusual today. It was generally expected among the older Fellows that Tutors should be not be married, and should live in College. Indeed, Tutorial Fellows elected whilst still single were not permitted to marry in their first seven years. There was also a requirement for four single members of the academic staff to live in College. Relations between students and tutors at Balliol were thus close and informal, and Dons and students were on first name terms, often using nicknames.

It was said that the Balliol community at this time was as diverse as any at the University. The public schools, both great and small, were well represented with Old Etonians in abundance. There were also grammar school boys, as well as significant numbers of undergraduates from overseas, in part because Balliol was a popular destination for the newly founded and funded Rhodes Scholars. There were thus also students from the British Empire, the United States of America and Germany. Famously, the new Prime Minister, HH Asquith, himself a Balliol man, attended a dinner at the House of Commons hosted by other alumni

Parliamentarians in July 1908, and spoke of 'the tranquil consciousness of effortless superiority'[40] which was the mark of the Balliol man. This might have been seen as mere self indulgence, on the part of one highly successful Balliol graduate, but outsiders too recognised the magic of the place. One such was John Buchan, a member of Brasenose, who drew parallels between the brilliant Balliol of his own time in the closing years of the nineteenth century, and the sparkling years before the Great War that Aidan was to witness.

> The Balliol generation of my time was, I think, the most remarkable in Oxford, only to be paralleled by the brilliant group, containing Charles Lister and the Grenfells, which flourished on the eve of the War. It was distinguished both for its scholars and its athletes, but it made no parade of its distinctions, carrying its honours lightly as if they fell to it in the ordinary processes of nature. It delighted unpedantically in things of the mind, but it had an engaging youthfulness, too, and was not above high-jinks and escapades.[41]

Aidan and his contemporaries were talented, usually rich and privileged, and had the clear-headed conviction that whatever they chose to do, they would do it well and be successful. It was a powerful self-belief that came from the knowledge that generations of Balliol men had been counted among the great and the good, and had served Great Britain and the Empire in high office. The expectations amongst the young men who arrived at Balliol in the autumn of 1908 were that they too would serve their country with distinction and reap their just rewards.

The lives of Balliol men were very carefully regulated during term. It was a requirement to present oneself under the gateway in academic dress before 8 am during the working week, where names were taken by the Head Porter, the popular Ezra Hancock. He had been appointed Under-Porter in 1878 and became Head Porter from 1891. A kind-hearted and tactful man, blessed with a prodigious memory, he was greatly loved and respected by generations of Balliol men.

Chapel was compulsory on Sundays, unless parents asked for dispensation, and it would seem likely that the Roman Catholic Aidan was excused from this particular part of the regime. Undergraduates had to remain at Oxford during term and leave of absence was formally required and granted only for very special reasons. Students were expected to dine in the Hall, but were permitted to sign off from time to time. Breakfast and lunch were less formal and usually taken in student rooms, the servants or scouts carrying trays of food and drink from the College kitchens. Additional or luxury items could also be provided, sometimes supervised by the College Butler, Mr Pusey. He did his best to offer the young gentlemen sage advice on the need for thrift and economy when at Oxford. Things might seem inexpensive, but the shillings could quickly mount, and he solemnly warned the young men that it was only too easy to travel in the direction of pounds. It seems unlikely that many in Aidan's set would have found it necessary to heed this well meant advice.

The rooms themselves were generous, normally comprising sets of a study/sitting room and an adjoining bedroom. They were fully furnished and lit by electricity. Heating was by coal fire, and water required for washing or shaving had to be carried in, or a journey taken to the invariably far-off bathrooms. While a far cry from the luxuries of the recently renovated Sherfield Manor, the comforts of Balliol, electric light aside, must have seemed remarkably similar to Stonyhurst.

Aidan was one of fifty-four new students listed in the Balliol Record for 1908/09. His tutor was the man who had examined him for entrance, Harold Hartley. Hartley had been educated at Dulwich College and went to Balliol as a Brackenbury Scholar, reading Chemistry and obtaining a First in the Schools of 1901. Before even obtaining his

27. Balliol Freshmen 1908. (Aidan, back row 6th from left.) Photo Balliol College.

degree he was elected to a Fellowship, so beginning a lifelong association with the College.* Another memorable figure was Neville Talbot, the Junior Dean. He was a giant of a man, who had distinguished himself in the Boer War before taking Holy Orders. Jolly, loud and very boisterous, it was not unknown for him to tip pitchers of water over late-rising students as they scuttled under his rooms on the way to the bathroom. And of course there was Sligger, who was to become a particular friend of Aidan's, as he was to so many Balliol men. Sligger's rooms, over the back gate, with massive bay windows overlooking the Protestant Martyrs' Memorial were one of the social centres of the college. He liked to talk, he liked people, and they liked him. There were tea parties, lunch parties and dinner parties. As Sligger remarked, '. . . there are not half enough meals in the day for it is only then that you can really meet people.'[42]

He was an extraordinary clever, decent and civilising force at Balliol. A pupil wrote of him:

The kind of history for which Sligger stood which you breathed when you came into his room, was the kind to appeal to young men of wide interest and eager minds. It was really humanistic: he put you on to the big French books with style and ideas and real culture behind them, and made you want to be an educated and civilised man.[43]

All students of whatever discipline were welcome, so that Sligger's rooms became a Balliol and Oxford institution. He held court night after night, sitting in a low chair or squatting cross-legged like some Eastern potentate on the stool before the roaring fire. Like many of his contemporaries he never married, nor did he contribute significantly to original thought as an academic. His calling was rather to shape and influence young minds. He enjoyed it immensely and his students did too.

In general he appeared more happily at ease with the young than with his contemporaries and seniors, and he had an almost miraculous gift – born of his own genuine interest and affection – of making the gulf of years vanish or rather never be perceived.[44]

But as well as a talker Sligger was a great walker. Indeed, while at Stonyhurst he was one of the very few people to have walked to the source of the River Hodder. His family had a chalet near Saint-Gervais in the French Alps, and year after year he would invite groups of students to summer reading parties in the Alps, teaching them the lore of the mountains.

The Master at this time was the classicist J L Strachan Davidson, who it was said never remembered the names of undergraduates, nor who they were or what they did. Stories abounded of confusing meetings in dusty corridors in which the kindly Master greeted his students by name,

* See Appendix Two, Notes in Persons Mentioned in the Text.

the wrong name, and then attributed to them inaccurate academic or sporting attainment, and mistaken countries of origin. ' Ahh, your name is Higgins isn't it?' 'No Master, Liddell.' 'You come from Scotland don't you?' 'No Master, Hampshire.'

It was the custom for undergraduates to dine formally with the Master in his lodge in groups. It was all carefully orchestrated and at precisely 9.20 pm the senior undergraduate would ask to take his leave, and his peers would rapidly follow. These dinners were not regarded as being riotously jolly occasions. However, Strachan Davidson did have a large cat called Tiberius, which was invariably present in the lodge. When conversation flagged, an oft-used filler was to comment 'My word Master, Tiberius is looking well today' while desperately searching for a suitably impressive follow-on remark.

Amongst the contemporaries who shared those few years at Balliol were many who would make their mark in the world. They included Philip Guedalla, a historian destined for the world of academe; Vincent Massey, a Canadian who was to become Governor General; Walter Monkton, lawyer, politician and confidante of King Edward VIII; Cyril Asquith son of the Prime Minister; and Friedrich von Bethman Hollweg, son of the German Chancellor. Others were Ronald Knox, who subsequently converted to Roman Catholicism, and translated the bible from the Latin *Vulgate* into English; the author Aldous Huxley; the poet Julian Grenfell; and Peter Wimsey, the second son of the fifteenth Duke of Denver.[*]

Aidan Liddell had proved himself an immensely likeable and popular young man at Stonyhurst College and he had the intelligence and personality to do equally well at Oxford. It was now that the family nickname Peter was adopted by an increasing number of his friends. Balliol was clearly a challenging environment and was certainly regarded by many as the epicentre of university life. Despite this, Aidan did not shine academically, and later Harold Hartley was to attribute his modest performance to his still unspecified poor health. He wrote to Aidan's mother in September 1915:

> Aidan always interested me, he had very unusual gifts, and I felt
> that he ought to do something big. While he was at Oxford he was
> never really fit, and I hoped that afterwards he would get stronger. I
> remember how anxious you used to be when he was ill.[45]

But despite the unspecific ailments there was certainly a wide range of cultural, sporting and leisure activities to occupy the undergraduates when they grew bored of their academic studies. There was a flourishing musical society, with five concerts a term, and special performances during Eights Week. No doubt this gave Aidan ample opportunity to continue his interest in music. Rowing was an immensely popular sport

[*] Lord Peter Wimsey became a distinguished detective and was the inspiration for Dorothy L Sayer's fictional creation.

at Balliol, exerting an almost religious fervour among its adherents, including many of the Old Etonians that Aidan soon began to count among his friends. There was also tennis, cricket, soccer and hockey, and Balliol fielded a particularly strong rugby side. But as at Stonyhurst, Aidan stood aside from team games.

One of his first activities was to seek out and join the Newman Society, which was the Roman Catholic society at Oxford, as indeed it still is today. Activities then centred around debates and guest speakers and in his first term there was a paper read by the Right Rev. Prior Cummins, OSB, entitled 'The execution of Darnley, a plea for Mary Queen of Scots'. No doubt this was a suitably uplifting evening for devout young Roman Catholics, but at the next session topicality returned with a debate on the motion that 'Conscription is the only remedy for unemployment'. Aidan spoke first against the motion and no doubt also attended the final meeting of the term – a motion condemning the Chancellor's contentious proposal to admit women to degrees at Oxford. The outcome is not recorded, but women seem to have figured hardly at all in the lives of the undergraduates and their mentors. They appeared for Eights Week and for Commemoration Balls but were otherwise rarely seen, and certainly did not intrude into the lives or rooms of the members. Topicality at the Newman Society was maintained the following year with a motion that 'The present government's naval policy is inadequate' – which was passed with only a single dissenting voter. The opposition were unable to convince the House of their argument that the German toast to 'Our Life on the Water' was no threat to Great Britain but simply a temperance motto. At another meeting Hilaire Belloc read a paper on 'The Church and Reality' and delighted the audience with his forcible arguments and clever wit. They were clearly stunned by the performance as the record of the meeting read 'the subject was a deep one and no very lengthy discussion was possible'.[46]

Aidan also joined the Oxford Union, and was co-opted onto the Library Committee over the period between Easter 1909 and Easter 1910. There he served alongside fellow Balliol men Arthur Macmillan, the brother of the future Prime Minister and Philip Guedalla the historian. Debating was a popular pastime, and the Oxford Union provided the showcase, with some particularly topical events attracting audiences of over 500. However, during his time at Oxford there is no record of Aidan speaking formally at any of the numerous debates.

There were also debating and dining societies within Balliol itself, although one suspects that there was rather more dining and carousing than serious discussion. The three in Aidan's time were the Annandale, the Brackenbury and the Arnold. It was said that the Annandale washed but didn't work, that Arnold worked but didn't wash, and that the

Brackenbury attempted to do both, albeit with no obvious success in either area of endeavour. Aidan was a member of the Annandale, a society that was much favoured by Old Etonians and had an outrageous reputation for wildly excessive parties. Nothing was safe or sacred on the evening of an 'Anna' dinner. A favourite trick was to arrange for a cascade of College crockery to tumble like a waterfall down the hall steps, causing vast amusement to the merry onlookers. Fortunately, the pockets of the members were deep and next morning they would cheerfully pay for the damage. The Honourable Charles Lister was one of the most excessive members of the Annandale/Eton set. He was eventually rusticated in 1908 for forcing the Dean of Trinity to dance with him around a bonfire following a party. His departure was marked with a lavish mock funeral and a memorial inscription was carved into the stone of his staircase.

There were of course activities for Aidan beyond Oxford, and at Easter 1909 he returned to Stonyhurst with his father John to attend the annual Visitors' Retreat. The event was led by the impressive Fr Bernard Vaughan SJ, and attracted an unusually large number of attendees, who followed his stimulating meditations and addresses with the greatest interest. He also preached, in St Peter's Church, both on Good Friday and on Easter Sunday. The church was crowded on both occasions, but the numbers that appeared on Good Friday were quite exceptional, with crowds gathering outside the church several hours before the doors were opened. A massed congregation of some 1200 crowded into every available nook and cranny, with many travelling from neighbouring towns in 'motors brakes and wagonettes'. The sermon was a huge success, one local man commenting in broad Lancashire dialect 'I could hearken to 'im while mornin'.[47]

That summer Aidan was invited by Sligger to be one of the guests for the forthcoming chalet party in the Alps. This was a coveted honour among the undergraduates, for Sligger chose the make-up of these groups with care. That year there were to be two groups and Aidan went with the first for the month of July, together with seven other 'chalet-ites' as they were dubbed. The regime was simple; rise at about 8 am, take a cold shower, work from breakfast to lunch, games or a walk in the afternoon, work again between tea and dinner, and after dinner talk. Meals were plain but plentiful, and largely vegetarian. There was often lentils and salad that Sligger dressed himself, and while there was water at lunch there was always '*vin ordinaire*' at dinner.

It was a magical place, with breathtaking views, and an ever-changing vista of mountains and clouds, as Sligger himself described.

I am writing this on the lawn, waiting for the sunset. It's a cloudy one. Great clouds with golden edges heaped up all along the Avaris

28. Sligger's chalet near Saint-Gervais. Photo Balliol College.

with rays here and there piercing through holes and making a great beam across the valley. Then there is the delicious mellow colour far away in the distance behind the Charvin and in the gap over Cluses.[48]

The rules of the house were clear-cut and simple. To make them absolutely clear Sligger wrote them down, in an extensive document that he dubbed 'The Perfect Chalet-ite'. Written with a kindly twinkle the 'PC-ite' as it was called offers a wonderful insight into the mind of the man, and into the leisurely and gentle experience of the young men who joined him for those holidays. He got straight to the point, stating without equivocation:

The perfect Chalet-ite, as he is a very intelligent and thoughtful young man, will realize that when a number of young men are gathered together, especially in a rather out-of-way place, there is a great danger of their getting slack and indifferent in many of the little observances of social life, and that it is important to react against this and keep up a certain standard: for instance, he will wear a coat at luncheon and, as a symbol of respect for the others he will wear a tie at dinner, he will be decent even in hot weather, he will not make too much noise when going to bed, remembering that the servants go to bed early and that the house is very 'transparent' to sound. A party keeps together on better terms and gets through more work if its members practise self-restraint in all these small but important things.[49]

This heartfelt and wise general advice was supplemented by a vast array of additional detail ranging from 'The "PC-ite" will not bump his head on the stair more than once' to 'The "PC-ite" will not burn down the Chalet. He will even be extra careful not to do so. Reading in bed with the candle on the pillow may be dangerous'. This was a masterly understatement for in 1906 someone did burn down the Chalet, necessitating a complete rebuild which was completed in 1909.

The 'PC-ites' in July 1909 were an outstanding group. Mervyn Bournes Higgins was from Melbourne and was reading jurisprudence. He went on to win his Blue in the bow of the victorious Oxford boat of 1910. There was Ted Kay-Shuttleworth who was reading history. The second son of Lord Shuttleworth, he was an extremely popular and strikingly good-looking Old Etonian, who was determined to enjoy his time at Oxford to the full, but had at the same time great strength of character and a deeply religious faith. Walter George Fletcher was another Old Etonian and had been Captain of Eton in his last half. Thickset and slightly ungainly, he was a young man of great patriotic fervour, and another accomplished oar. He rowed for Leander and spent some time in Germany after graduation. Hugh Martin had been educated at Edinburgh Academy and played rugby for Oxford and Balliol. Alexander Cardew was a Repton man and a fine cricketer who captained the College XI. The other two, Cardwell and Bunkway, who appear with Aidan in a holiday photograph (see right) were not from Balliol and so there is no record of their background.

29. *Aidan at the chalet with Cardwell and Bunkway. Photo Balliol College.*

Contemporary photographs portray a most enjoyable Alpine interlude, with long walks along rushing mountain rivers, studded walking boots, wide-brimmed hats, high-buttoned tweed jackets, snow fields and stout sticks. There was also cricket and golf, both played to heavily modified local rules, which included frequent warnings as to the vulnerability of the Chalet to a misjudged shot. Inside the Chalet, the look was shabby but comfortable. Some 'Chalet-ites' returned in other years, but not Aidan. Perhaps he was not perfect enough for Sligger, or maybe there were other calls on his summer time. Whatever the reason, the Alpine interlude of 1909 was clearly a great success, although the sad footnote is that of the eight young men who gathered at Saint-Gervais that July at least four did not survive the Great War.[*]

There is little recorded of Aidan's academic work, but we know he was a capable scientist with a deep interest in the natural world. Responsions[**] gave way to his Natural Science Preliminaries, and armed with his own large brass microscope, a keen investigative mind, and a wonderful skill as a draughtsman, he published a paper describing a new genus of microscopic parasite that he had discovered on the King Crab *Limulus*.

Away from his studies and the excesses of the Annandale Society, Aidan continued to develop his interest in modern technology, engines and speed. He now had his own car, and enjoyed a reputation as a dare-devil driver. Harold Hartley alluded briefly to this writing, 'He was of a very friendly, easy going disposition, and only his intimate friends, perhaps, and those who had motored with him at night, realized the nerve and grit that was in him'.[50]

He was also a keen motorcyclist, and a very active member of the Varsity Motor Cycle Club, serving on the Committee and competing in their many events. His own bike, or at least the one he is pictured riding (see page 76), is almost certainly a Kerry with a Kelecom engine, dating from around 1908. DR15 on the mudguard is not a registration number, and was probably for racing purposes. Other records of his riding prowess are sketchy, but we know that he finished fourth in an event known as the Dashwood Hill Climb, travelling at an average speed of 36 mph. He suffered an injury to his knee in autumn 1909, which left him 'laid up' for some weeks. It would seem likely that the Kerry motorcycle was in some way responsible for the damage. As well as riding, there was also the question of motor-cycle maintenance. At Stonyhurst Aidan had developed a deep interest in all things mechanical, and this endured at Oxford. It was in part a necessity. The early motorcycle was an extremely exclusive machine. Garages were scarce and mechanics even rarer, so that the enthusiast did much of the repairs and maintenance himself. 'Oozy' Liddell revelled in it.

---

[*] Aidan, Kay-Shuttleworth, Higgins and Fletcher all died in the war. Cardwell and Bunkway were not from Balliol and so their fate is not known. The gloomy odds are perhaps not quite as surprising as they might at first seem. Of the 900 or so Balliol men who served in the Great War almost 200 were killed and another 200 were wounded. The War was to have a profound effect on the College as it did on so much else in England.
[**] The first examination for BA degree at Oxford University.

30. Aidan on his Kerry racing machine. Photo Mark Liddell.

In 1912, at the end of Aidan's final term, there was a particularly memorable Annandale Society dinner, which was described in great detail in a letter penned by ETN Grove to his girlfriend in the aftermath of the event. He offered the following general background:

There is in Balliol a society called the Annandale Society which consists of the 20 jolliest men in the college – in fact the only jolly men in the college. Mostly Etonians. The rest of the College who are pigs and unpleasant, who wear dirty shirts and come from Dulwich hate the Annandale Society because they say they are arrogant, offensive and exclusive.[51]

The Annandale Society included among its members Cecil Asquith, the son of the Prime Minister; Billy Grenfell, the younger brother of the poet Julian; Walter Monkton who would play the role of confidant to King Edward VIII during the abdication crisis; and of course Aidan. The great event was dubbed the 'Anna Two Thousand Years Ago Dinner' and was a prehistoric event. Costumes were brought in from London, and all the diners wore immense skins, huge red wigs and beards, and carried prehistoric clubs. Their faces were liberally daubed with woad and vermillion. Because it was prehistoric, knives and forks and spoons, although obligingly laid up by the College staff, were disregarded and soup was lapped, and meat torn. Conversation was conducted in

31. *Cavemen at the Annandale 1912 dinner. Photo Balliol College.*

guttural grunts.   ETN Grove takes up the story:

> After dinner we adjourned to College, feeling extraordinarily prehistoric, and preceded to business. We systematically broke the windows and heads of all the people who had taken a prominent part against the society. Also we threw their beds out of their windows onto the street. The College fled at our approach and indeed 20 desperate prehistoric men all blue must have seemed a bit awesome. But never the less it was the great fighting there was. When we had done our job we whooped around the quad and smashed a few lights and then went to our caves. Next morning there was trouble. . .[52]

The trouble was that three of the cavemen, including Grove, were sent down for a term. Billy Grenfell, who had set about a senior don with a papier mâché club, was sent down for a year. As Grove so cloquently put it 'Sorrow descended on the Annandale Society'.

Shortly thereafter Aidan graduated with Third Class Honours in Zoology. He had spent his time at Oxford in the company of some of the most talented young men of his generation. Clubs, societies, debates and dinners, were very much the order of the day, but while many of his contemporaries burned off their excess energy on the sports field or the river, for Aidan his particular interest was in technology and speed. For

77

a short time though he considered continuing with his scientific endeavours and was offered a travelling scholarship to investigate the fauna of Krakatoa in the Straits of Sunda, which had been devastated by the violent volcanic eruption of 1883. In the event, he decided to remain at home at Sherfield Manor where he was now the young Squire.

Chapter Six

The Young Squire

Krakatoa must have seemed a very long way away, whereas Sherfield manor offered the comfortable prospect of friends and acquaintances, and the opportunity to enjoy the proximity of the close-knit Liddell family. There was also much work to be done about the house and particularly in the garden, where Aidan and his mother worked very hard to lay out the grounds to their own requirements. This was the time that Aidan began to plan and set out his own section of the grounds, which for many years afterwards was to be known as 'Peter's Garden'.

Aidan had made another notable decision that summer. Oxford had an extremely active Officer Training Corps, with seven or eight hundred members. This was far larger than Cambridge, but was a clear reflection of the patriotic fervour that was sweeping the country in those last few years before the Great War. Aidan had never joined, but many of his friends were with the Oxford University Officers' Training Corps, and he now determined that with time on his hands it was right that he should do his bit. His young brothers both aspired to military careers. Lance was a midshipman at Osborne, and Bertie, who had recently passed out of Sandhurst, was now a cornet in the 15th Hussars. He had sailed for South Africa in December 1911 to join his Regiment at

32 Portrait in dinner jacket. Photo Mark Liddell.

Potchefstroom. While Aidan did not see military service as a long-term career, it offered the prospect of excitement and a focus for a few years, and what is more it was something worth while. In his own words, 'not wishing to be a slacker', he joined the Special (Reserve) of Officers, and in June 1912 was granted a commission with the 3rd Volunteer Battalion of the Argyll and Sutherland Highlanders (A&SH).

Why Aidan Liddell, son of a Hampshire landowner with an estate near Basingstoke, should choose to join a Highland Regiment with its Depot in Stirling Castle remains something of a mystery. His maternal grandfather had been an officer in the Cameronians, but that rather tenuous link is about as far as the Scottish military antecedents can be stretched. Oxford connections would seem to offer the most likely explanation, and through the good offices of one Colonel Ferguson his place was secured. The shooting and fishing in Scotland, it must be remarked, also enjoyed a superlative reputation!

It would be very wrong though to suppose that Aidan's commission was a small matter, lightly acquired and of no lasting consequence. On the contrary, it was a serious undertaking that required considerable commitment. In 1908 the old Militia units ceased to exist in their previous form and were replaced by Special Reserve Battalions, still linked to regular infantry regiments. For Special Reserve officers, training was given in the main by lengthy attachments to regular battalions. After

33. *Aidan in the full dress uniform of the Argyll and Sutherland Highlanders. Fort George circa 1913. Photo Mark Liddell.*

appointment, most of the first year would be spent with the appropriate regular unit, and Aidan was to find himself spending much of his time with the 2nd Battalion of the Argyll and Sutherland Highlanders. The second year was perhaps not quite so demanding, but six months with a regular battalion was not unusual, together with a variety of courses and camps. It was all rather different from Oxford.

Thus it was that Christmas 1912 found Aidan at Fort George, on the southern shores of the Moray Firth, a little to the east of Inverness. He was attached to the 2nd Battalion, Argyll and Sutherland Highlanders, or the old 93rd, as they were still known. These soldiers were the successors of the 93rd Sutherland Highlanders who at Balaclava in 1854 were among the few British troops defending the town against a major Russian assault. The orders had been to stand and fight and the 93rd faced a mass Russian cavalry charge. The 93rd fought in an extended line only two men deep and fired in controlled volleys from 600 yards until the charging horsemen broke. A Russian cavalryman is said to have explained their defeat by saying 'We expected to fight soldiers not red devils'. The 'thin red line' of the 93rd at Balaclava became a Victorian legend.

Aidan wrote home to his sisters Dolly and Monica at Sherfield Manor on 2 January describing regimental life. As a forerunner of things to come, the family were already keeping him supplied with little extras to ease the discomfort of soldiering. The scarf the girls had provided was particularly welcome, especially as on 2 January the 93rd had conducted a 'regimental exercise'. All the officers had assembled on 'some blasted heath' and 'pretended that the enemy were going to try and capture the place, which no one but a lunatic would want. . .' The newly acquired garment made all the difference though, for as Aidan remarked 'It was very windy and cold and the scarf saved my life, as we were standing about for about four hours'.[53] But of the outcome of the exercise, one can only assume that it was not remarkable enough to deserve a mention.

Much more memorable had been the Christmas and New Year festivities shared notably with the Sergeants' Mess.

> We have had great times here. There was a Christmas tree for the soldiers' children. I never knew there could be so many in such a constricted spot. On New Year's Eve there was a smoking concert in the Sergeants' Mess. At 12 midnight they came across to the Officers' Mess where we all consumed quantities of Athol brose, a Scots' emulsion-like product made of cream, honey, oatmeal, whisky and any other liqueurs the Mess Sergeant fancied. After that we adjourned to their mess for the concert where there were innumerable other drinks with all the sergeants in the company. I am the only officer in A Company left here so it fell very heavily on me, and I haven't recovered yet. Added to which (at) the men's New Year Dinner yesterday which had to be attended, more healths drunk in beer and port, so that it will be days before I am myself again.[54]

As Aidan's letter implies, the 93rd were a close-knit military community, at that time living in the massive Hanoverian fortress of Fort George. Built soon after the Jacobite defeat at nearby Culloden Moor, the fort was conceived as a vast defensive base, providing accommodation for a garrison of two infantry battalions and an artillery unit.

Isolated and austere, the military community in 1913 was largely self contained. Regimental routine at Fort George went on much as it had for 150 years, regulated by pipes and drums, with platoon, company, and regimental exercises and, as was the way of British infantry, considerable emphasis on musketry. Marching soldiers, swinging kilts, and when in full dress uniforms, gorgeously apparelled officers were much in evidence. The full dress uniform of an officer in the Argyll and Sutherland Highlanders was extremely elaborate. Topped off with a feather bonnet with white plume, it consisted of a high-collared red jacket with white belt and cross-belt, a scarlet sash, kilt with dress sporran, hose, spats and black shoes. It was completed with a plaid and brooch, and a highland broadsword. The overall, and somewhat dramatic effect, can be seen in the picture of Aidan taken at about this time opposite the main gate and guardroom to Fort George (see page 80).

A life regulated by bugle calls, and with the ever present skirl of the pipes, was a far cry from the languid days at Oxford. Reveille was at 6, Cookhouse Call, which heralded breakfast, at 7, with the other meals and significant occurrences of each highly organised and well ordered day being appropriately signalled by a different call. There was a call to turn out the quarter guard, one for the CO's Orderly Room, and others to summon the Orderly Sergeants and Orderly Corporals, with special subtleties to indicate which Company was involved. At 4 pm in the winter and at 6 pm in the summer the Retreat was sounded at sunset, but the regimental day continued. Thereafter, there was an hour's pack drill for defaulters, followed at 10 pm by a parade or tattoo taken by the Orderly Officer and attended by the Company Orderly NCOs. The men were counted in at 9.30 pm each night, and at 10.15 pm the bugler and a piper signalled lights out.

The band were a very important part of regimental life, playing at events in the Officers' and Sergeants' Messes and at other social gatherings. At Guest Nights in the Officers' Mess six pipers marched clockwise around the tables at various stages of the meal displaying the Regimental badge on the banners of their pipes to the diners. Finally though, for the Regimental March, they reversed direction and paraded anti-clockwise, to display the Colonel's badge and that of the Company Commanders on the reverse of the banners.

The Bandmaster of the 93rd at this time was Joseph Ricketts, who composed under the pseudonym of Kenneth J Alford. He was later to become famous as a great Bandmaster whose best known works included 'Colonel Bogey ', 'The Thin Red Line' and 'The Great Little Army'. Indeed, he composed 'Colonel Bogey' while at Fort George, and is said to have received his inspiration for the melody from a round of golf he played with the colonel. Instead of shouting fore, the colonel was in the habit of loudly whistling two notes to warn those playing on ahead of the dangers of an errant ball. Ricketts added additional notes and named the resulting piece 'Colonel Bogey' in honour of his whistling golf partner.

Henceforth Aidan was to spend much time in Scotland with the 93rd, and his brothers also advanced their military careers. The 15th Hussars had returned to England after fourteen years of Foreign Service at the end of 1912 and became part of the Aldershot Command, where they were detailed as Divisional Cavalry. The brothers were therefore able to see each other when Aidan was at home in Sherfield. Similarly, Lance moved on from Osborne in the autumn of 1913 and was appointed a midshipman on the new dreadnought battleship HMS *Monarch*, conveniently serving with the 2nd Battle Squadron at Portsmouth. This was at about the same time that Aidan was sent on a Maxim gun course at the School of Musketry at Hythe from 22 September to 10 October.

The machine-gun was still a very new weapon in the British Army, and an infantry battalion only had two in its order of battle. Aidan, with his interest in technology and innovation, must have relished the prospect. Indeed, from the results, it is clear that he performed exceedingly well and greatly impressed the 93rd. Nine officers from the Scottish Command took part, and of these only two, one of which was Aidan, obtained a distinction. In forwarding the course results the Adjutant at the School of Musketry added a personal handwritten note.

I am very pleased to state you have passed successfully with 'Distinction'. You have distinguished yourself in two ways, one on your certificate, and the other, in that you are the only Special Reserve Officer who gained distinction'.[55]

Another participant on this course was Lieutenant GS Hutchison, who was another Special Reserve officer from the 3rd Battalion. He was to become a particularly close comrade of Aidan's, and would eventually become a distinguished member of the Machine-Gun Corps.

In between the excitement of soldiering, were the demands of life at Sherfield. There were Oxford and Stonyhurst friends to keep up with, a continuing interest in cars and motorcycles, and Aidan's favourite country pursuits of shooting and fishing. And of course there was the garden! A letter to his mother gives the flavour of Sherfield life in the spring of 1913, beginning, 'Just a line, although there is nothing to tell you. I have little to do except prune laurels and play billiards'. This was not altogether true for the Sherfield fisheries were well stocked and that week he and a chum 'had a great time larking about and managed to take 330 trout out of the little ponds, 181 of which were three year olds, and some as large as $1^3/_4$ lb'. Many of these were then, he explained, released into the lake.

Aidan also supervised and encouraged the work of the gardeners,

34. Although not keen on hunting, Aidan shot and fished regularly. Photo Mark Liddell.

which in the case of one Mr Learmouth, was not always a straightforward task. 'Today's grouses' he recounts were '1. The bullfinches have eaten all the buds off a) the lilac, b) the prunus, c) the apples, and I'm not sure that they haven't swallowed the gooseberry bushes whole. 2. He won't be able to do the log garden this spring. Otherwise, he seems cheerful.'[56] Bertie was also managing to get across most weekends and Lance had visited a couple of times too. The next trip out for Aidan was to watch Bertie win sundry point-to-point races at Alton. He also reported on the return of his camera from its 'spring clean' and enclosed some examples of his recent experimentation in 'Autophotography', ending more or less as he had begun, with the reminder that 'There is absolutely nothing exciting in the way of local happenings'.

But there was another burgeoning interest that was taking up more and more of Aidan's time. The last few decades of the nineteenth century had been a time of massive technical achievement, and saw the dawning of a new and increasingly sophisticated age. Railways, the electric telegraph, the telephone, bicycles, electric light, the motor car, wireless, photography and the cinema were just some of technological wonders that had changed or were changing the world. These things fascinated Aidan. There seemed to be no limit to the ingenuity of man, and it was in this progressive and inspirational atmosphere that the early air pioneers were striving to push forward the boundaries of flight. Progress had been extraordinarily rapid. On 17 December 1903 Orville Wright piloted his Flyer aircraft in a fifty-nine-second hop, that was the first manned flight by a powered aircraft. By September 1905, the year of Aidan's Spanish expedition, Wright was able to stay airborne for forty-five minutes and covered almost twenty-five miles. In July 1909 Louis Blériot flew across the Channel, crossing

35. Aidan in reflective mood with pipe. Probably Autophotography. Photo Mark Liddell.

from Calais to Dover in thirty-seven minutes. In one sense Britain was no longer an island!

Flying held an extraordinary fascination for many people, and it is important to understand the place that aviation had won in the national consciousness from the very outset. Indeed, numerous popular authors had for years been producing predictive fiction with such tantalising titles as *The Battle of Dorking* (1871) and *By Aeroplane to the Sun* (1910), and the success of the Wright brothers merely increased both the popularity and the productivity of their efforts. Perhaps the most celebrated British example was HG Wells' *The War in the Air* (1908). In addition, the pioneer pilots in the first decade of the century made headlines, sold newspapers and were fêted as national heroes. Among the air-minded readership were the young men who were not just content to read and marvel, or even to visit the air shows and races, but wanted to be a part of it.

Many of these early pioneers developed their enthusiasm through an interest in the challenges of engineering, technology and speed. It is no surprise that Wilbur and Orville Wright were bicycle engineers. The Belgian wartime ace Willy Coppens enjoyed kite flying as a child, and as a teenager built and raced sand yachts. Immelmann, one of the most famous early German aces, owned motorcycles and rallied motor cars; Hugh Trenchard, the RFC's most celebrated senior commander, was a bobsleigh enthusiast who had competed on the Cresta Run; and the high scoring British ace James McCudden was an ex-RFC mechanic. It is not hard to see how Aidan fitted into the pattern, with his interest in scientific innovation, his practical engineering skills, and his fascination with speed. He was also wealthy, and now a soldier.

Indeed, military men had been quick to appreciate the potential of the aeroplane, although in Britain among the many sceptics was Sir William Nicholson, the Chief of the Imperial General Staff, who famously described aviation as a useless and expensive fad. Despite this less than effusive support, the enthusiasts eventually had their way and on 1 April 1912 an air battalion was formed within the British Army. Tested for the first time during the annual manoeuvres of 1912 the infant Royal Flying Corps made a decisive contribution, and within a few hours General Grierson had valuable air intelligence that enabled him to outmanoeuvre the opposing forces under General Haig. The lesson was not lost on either commander and Grierson's clearly saw that success in war would be impossible without control of the air. So, despite some sceptical senior soldiers who still doubted its utility, military aviation had become a reality.

Aidan's interest in aviation probably began at Oxford, although it has not been documented. Indeed, other than his favoured stunt of leaping from first floor windows clutching an open umbrella, there is no evidence that he took to the air. He did visit aerodromes however, as a series of photographs taken by him at Brooklands testify. These were probably taken in 1912, and were of a particular air event, with the various aircraft numbered for competition. Most of the pictures are identified by Aidan's pencilled commentary on the reverse, and on some the aircraft sheds and banked track are clearly visible. Two other Stonyhurst men were involved with aviation at around this time, and both flew with the Vickers School at Brooklands. Edward Corballis, who had gone to Stonyhurst in 1901, had become a Lieutenant in the Royal Dublin Fusiliers, and obtained his Royal Aeronautical Club (RAeC) Certificate (No.378) on 17 December 1912. This was in effect a licence to fly. Richard Creagh, an exact contemporary of Aidan's, had started at Stonyhurst in 1900, and had been at the Easter Retreat of 1913, which both Aidan and his father had attended. Between prayers and righteous contemplation, no doubt the young men's thoughts turned heavenwards in an entirely different way, as they compared flying notes and airborne aspirations. Richard Creagh attended the Vickers School in February 1914, gaining Certificate No.737, and acquiring his own aeroplane. He promised to fly it to Stonyhurst for that year's retreat, but there is no evidence that the airborne visitation ever took place. It therefore seems very likely that Aidan himself would have taken to the air, perhaps during 1912, but almost certainly during 1913, and shortly after Richard Creagh's success at Vickers.

36. *The Vickers sheds at Brooklands photographed by Aidan. The banked motor racing track is clearly visible. Photo Gillian Clayton.*

37. *(Top) Cody's Biplane, photographed by Aidan. Photo Gillian Clayton.*

38. *(Above) Barnes on his Humber, photographed by Aidan. Photo Gillian Clayton.*

39. *(Left) Rawlinson alighting, photographed by Aidan. Photo Gillian Clayton.*

A contemporary advertisement for the Vickers School read 'A thoroughly graded course of tuition is given upon machines of sound construction, and of up to date design by experienced and capable instructors'.[57] An advertisement in *The Aeroplane* read 'The new Vickers School biplane (50 hp Vickers radial engine), designed to protect pilot and pupil, who sit side by side, in cold weather. Its speed is about 50 mph, and the engine is giving excellent service'.[58] The advertisement also noted that special terms were offered for naval and military officers. It was not surprising then that on 19 April 1914, Aidan reported to the Vickers School at Brooklands to commence flying. The requirement for the eventual test was as follows:

> Two distance flights, consisting of at least five kilometres (3 miles, 185 yards), each in a closed circuit, marked out by two posts situated not more than 500 metres (547 yards) apart, the aviator changing his direction after going round each post, so that the circuit shall consist of an uninterrupted series of five figures of eight.
>
> One altitude flight, consisting of a minimum height of 100 metres (328 feet), but this must not form part of one of the two flights prescribed above. The method of alighting shall be with the motor cut off at the height of 100 metres, and the aeroplane must come to rest within a distance of fifty metres (164 feet) from a point indicated previously by the candidate.[59]

It was to take Aidan until the middle of May to obtain his certificate, but the process could be accomplished rather more swiftly. In the previous September the eccentric industrialist, aviation enthusiast and politician Noel Pemberton-Billing had wagered £500 that he could obtain his Royal Aero Club certificate within twenty-four hours of first sitting in an aircraft. To assist him he elicited the help of Mr Robert Barnwell, an instructor at the Vickers School, and purchased an old Henri Farman biplane because no school would lend him one of theirs. His account of this extraordinary feat gives some idea of the challenges that faced a trainee pilot at Brooklands.

> After four minutes taxiing Mr Barnwell gave the sign to shove her up in the air. I did so and we attained a height of 200 feet flying steadily. Mr Barnwell accompanied me for about twenty to twenty-five minutes in the passenger seat, during which time I succeeded in doing some dozen circuits of the aerodrome. Several figure eights, two or three *vol planés*[60] landings, and some landings under power were carried out, and as it was raining, and the machine was sodden and sluggish in consequence of carrying two thirteen stone men, this made the landing rather speedy and much more difficult in consequence. At the end of twenty-five minutes Mr Barnwell left me, and told me to get up and get on with it. I immediately started

* Flying without the engine.

LEARN
TO
FLY
AT THE
VICKERS FLYING SCHOOL, Brooklands.

VICKERS Flying School, Brooklands

Instruction on the Biplane

Instructing Pupils in Aero Engines

VICKERS, Limited,
AVIATION DEPARTMENT,
VICKERS HOUSE, BROADWAY,
WESTMINSTER, S.W.

Chief Pilot Barnwell

Assistant Pilot Knight

40. A Vickers School Advertisement, The Aeroplane, April 1914.

away without any taxiing, rose straight in the air at an exceedingly dangerous angle, amid the yells and shrieks of the spectators.

I did a half circle and landed successfully, got up immediately and did a circle and landed successfully, and then rose again and did five circuits. It was my intention to do twelve, but the petrol running out brought me down, the idea of coming trouble dawning upon me by the missing of the engine and the frantic waving of petrol cans by agitated spectators below. The rain had then set in so heavily that I was obliged to put the machine away for half an hour, at the termination of which time the machine was brought out again, and Mr Barnwell went once again as passenger for three or four minutes to test my right-hand turns before allowing me to essay the figure eight alone. Immediately on descending, Mr Barnwell jumped out of the machine, and I took her up at once, doing three successful eights. During the right-hand turns of these I managed to execute the most alarming banks, and, from inexperience, startled by the angle, at first hung onto the struts. When I had descended from this stunt, on Mr Barnwell's orders, I proceeded to practice *vol planing* from an altitude of about one hundred feet, with the engine cut off, which experience I found the most arduous of all.

Barnwell then judged Pemberton-Billing to be ready for the test. The RAeC official observer Mr Rance was found and very reluctantly agreed to judge the performance. The would-be pilot continued:

I then rose in a very steep climb to a height of about 250 feet, so as to make sure of the altitude test once and for all. Then I came round with a left-hand bend, and proceeded on my first five figure eights. The five, so I was told afterwards, were good sound flying of an experienced airman, although the fifth right-hand turn proved an alarming one. I was flying over the paddock, where my wife was watching very anxiously, and to give her confidence I waved my hand to her, taking my attention off the elevating plane for the moment. The machine, as machines will do on right-hand turns, shot up, throwing me back on my seat. The position was rendered more hopeless, undoubtedly, by my grabbing hold of the 'joy stick' to recover myself, which caused her to stand on her tail. She stopped dead in the air, about 200 feet up, and then fell about 100 feet tail first.

From the looseness of the control, caused by the machine being stationary, I jumped to the conclusion that the wires were broken, and tried to save the position by throwing all my weight forward, with the result that when about fifty feet from the ground the machine righted itself and dived head first. This, of course was not attributable so much to my throwing my weight forwards as to the fact that with me also came the joy stick, bringing the elevator down and causing the machine to dive, which immediately tightened up the controls.

I instantly realized that I had the control of the machine again, and, thinking I would be disqualified for this stunt, saved her from landing about twenty feet from the ground, climbed up again to 160 feet, and did an extra figure of eight to make sure. Then followed a *vol plané* landing, and after listening to Mr Barnwell's illuminating and very forcible remarks on my right-hand turns, I started off for the last half of the test, which was accomplished most successfully, finishing off with a *vol plané* from 100 feet with the engine cut off, and brought the machine to rest without switching on again, with the elevating plane over the heads of the observers, thus succeeding in obtaining my pilot's certificate before breakfast on the morning when I had for the first time in my life sat in a flying machine that flew.[61]

Actually, the process had taken a little over four hours, and Mr Pemberton-Billing won both his £500 and Royal Aero Club Certificate No.632. Aidan's achievement took rather longer and was accomplished

41. Aidan at Brooklands in the Vickers Biplane, May 1914. Photo Mark Liddell.

between 19 April and 14 May 1914, when under the expert tutelage of the Vickers team, and flying in the large and stable Vickers Boxkite he successfully passed his test and obtained Royal Aero Club Certificate No.781. While no detailed descriptions of this achievement survive, the account of instruction and testing provided by Pemberton-Billing in a broadly similar machine, and also under the instruction of the Vickers School, does offer an insight into the challenge that confronted Aidan. Despite the dramatic account, although minor crashes were very common, serious injuries were rare because of the slow speed and low wing loading of the aircraft. That said, a pilot was killed at Brooklands the week before Aidan's arrival when, having failed to strap in, he fell out of his aircraft during a steep turn.

Brooklands was a convenient distance from Basingstoke, and there is little doubt that Aidan was planning to spend more time there. As well as being an active airfield and motor racing circuit, it was also at the forefront of modern technology, with new aircraft and engines being developed by companies such as Vickers, Martinside, Bleriot, Sunbeam and Armstrong Whitworth. It was in many ways the epicentre of the burgeoning British aviation industry, and an exciting place for a young man. He must have wondered too about the prospect of military aviation, and carried his rank proudly on his Royal Aero Club Certificate.

42. Aidan at Brooklands in the Vickers Biplane, May 1914. Photo Mark Liddell.

Chapter Seven

War

The spring of 1914 moved slowly towards summer and on 20 May Empire Day was celebrated. Across the country streets and buildings were decked with flags and bunting as the people fondly remembered Queen Victoria, whose birthday it had been, and rejoiced in the power and prosperity of her great British Empire. Midshipman Lancelot Liddell was looking forward to the Royal Navy's King's Review planned for Spithead in July, and he eagerly anticipated taking part in the great events aboard the dreadnought HMS *Monarch*. In the Aldershot garrison Ensign Cuthbert Liddell faced the exciting prospect of regimental manoeuvres with the 15th Hussars. These were to be their first full regimental exercises since their return from South Africa in the winter of 1912. At Sherfield Manor, Aidan and the other members of the Liddell household looked forward to the summer and the season, albeit that the news from Ireland was somewhat troubling. Prime Minister Asquith was attempting to negotiate his way through the minefield of Irish Home Rule and reconcile the competing demands of the Irish Nationalist Party and the Unionist opposition. Certainly, war in Europe, despite all the talk of the past ten years, was the last thing on anybody's mind.

In June the Kaiser reopened the Kiel Canal, which had been deepened to accommodate the new and larger German battleships. There was to be much pomp and ceremony, and a British squadron of four battleships and three supporting cruisers paid a courtesy call to honour the splendid occasion. The Royal Navy moored alongside the German High Seas Fleet, and the Kaiser, in the full dress uniform of a British Admiral of the Fleet, toured the flagship of the squadron, HMS *King George V,* and displayed great enthusiasm and interest. The German and British navies enjoyed such exchanges and showed great professional interest in each other's warships and equipment. Indeed, the senior British diplomat at this convivial occasion, Sir Horace Rumbold, from the British Embassy in Berlin, remarked on the warmth of Anglo-German relations during this naval jamboree and throughout the Elbe Regatta which was also taking place. He made his observations despite being personally ticked off by the peppery Kaiser who took exception to him wearing a top hat on the battleship *King George V*. The Kaiser clearly took his duties as the senior British Admiral at the event most seriously!

43. *The most widely reproduced portrait of Aidan, taken on 14 May 1914. Photo Mark Liddell.*

The next day, as part of the regatta, Kaiser Wilhelm was competing in a race in his yacht the *Meteor*. A fast launch sped out into Kiel Bay, and a vital telegram, placed in a cigarette case by an aide, was tossed across the water to *Meteor* for inspection by the Kaiser. It was clearly an important message and contained the appalling news that Archduke Franz Ferdinand, the heir to the Austro-Hungarian throne, had been assassinated in the Serbian capital Sarajevo, along with his wife. The Kaiser, who had been the guest of Franz Ferdinand at Kanopischt only two weeks earlier, was profoundly shocked. The race was immediately abandoned, and shortly afterwards the rest of the regatta was cancelled. Kaiser Wilhelm returned at once to his palace at Potsdam.

The news spread rapidly across Europe, although at first the significance of the event and its profound consequences were not apparent. On 4 July *The Hants and Berks Gazette*, the local news-sheet for Sherfield-on-Loddon, carried the story under the heading 'Assassination of the Austrian Heir' and sketched out the bare facts.

> The Archduke Francis Ferdinand, heir to the Austro-Hungarian thrones, and his wife, the Duchess of Hohenburg, were assassinated in Sarajevo, the capital of Bosnia. The perpetrator of the outrage was a student who fired shots at the couple from a Browning pistol as they were driving through the town. The Archduke and his wife died almost immediately, expiring in the motor car as they were being taken to the Government House. Earlier in the same morning an attempt had been made on their lives by a man who threw a bomb at them. The Archduke, however, warded off the bomb with his arm, and it exploded only after the royal car had passed, wounding two people of the suite in the next carriage and a number of people in the crowd.[62]

The journalist went on to explain that while the captured terrorists showed absolutely no remorse and were reluctant to answer questions, they 'do not deny that they received the bombs from Belgrade. . .' Blame was clearly being apportioned, and a smarting Austria resolved to teach Serbia a lesson, so starting the process that was to gradually unravel the delicate fabric of European peace. However, few grasped the implications of this Balkan affair, and in *The Hants and Berks Gazette*, the assassinations in Sarajevo shared the page with news of a destructive storm in the north of England, floods in Bradford and a dust storm in Bristol!

Plans for the Royal Review at Spithead proceeded apace with full mobilisation of the Royal Navy commencing on 2 July. This was unrelated to the crisis developing in the Balkans, for it had long been planned to combine the complex and expensive process of a test mobilisation with the preparation for and execution of the Royal Review and the subsequent manoeuvres at sea. A total of 20,000 naval reservists were recalled to the colours, and the ships' companies of the Grand Fleet were brought up to full strength. An enormous concentration of warships gathered at Spithead, in numbers that today are hard to comprehend. There were fifty-nine battleships, twelve squadrons of the smaller more lightly armed and armoured cruisers, one hundred and eighty-seven torpedo boat destroyers and fifty-nine submarines. It was the largest and most powerful navy in the world, and ship by ship, squadron by squadron, it made steam and ploughed past the Royal Yacht at anchor far out in the English Channel. Bands played, flags flew, sailors removed headdress and cheered lustily, and His Majesty King George V looked on as ship after magnificent ship saluted. It took six hours for the steel columns to pass him by, and thereafter the huge armada steamed out to sea for the long-planned exercises. It was a unique and massively impressive occasion, a warm and patriotic tribute to the sailor King and an unforgettable experience for the tens of thousands who participated, but also a clear signal of Britain's naval might to the Kaiser.

But Lance on HMS *Monarch* was not the only Liddell delighting in service to King and country that month. On 23 July the 15th Hussars encamped at Nursery Camp Aldershot and took part in an extensive regimental field day. It was their first exercise on this scale since their return from Potchefstroom, and the Hussars deployed and exercised as a full cavalry regiment. It was judged a successful day, and was much enjoyed by the participants including Ensign Bertie Liddell of B Squadron. The tired troopers, trotting back to their lines after a hard and hot day in the saddle, were oblivious to the deteriorating international situation. Austria had issued an ultimatum to Serbia. The next time the 15th Hussars would march together would be to the sound of German guns in the Ypres salient.

When the Grand Fleet returned from its manoeuvres on Monday 27 July Winston Churchill, the First Lord of the Admiralty, agreed with the Chief of the Naval Staff that the international situation was sufficiently grave to delay the planned dispersal of the fleet to peacetime stations, and that they should keep the Royal Navy concentrated. The following day, Austria declared war on Serbia, and on 29 July the Admiralty ordered the Grand Fleet north, to its war station at Scapa Flow in Orkney. On 31 July Austria, Belgium and Russia mobilised, and in the space of barely a week war had become almost inevitable.

Despite frantic last-minute efforts to avert disaster the awful sequence of events continued to unwind. On 1 August Germany declared war on Russia, and France mobilised. The following day Germany issued a demand to neutral Belgium to allow the passage of German troops across her territory. On 3 August, a sunny Bank Holiday Monday in London, a brief notice appeared in the Personal column of *The Times* entitled 'German Mobilisation'. Issued by the German Consul, it instructed all those eligible for call-up in the German military to return home immediately. Later that day the ticket barriers at Victoria were thronged with German men clutching bags and cases, as they struggled to board the boat train home. On that same day, with her troops already in action on French soil, Germany declared war on France, and Britain mobilised. Pre-prepared telegrams were sent to every army reservist and to police stations and military formations across the British Isles. The following day Germany invaded neutral Belgium and Britain declared war on Germany. Thus it was that by midnight on 4 August 1914 the five great European empires of Russia, France, Great Britain, Germany and Austro-Hungary were at war. The Ottoman Empire, already mobilised, would join the combatants on the side of the Central Powers in November.

It was a time of wild excitement and uncertain expectations. There had been no major war in Europe since the Franco-Prussian War of 1871 forty-three years before. Although Britain had her colonial experience and that of the South African War, and in 1904/1905 Japan had fought the Russians in the East, the truth was that very few of those who were likely to command or even to fight had any relevant experience to draw from. The common expectation was of rapid mobilisation, swift and decisive campaigns, and a war that would probably be over by Christmas. Few appreciated that the modern technology of the industrialised nations would so significantly change the battlefield. The war was welcomed by young men everywhere as a patriotic duty, and a great adventure with swift victory almost a certainty.

On the streets of Europe the people cheered and roared their approval. In Berlin the Kaiser, dressed in a symbolic field-grey uniform, appeared on the balcony of the Potsdam Palace to tell the enormous crowd that the sword had been forced into Germany's unwilling hand, and that they must all now pray for their soldiers. In Bavaria huge crowds gathered in the Odeonsplatz, including one Adolf Hitler who was overcome with the emotion of the occasion. St Petersburg witnessed enormous crowds in the Winter Palace Square, with the people carrying banners, religious icons and portraits of the Tsar. When Tsar Nicholas appeared on the balcony the people fell to their knees and sung the Russian national anthem. In Paris, troops marching through the streets to the railway stations as part of the mobilisation plans were cheered and garlanded by the enthusiastic Parisians. In London there was a protest for peace in Trafalgar Square, and some clashes with the patriotic-flag waving crowds.

44. Aidan at Sherfield on the morning of 5 August 1914, before departing for duty to Stirling Castle. Photo Mark Liddell.

In Britain the War Book set out the blueprint for mobilisation. It was a highly detailed series of documents that had been drawn up over the previous three years as it became increasingly clear that one day such a plan would be required. It proved to be a triumph of organisation and worked extraordinarily well. The details of mobilisation were familiar enough to most military officers, in part because they had been for many years a favourite question in army examinations. The procedures had been carefully rehearsed and practised regularly by brigades, battalions and regiments across the United Kingdom. Troops deployed smoothly to key points and mounted armed guard, war reserves were broken out, and accommodation, transport and horses were sequestered by the military. Across the country, kit bags were hastily stuffed, railway warrants issued and Reservists and Territorials hastened to their assembly areas.

Aidan had watched the deteriorating political situation that August from Sherfield Manor, and now as a Special Reservist he was ready to respond. Like tens of thousands of others he received his mobilisation telegram and was summoned to do his duty. Few others can have had such a lengthy journey, for his assembly point was the Regimental Depot at Stirling Castle. So, on Wednesday 5 August he dressed in service dress and kilt, gathered up his valises and other equipment and prepared to depart for Basingstoke station. There was time for a final photograph on the terrace before family farewells, firm handshakes, hugs and kisses and the inevitable Godspeed. Family and servants waved him off, and then suddenly he was being driven down the long drive and onto the Basingstoke road to connect with the 11.07 am London train. Leaving Euston at 2 pm, he arrived at Stirling eleven and a half hours later at 1.30 am on the Thursday morning.

Another part of the War Plan was the requisition of horses for the military, and after Aidan's departure the army came to select the most suitable horses from the Liddell stables. The pony with the leather shoes that pulled the lawnmower was safe enough, but Dorothy was particularly saddened to lose her beautiful grey hunter, which she considered quite unsuitable for military service, as its gleaming white coat would make it stand out at night. But that did not convince the army, and as at great houses, livery stables, farms and hunts across the country, the soldiers had their way. The plan called for the mobilisation of some 120,000 additional horses. In return for her prized hunter Dorothy would have received up to £75 – a not inconsiderable sum. It was all laid down in the War Book.

For Aidan, as for any soldier going off to war, there was now time to ponder, to consider the future and what might be, and to think of family and friends. There must have been the almost inevitable feeling of unreality, and the sense of disbelief that invariably accompanies great and tragic events. The long railway journey would have provided plenty of time to think things through, and emotions must have been highly charged and feelings very mixed. He was all but a professional soldier, and like every soldier he would have had the desire to do the job he had prepared and trained for. There would be pride in unit, and pride in being a soldier and wearing the King's uniform at such a dramatic time in the life of the nation. No doubt he also felt self-conscious, although uniforms were much more commonplace than today, and was aware of the eyes of fellow travellers upon him, and of the need to appear calm, assured and resolute. His thoughts must have also have been with his brothers who like him both faced the perils of the German War, and of the family that had to wait and worry about all three of them. Perhaps the biggest question of all, and the one that no one could answer, was what was going to happen.

There had never been a war like this before, so there was no relevant experience to draw upon. Would it all be over by Christmas as so many predicted? Would it all be over before he got there? And the awful imponderable questions that every soldier thinks of in his heart. Is this a cause worth dying for? How will I handle myself and my men? Am I up to the job? How will I react under pressure and when things start to get tough? How will I react under fire? As a deeply religious man, he would also have prayed for guidance and protection, for himself, for his brothers, for his friends and family, and for his country. But above all he must have felt that sense of disbelief and unreality. To be jerked, in the twinkling of an eye, from the prospect of a long, hot and peaceful English summer to the prospect of total war in continental Europe was going to take some getting used to. No doubt the stories of German atrocities against 'plucky little Belgium' that were already starting to circulate helped stiffen his resolve. That and the fact that his Regiment and his friends needed him. In addition, travelling on trains packed with other soldiers, he must have felt very much a part of a great and growing national endeavour.

But churning brain and profound uncertainties aside, the journey was extremely hot and uncomfortable. Euston was more or less impassable, and full of drunken reservists, no doubt encouraged in their insobriety by enthusiastic and patriotic members of the public who were delighted to do their bit by buying Tommy, Jock or Jack a drink. The train was also extremely crowded, although Aidan did just manage to find himself a seat. Arriving in 'the wee small hours' he naturally enough decided to stay at the nearby Station Hotel, rather than trudge through the darkened town with his mass of kit. Although he complained that the hotel was full of 7th Battalion Territorial Officers, he was again lucky and managed to secure a room for the night.

The next morning Aidan rose early and climbed through the narrow streets of Stirling to the castle, high on its massive basalt crag above the town. The castle was home not just to the Regimental Depot of the Argyll and Sutherland Highlanders, but also Aidan's 3rd (Reserve) Battalion and 1/7th Battalion (Territorial Force) which had its Regimental Headquarters (RHQ) and A Company based within the walls. The great esplanade and the various squares and closes within the fortifications were already a hive of noisy activity with troops drilling, bugles calling, equipment being checked and counted, and reservists and territorials arriving breathless from the climb. Like Regimental Depots across the length and breadth of Great Britain, the activity was intense and the level of excitement high. Armed sentries patrolled the ramparts and guarded key points, and the old walls echoed to shouted orders, bugle calls and the rattle of hobnailed boots on cobblestones. Despite the sea of urgent activity Aidan sensibly decided that his first priority should be a proper breakfast, and his second to secure somewhere to sleep, for the castle was not large and already bursting at the seams. Finding a room proved to be a real struggle, and in the end he doubled up with another subaltern Lieutenant Ure. He dashed back into the town where he managed to buy a collapsible bed from Graham and Morton's that could be squeezed into a corner of the room. Creature comforts addressed, he found himself placed in command of the machine-guns as Warren, the Machine-Gun Officer was sick.

The plan was for the 3rd Battalion to deploy to Woolwich Arsenal, not very far from Basingstoke as the crow flies, but it was not clear precisely when the great move south would take place. But whenever it was they had to be ready, equipment had to be prepared, officers and men assembled and transport arranged. Suddenly, Aidan had significant responsibilities and a great deal of work to do. On Friday 7 August he took over the two heavy .303-inch Maxim machine-guns that equipped each British infantry battalion, together with 8000 rounds of ammunition and their horse-drawn cart and limber. The ammunition was boxed and the machine-gun belts needed filling. It was a great struggle to raise a fatigue party as the battalion sought to complete scores of vital tasks in double time, and the newly arrived 2nd Lieutenant Liddell was hardly the most influential man in the battalion. But he stuck to the task, called in favours and in the end secured a fatigue party of soldiers who were able to complete the task in only three quarters of an hour. In the afternoon Aidan patiently assembled the leather harness for the horses that would pull the gun transport, limber and ammunition wagon. Another fatigue party had proved impossible to raise, and he probably also doubted the Jocks' proficiency with harness and tackle. 'All in small pieces and very complicated' his diary dryly remarked. But by evening the massive jigsaw puzzle was complete. Meanwhile, in France the first elements of the British Expeditionary Force (BEF) were landing, safe behind a protective screen of Royal Navy battleships. In London, Lord Kitchener, now Minister for War, publicly called for 100,000 volunteers. There was growing recognition in high places that Britain's little army was likely to be severely tested.

It had been an exhausting day for Aidan, and he was pleased to fall into his newly acquired collapsible bed, but it was not to prove the comfortable night he had anticipated. Early the following morning he was rudely awakened by a vigorous shake. It was pitch dark, still only 0245, and the battalion had just received orders from Perth to be ready to move in an hour! Having dressed hurriedly with adrenaline racing, it soon became apparent that details of what was actually required of the battalion were sketchy. While clarification of the orders was sought Aidan packed up his bed, and then curled up on the anteroom sofa to try to complete his night's sleep. It was, he noted in his diary 'too short, no good'. Later in the morning the castle was a scene of frantic activity, even more so than on the previous day. Aidan anxiously awaited the arrival of his machine-gunners to help him pack and load the guns and equipment, but they did not appear. Soldiers were being pressed into sundry vital tasks across the castle at the behest of the Colonel, the Adjutant, the Regimental Sergeant Major, and various other personages, each far more influential than Aidan. He waited patiently, but the machine-gunners never arrived, and by 1400 he decided to raise his own fatigue party. It was a good idea, but by 1500 he realised grimly that this was an impossible task, and decided that the only option open to him was to do the work himself. As his diary recorded, '. . .had to pack guns, stores, harness, myself and got guns taken to station. Paraded at 10.45 for move. Left in first train about midnight. Slept on floor'.[63] The travellers breakfasted at Crewe, and arrived at Woolwich Arsenal station shortly after noon. They were to be quartered on Plumstead Marshes. They had the dual role of guarding the riverbank and the Royal Arsenal and training recruits.

The conditions were not ideal, and the ground they occupied was dreary in the extreme. Bordering the wide grey Thames and separated from the murky waters by a large dike, the Highlanders found themselves camping below the level of the river, on what in wet weather conditions became a bog. It was also extremely crowded with twenty or twenty-four soldiers sharing a muddy bell tent designed to accommodate only fourteen. Aidan described these uncertain delights in more detail in a letter home:

> The camp is bordered on the south by the main Thames sewer, with ventilators at intervals and very noticeable. On the west is an experimental electric railway, with a dangerous live rail, and all the rest is magazines with thousands of tons of Lyddite and Cordite, and testing ranges where they fire all sorts of big guns up to 15 inch at uncertain intervals. One hardly notices anything less than 12 inch, but the 15 inch fairly hurts, it makes such a blast of air on one's ears. We're very nearly half a mile away from it, and it shakes the ground and bulges the walls of the tent even from there. There's supposed to be enough Lyddite here to kill everyone within five miles if the main magazine blew up. Belgium sounds comparatively safe compared with this.[64]

It was clearly not a pleasant place, and the Highlanders were a tough bunch too, requiring firm handling. Most were old soldiers, many with memories and ribbons from India and South Africa, and there was a sprinkling of militia men too. After hard years of service with the Colours some had lived even tougher lives since and looked upon the war as an opportunity to be made the best of. A soldier's routine on the marshes was unpleasant and uncomfortable, and it was not long before the old soldiers found their way to the comfort of the pubs and bars of Woolwich. August 1914 was a time when the public wanted heroes, and the canny Jocks were only too pleased to oblige. The hospitable munitions workers of Woolwich were happy to dig deep into their pockets to toast the health of the kilted warriors. It was a difficult time for officers and NCOs reintroducing reservists to the rigours of military discipline. All the while the camp got fuller, conditions grew worse, and the seemingly endless process of drilling, issuing kit and basic training continued.

It was the same across the whole country. The dates for the BEF's departure had been a closely guarded secret and at Longmoor Camp the 15th Hussars had experienced several false alarms. Squadrons had paraded ready and had been equipped to march, only to be ordered back to their lines. But eventually it became clear to Bertie Liddell and his brother officers that during the night of 15/16 August the Regiment would move to its port of embarkation. That evening the officers dined formally together for the last time at Longmoor, dressed in wartime khaki, with the regimental portraits looking down upon them and the regimental silver and gold plate on the table. A final stirrup cup was taken, and then they buckled on their equipment and marched away to war, C Squadron at midnight, B Squadron at 0400 on 16 August and A Squadron at a rather more sedate 0930.

With his brothers already deployed to war, Aidan's most pressing personal concern at Woolwich was to ensure that he was properly equipped. It was not clear how many officers would be wanted to go to France, or what the basis for choosing them might be. By the end of August the Battalion had grown to around 1300 men, and the first draft of an officer (Purves), eight NCOs and ninety-seven men had departed on 26 August to join the 2nd Battalion, the 93rd, in France. Training aside, Aidan had been preparing himself:

> I've been very busy buying valises and all sorts of fitments. It's an expensive job, as one has to be prepared to stay here indefinitely and also to move off at a moment's notice with all one's luggage weighing 35 lb.[65]

The details of how an officer of the Argyll and Sutherland Highlanders went to war are extraordinary. The headdress was a Glengarry with the red and white check band and black ribbons down the back, and on his feet the officer wore brown brogues and khaki spats beneath red and white hose tops. The kilt was covered by an all-around protective khaki apron, which had four pleats and was stiff and cumbersome, and to many, ugly. Above the waist he wore a khaki service dress jacket with shirt and tie and buckled over it the leather Sam Browne belt. An additional cross belt was added to the Sam Browne with four brass D rings, for attaching two rolls at the back, one above the other. The first was for the greatcoat, and the second for waterproof cape, spare shirt and socks, washing and shaving kit, housewife* and other personal items. In addition, he carried holster and revolver, ammunition pouch, water bottle, compass, torch, field glasses and the heavy Highland broadsword or claymore, with a modified cross hilt instead of the customary basket. Then there was the haversack, with knife, fork, spoon and mug, map, notebook, paper and indelible pencil, and finally rations. At the beginning of the war this included the 7-lb bully beef tin that was the daily ration for seven men. The beef was of splendid quality, but the large, heavy and very awkward tin was an almost impossible burden. Everyone took their turn in carrying it, including the officers. This then was the proverbial 'Christmas Tree' that was the well dressed British

---

* The housewife was the wallet of needles, thread, spare buttons etc. that enabled the soldier to repair his clothing in the field.

officer in 1914, and one is forced to conclude that the Highlanders seemed to have had it rather worse than other regiments.

There was one other curious practice that was adopted by many kilted regiments. Officers often had ten gold sovereigns sewn singly into the inner panel of their kilts, in case of capture. It was a legacy of colonial warfare. This resulted in the story of a Black Watch captain who was wounded in the stomach. An astonished surgeon dug a twisted and bent sovereign from inside him, and when the captain came round told him that it had undoubtedly saved his life.*

In the event, Aidan did not have long to wait at Woolwich. Writing hurriedly to his mother on Sunday 30 August he explained 'Only time for a little line. I wired you that I have been detailed for a draft. We start at 7.50 from Woolwich tonight. 100 men and self'.[66] With personal kit, two rolls, weapons and valises, Aidan must have staggered off to war weighed down by his equipment and the gold that it seems likely would have been concealed about his person.

*The practice among Highland officers of sewing sovereigns into their kilts and the story of the Black Watch captain is described in *The Memoirs of Brigadier JC Cunningham MC*, a personal friend of Aidan's. The typescript is held in the IWM.

Chapter Eight

France and the 93rd

Aidan and his men had spent much of the day packing and preparing for the journey before parading at 0645 and leaving Arsenal station at 0740. It was a crowded occasion with the station already packed with civilians and large numbers of soldiers on pass who tried to press drinks on the departing Jocks. When the train arrived, the Gloucesters were found to have taken up more than their rightful share and that further compounded the problems for Aidan. None the less, the draft boarded the train in under five minutes and steamed off to Southampton via Guildford and Woking. Arriving at 0030, they drew five days' rations and field dressings and at 0230 on 31 August went aboard the very crowded SS *Lake Michigan*, where the men were crammed five to a 25 ft by 8 ft horse stall. Aidan was somehow able to slip ashore for a last swift but hearty supper in England, through the good offices of a nearby hotel. He was safely back in bed at 0415 for the start of a very foggy crossing to France. The next morning there was time for a brief and reflective note to his father:

I never thought a month ago that I would be doing this job instead of shooting partridges today. I got my draft safely on board, and we're now sailing to some place on the West coast of France, but we haven't definitely heard the name. Anyway we don't know what is going to happen even if we do land. There are about 3000 troops on board and about 36 officers. Thank heavens it's been fine.[67]

The unnamed port turned out to be St Nazaire, where they lay off outside until 0200 on 2 September. Then the *Lake Michigan* entered harbour and began the lengthy disembarkation that was completed by noon. Thereafter, the draft marched off to a designated Rest Camp, which was actually a ploughed field overlooking the sea, with no tents, no food and no water. The staff had only arrived to set up the camp the previous day, but already men were pouring in and there were said to be 12,000 in the vicinity. That morning as Aidan munched on hard tack and contemplated his extraordinary experiences since mobilisation, he can have had little comprehension of the momentous events that had already overtaken the 93rd. Of course, he knew the men well from happier days at Fort George, and it was there that the war had begun for his new battalion, in much the same way that events had unfolded at Stirling.

The 93rd received their orders to mobilise at 1730 on 4 August, and with remarkable speed the Reservists recalled to the Colours began to flood in. By mid-afternoon on 6 August the process was complete and the battalion had been augmented by 700 men, and the process of preparing for deployment had begun in earnest.

The 93rd was at this time almost entirely Scottish, although there were relatively few native-born Highlanders among them. Many though were of Highland blood, although they had been born and brought up in the Lowland cities of central and south-west Scotland. As for the officers, almost all were Scottish (although few were true Highlanders), a fact that adds to the mystery as to why the very English Aidan should have chosen this particular regiment.

The first encounter with the enemy for the 93rd was not slow in coming, for the Royal Navy had intercepted a German fishing fleet in the North Sea. On 6 August ninety-one prisoners-of-war were brought ashore and confined in the casements at Fort George. They were German, Austrian and for some reason Dutch, and were said to have been signalling by radio and carrier pigeon when they were picked up by a British cruiser. Despite their incarceration, they seemed remarkably cheerful and were allowed to exercise in the dry moat during the day. But German prisoners were not the priority, for the real task was rapid deployment south to the embarkation ports, for the 93rd had been designated as a line of communication battalion with the role of facilitating the deployment of the BEF.

Mobilisation had gone well, although there had been difficulties fitting boots for many of the Reservists* and a new type of harness for the horses was troublesome – when fitted the animals seemed reluctant to pull. Problems notwithstanding, the 93rd moved out from Fort George on the evening of 9 August and travelled south by rail to Southampton on four trains. They shipped to France on the SS *Seahound*, SS *Bertha* and SS *Empress of India*, and by 14 August the 93rd were assembled in Boulogne.

That was also the day that the Commander-in-Chief of the BEF, Field Marshal Sir John French, arrived in France. He too landed at Boulogne, before moving north to his HQ at Le Cateau, close to the BEF concentration area at Valenciennes where A Company had already been dispatched to unload trains. 'Johnny' French was a much decorated Boer War hero, and a successful cavalry general who had proved his valour in action. Red-faced, small and stocky, he was a quick-tempered and mercurial individual who tended to act on instinct and did not respond well to pressure. Until a few months previously he had been Chief of the Imperial General Staff, but he himself was no staff officer or strategic planner. He found it difficult to relate to the French high command, and

---

*This was a common problem and attributed to soldiers' failure to be measured properly at the annual camps.

44A. *The 93rd land in Boulogne. 12 August 1914. Photo: Taylor Library*

although reckoned to be a decisive man of action was deeply conscious of his custodianship of most of the irreplaceable British professional army. For much of the campaign French appeared understandably cautious and to some out of his depth.

But for the 93rd, generals must have seemed remote and distant, although on 19 August they had the sad task of attending to the carriage of the body of Lieutenant General Sir John Grierson, the commander of the British II Corps, who had collapsed and died on a train as he moved to the front. There were rumours that he had been murdered by spies or saboteurs! The 2nd Battalion the Royal Welch Fusiliers (RWF), another Lines of Communication battalion with whom the 93rd were soon to become very familiar, also had dealings with the late Sir John. Major Geiger, commanding A Company 2nd Royal Welch Fusiliers, was tasked with providing a Guard of Honour and 'any other relevant duty'. To him there was no mystery or skulduggery about the death:

There were a lot of stupid rumours about General Grierson's death. I have the best of reasons for knowing that he died of bursting a blood vessel, probably brought on by the heat and a heavy meal. He was a man of full habit, the weather was torrid, and the Staffs of higher formations were at that time living exclusively on hampers supplied by Fortnum and Mason – purveyors of edible and potable delicacies.[68]

The evidence was of a heart attack and late on the evening of the 19 August all officers and C Company of the 93rd attended as the General's body was conveyed from train to ship. A French Guard of Honour gave the salute as eight Argyll and Sutherland NCOs bore the coffin on board while pipers played 'The Flowers of the Forest'. This unexpected death was a pity. Sir John Grierson was highly regarded and forward thinking, as evidenced by his enlightened views on the use of aircraft. He was also an acknowledged expert on the German Army. Fortunately, however, his replacement, Sir Horace Smith-Dorrien, was to prove an excellent successor, although he was not the choice of Sir John French.

Sad ceremonial aside, there was much hard work for the 93rd as they fulfilled their role as Lines of Communication troops, which for the moment meant camp and dock fatigues. Bugler Ditcham, a boy soldier who was too young to carry arms, summed up the situation:

My company was one of the companies that was putting tents up. Other people were doing dock fatigues and unloading various units' transport and stuff that was coming up behind us. We were the general factotums of this particular part of the British Expeditionary Force.[69]

But the task of general labouring finished abruptly when the battalion deployed north to the BEF concentration area at Valenciennes, arriving at 0700 on 23 August and billeted in a school. It was at this point that the four Lines of Communication battalions were formally reconstituted as 19th Brigade, and this independent formation was effectively the only infantry reserve formation for the BEF. It comprised 1st Middlesex, 2nd Royal Welch Fusiliers, 1st Cameronians (Scottish Rifles), and 2nd Argyll and Sutherland Highlanders, together with supporting arms. Rushed hither and thither to plug gaps and cover flanks it was soon to earn the nickname 'French's Flying Brigade', but that was in the future.

For the moment it was still smiling faces, cheering crowds and bunting. The reception given by the French to the British was remarkable, and the Highlanders were greeted as heroes wherever they went.   As the first British Battalion to arrive in Boulogne, the 93rd had been welcomed loudly and enthusiastically, and there was great demand for British buttons, badges and collar dogs.   For a time it had seemed that the British might not deploy their Army to France, and in the event only four of the six regular infantry divisions were despatched, together with the Cavalry Division.   The other two divisions were for the present retained for Home Defence and to keep a nucleus of the regular Army out of harm's way.   Although not as numerous as might have been, the arrival of British fighting men was particularly welcome to the French, for the continental war had begun in deadly earnest.   While the British had been mobilising and deploying, the French, Belgians and Germans had already been fighting and dying.   There was no 'phoney' war in 1914, just the conflagration of massive armies and the testing of rival battle plans, and the BEF had a part to play on the left of the French line.

France had planned an aggressive offensive campaign of massed infantry attacks, supported by the mobile firepower of their quick-firing '75' field guns.   The French believed that the courage, character and tradition of their soldiers would give them the moral ascendancy on the battlefield and avenge the defeat of 1875.   French *élan* and the *offensive à l'outrance* would, they believed, win the day.   They called it Plan XVII, the latest in a series of plans developed by successive commanders to defeat the Germans, and regain *La Gloire* and the lost laurels of French militarism.

The French field army numbered some seventy Divisions, grouped into five armies with First Army on the right and Fifth Army on the left. First and Second Armies faced the Germans in Alsace and Lorraine, with the purpose of liberating the lost provinces seized by the Germans in 1875 and driving the Germans back to the Rhine.   There was a special assault group, part of First Army, intended to spearhead the attack into Alsace.   Third, Fourth and Fifth Armies made up the centre, from the fortress of Verdun to the Ardennes, with Fifth Army turned to face into the rugged country of the Ardennes.   The French left was also supported by the large Cavalry Corps, but the long French frontier with Belgium was undefended.   When the plan was devised Belgium was neutral, and even after the outbreak of war the French still did not envisage a significant German attack through Belgium.

But in any case the plans had been laid, mobilisation and deployment were underway, and Belgium with its massive fortresses seemed a secure bulwark on which to anchor the French left.   The forts around Liège and Namur had been built in the 1880s.   Positioned on high ground around each city they were designed to provide all-round defence, as befitted Belgium's neutral status, and were intended to hold the passage of the Meuse against attack from either bank.   Liège had twelve forts and

Namur nine, each protected with armoured gun turrets that could withdraw into their concrete emplacements. There were underground magazines, barracks and command centres, and the forts which were protected by dry moats, had observation towers equipped with searchlights. The principal eight-inch gun batteries, the most powerful available when the forts were built, were protected by smaller quick-firing guns and machine-guns, and the plan was for the gaps between the forts to be protected by the Belgian field army. At Liège the defences had over 400 guns.

The German war plan was an adaption of that prepared by the great German strategist Count von Schlieffen and was based around the need to reach a decisive conclusion in the west before Russia could fully mobilise. Germany believed herself unable to sustain a war on two fronts indefinitely, and recognised that while France would quickly mobilise and attack, it would take the Russians much longer. The German plan was to envelop the French forces with a sweeping right hook that would swing through neutral Belgium and take the French armies clustered along the common border in the flank and rear. The plan meant concentrating the great weight of the German armies in the west, while fighting a holding campaign against the Russians. With France subdued, the Germans would then turn their attentions east.

After mobilisation seven German armies, totalling more than 1.5 million men, were ready to move on the Western Front. The First, Second and Third Armies consisting of thirty-four divisions were the hammer blow that made up the German right wing, which was intended to sweep through Belgium and roll up the French line. The Fourth and Fifth Armies made up of twenty divisions were in the centre, and the Sixth and Seventh Armies comprising sixteen divisions were on the left of the German line. In support of the right wing were two cavalry corps totalling another five divisions. The plan allowed forty days from mobilisation for the Germans to achieve a decisive victory in the west.

The Germans anticipated little resistance from the Belgians and had expected to be allowed safe passage for their armies or be offered only token opposition. In this they had miscalculated badly. The energetic and patriotic young King Albert was from the beginning determined that his nation should resist. Even before the commencement of hostilities he had pressed for the concentration of Belgian forces and sought to deploy his field army in defensive positions along the Meuse to block the threatening Germans. However, such sensible precautions were felt to be potentially provocative, and so the army remained dispersed to provide all-round defence against all possible threats thus underscoring their neutral status.

The Belgian army was small, only six divisions, and poorly equipped with inadequate artillery and few machine-guns, the latter famously pulled by giant dogs. It was an old-fashioned army with nineteenth century uniforms that would not have looked out of place at Waterloo. The infantry wore dark blue uniforms and shakos, while the cavalry had red trousers and fur busbies or Polish lancer caps. The militia, the *Garde Civique*, were even more old-fashioned, and dressed in bright green uniforms set-off by tall top hats. The Belgian forces were poorly trained, and lacked a wide range of equipment that was necessary for modern warfare, ranging from field kitchens and entrenching tools to transport and tents. They were certainly not ready to take on the most formidable military machine in Europe. Notwithstanding the inadequacy of their forces, when the Belgian Government did not simply give in to German pressure, their old-fashioned army fought with great gallantry under the dynamic leadership of their young King who on 3 August also became their Commander-in-Chief.

Liège was the key to the German flanking attack through Belgium. The ring of Belgian forts protected the five bridges over the Meuse, and an important railway junction connecting Germany and Belgium to the north of France. At 0800 on 4 August the German Army crossed the border into Belgium screened by cavalry, and their advanced guard was fired on by Belgian *gendarmes* manning the sentry boxes at the border crossings. Six infantry brigades supported by a cavalry corps and other supporting arms led the assault and raced to Liège to seize the Meuse crossings. There they found the bridges already blown and when the German engineers rigged pontoons they came under heavy fire and took casualties. It was a surprise to the Germans, but the battle for Liège had begun and it proved to be costly, with the initial German attacks being bloodily repulsed.

However, the Belgian forts, although formidable, were old by contemporary standards and had not been upgraded. Nor had the Belgian infantry been allowed to dig in and wire the intervals between the forts, as had been planned, for fear of compromising Belgian neutrality. Most significant of all, the Germans had been building specialist siege artillery, designed to quickly smash the Belgian forts into submission. These secret weapons were bigger than the guns of the latest battleships in the High Seas Fleet and were quite simply the most powerful artillery in the world. Krupp's had built a massive 16.5-inch cannon in their Essen foundry, that weighed almost 100 tons and had a range of nine miles. It required a crew of 200 men, fired an 1800-lb shell and had to be transported by rail, in two parts each pulled by a separate locomotive. In addition the Austrian armament firm Skoda built smaller and much more manoeuvrable 12-inch siege mortars. These formidable weapons had been literally years in the making, and by the beginning of the war there were five of the massive Krupp's cannon and several of the Austrian Skoda mortars available to the Germans. Although not initially deployed, these siege weapons were called forward when it became apparent that the Belgians would make a fight of it. The great guns arrived on 12 August, and by 15 August the forts of Liège had been smashed into submission.

In Lorraine the French offensive had opened on 14 August and for four days the Germans fell back before the apparently successful French, who advanced with bugles blaring and drums beating. They must have made a magnificent martial sight, in their closely packed formations with their old-fashioned imperial-style uniforms. The infantry were still dressed in red trousers, high boots and turned-back coats, while the heavy cavalry wore plumed brass helmets and breast plates, and the light cavalry frogged jackets and scarlet pants. But on 19 August the Germans counter-attacked and drove the French back to their start line. In the centre the French Third and Fourth Armies had attacked into the Ardennes and met directly with the two German armies, Fourth and Fifth, marching to attack in the opposite direction. German reconnaissance was superior, however, and they gained the advantage in heavy fighting, driving the French Third and Fourth Armies back beyond the Meuse. By 24 August Plan XVII was in disarray, with the two major French offensives repulsed and countered and the German right hook through Belgium progressing well. The Belgian field army had been defeated and had fallen back on Antwerp. Brussels had been evacuated by the Belgian Government and had fallen, and the Germans were assembling their siege artillery at Namur, which would quickly succumb to the great guns.

The Germans had not anticipated Belgian resistance and when it came they dealt harshly with the civilian population. Terror had become a tool of modern war and Liège was threatened with air attack. When the city refused to surrender, a Zeppelin was dispatched from Cologne to spread panic. It bombed the city, causing nine deaths. There was no organised non-military resistance by the Belgians, but the evidence of heavy-handed treatment and then atrocities against civilians by the Germans are well documented. The 'Rape of Belgium' was not simply Allied propaganda, but a harsh and unnecessary reality, and it got worse as the invasion went on. Priests were shot and other individuals executed, but there were also organised massacres, carried out by regular army units who rounded up unarmed and helpless civilians, including women and children, and shot them. The small Belgian towns where hundreds were murdered in this way included Seilles, Tamines, and Dinant, where there were some 600 dead.

On 25 August the German occupiers of the ancient university town of

Louvain panicked during the night, apparently believing that they were under attack from Belgian irregulars. The Germans tried to burn out their attackers, and in the three chaotic days that followed much of the ancient town was destroyed, including the library and its priceless contents. Some 200 civilians were killed, and the population of 42,000 were forced to flee. Newspapers around the world told of the desecration of Louvain in what was a propaganda disaster for Germany.

The French Commander-in-Chief, Marshal Joffre, had not believed that the Germans would make any significant incursion into Belgium to the north of the Meuse, and perversely clung to this view until the middle of August. Only then, on realising his serious error, did he direct General Lanrezac's Fifth Army to advance north into Belgium between the Meuse and the Sambre to cooperate with the BEF in operations against the German left wing. Lanrezac, however, was cautious and realised that the loss of his army could have a calamitous effect. Rather than advance into Belgium he chose to occupy the strong defensive line of the Sambre where he planned to block the advance of the German Second and Third Armies. But the Battle of the Sambre was not the success that the French had hoped, with the Germans exploiting undefended bridges over the Sambre to force a crossing on 21 August and drive a significant wedge into the French positions. Bloody French counter-attacks on 22 and 23 August could not dislodge them, and after sustaining very heavy casualties Lanrezac decided to withdraw in the face of renewed German advances. He had now lost contact with Fourth Army on the Meuse, and had failed to link up with the British. Sir John French and the BEF had joined the action at the critical point, at exactly the time that the Germans were breaking out of Belgium and executing their sweeping right hook, intended to roll up the French armies and bring the Germans to the gates of Paris and victory.

II Corps of the BEF was by 23 August deployed on a twenty-mile front to the left of Lanrezac's Fifth Army, at Mons, along the line of the Mons-Condé canal. It was covering the canal and the town itself and the salient to the north defined by a loop in the canal at Nimy. I Corps was on the right to the south of Mons and facing east. This proved to be well out of the line of the main enemy advance. Sir John French had expected to move north into Belgium in step with Lanrezac's Fifth Army to his right, but their defeat changed all that. However, on receiving a request that he attack the German flank to assist the battered Fifth Army, he demurred but agreed that the BEF would hold its position for twenty-four hours and block further German advances. His caution was justified for there was actually no exposed German flank to turn, and instead II Corps faced the might of General von Kluck's First Army of fourteen divisions approaching rapidly from the north.

The Germans did not know the British were there. II Corps were now under the command of the newly arrived General Sir Horace Smith-Dorrien who had been with them for only a day. They were occupying strong defensive positions along the canal, in a mining area of slag heaps, coal yards and industrial buildings that leant itself to defence. Initial contact was made at around 0600 as British soldiers found themselves in action on mainland Europe for the first time since Waterloo in 1815.

After the first screening cavalry contacts the Germans came forward in massed ranks of infantry, and the battalions of II Corps demonstrated their skills in musketry with the Lee Enfield rifle and their ability to fire fifteen aimed rounds a minute. The serried field-grey ranks were greeted with a storm of highly accurate and concentrated rifle fire that led them to believe they were under mass machine-gun attack, although the British had only the regulation two Maxim Guns per battalion. It was the marksmanship and sustained rate of fire of the British regulars that broke down attack after attack.

The 19th Brigade had been placed on the extreme left of the II Corps area, with the Cameronians and the Middlesex forward on the canal, the RWF holding the open flank and the 93rd well back in reserve. This flank of the BEF was not seriously threatened and although the Middlesex were probed by the Germans in mid-afternoon these attacks were easily beaten back. However, the pressure at Nimy was too great and by mid-afternoon the bridges at Nimy and several other locations were blown and the British withdrew to pre-arranged positions to the south of the canal line.

The Germans were in no condition to follow up, having already suffered an estimated 5000 casualties, while the British had lost some 1600 dead, wounded and missing. Almost all of these were from General Smith-Dorrien's II Corps, while General Haig's I Corps was scarcely engaged. In the evening the Germans did not attempt any further attacks and their exhausted troops simply lay down to sleep and await the dawn and the prospect of trying to force the canal all over again. But that night the British learnt that the French Fifth Army to their right was withdrawing from its untenable position. The British had no option but to do the same.

The retreat from Mons had begun. It would last for two long weeks, cover some 250 miles of hard marching and bring the BEF with the Germans at their backs to the gates of Paris. For the enemy, decisive victory in the west within forty days now seemed a distinct possibility. The French armies in northern France were withdrawing not in disarray, but to regroup and reorganise, at what everyone now recognised as being the critical point of the campaign. It was to be a fighting withdrawal, but retreat under any circumstances saps morale and is hard to stomach. The triumphant Germans were pressing hard, and as the French pulled back the BEF and the 93rd marched with them on the left.

Extricating themselves from Mons, the 93rd faced a march of forty miles on 24 August in the sweltering heat before they were finally able to occupy old French trenches for the night. They had only tea and biscuits to sustain them until the regimental transport eventually arrived after 2200, and their pickets had suffered two dead and thirteen wounded or missing. This was their first contact with the enemy.

On the following day, again sustained only by biscuits and tea, the exhausted battalion arrived at Le Cateau at 2200 and were billeted in an old factory near the station. It had been an eventful march, with transport wagons pulled by exhausted horses that were unequal to the task. Perhaps it was in part the new harness that prevented the horses pulling properly, but even when the load was lightened by abandoning equipment by the roadside, the horses could not manage and one wagon upended. When it could not be righted, the animals were cut loose and the wagon, which contained much of the officers' kit and the Adjutant's box, was set on fire to prevent it falling into enemy hands. Among the papers lost were the Battalion War Diaries and these had to be painfully reconstructed over the coming weeks. But the men of the 93rd were better off than many, for exhausted units of II Corps were streaming into Le Cateau all through the night, finding little food, no billets and being forced to sleep where they could. Captain Jack, Staff Captain of 19th Brigade described the spectacle in his diary:

> It is heartrending to witness the exhaustion of all ranks after their march of almost 23 miles in steam-heat and heavily loaded, besides going into action about Romeries and Haussy in support of the cavalry. The men have been scarcely off their feet for three days besides having had no more than snatches of sleep or scraps of food because of transport delays through road-blocks. The last battalion to report, the Royal Welch Fusiliers, drop down on the cobbled square saying they can go no further. . .[70]

Although ordered to continue the retreat, General Smith-Dorrien realised that II Corps was in no condition to move out and that he had no choice but to stand and fight. Major-General Allenby, commanding the scattered and exhausted Cavalry Division, agreed to act under his command, as did Major-General Snow with his newly arrived 4th Division. General Smith-Dorrien planned to check sharply the German pursuit, and then continue his withdrawal as the enemy regrouped. He hoped that General Haig's I Corps would be close by to render support, but as at Mons that was not to be.

II Corps was stretched over a ten-mile front with the right wing anchored on the town of Le Cateau, and broadly covering the line of the Cambrai to Le Cateau road. The 4th Division was on the left, well back from the road and facing north-west to cover the flank, and they were also in touch with the French Cavalry Corps. The 3rd Division held the centre and the 5th the right. The line swung round below Le Cateau with the final units facing east. Allenby's cavalry deployed to the south, behind the infantry. General von Kluck, commanding First Army, believed he was facing the entire BEF, and was to attack initially with three infantry divisions and three cavalry divisions, and then be reinforced with two more infantry divisions later in the day. 'Old One O'clock' as the Tommies and Jocks called him, planned a two-pronged attack to turn the British flanks, and the weak point for the British was the right wing where General Smith-Dorrien had been hoping for support from I Corps.

It was here that 19th Brigade, the only infantry reserve for II Corps, was to be deployed. The 93rd had stood to arms at 0400 on 26 August and then been issued tea and bully beef. But having roused themselves, there was nowhere to go, for the town was crammed with soldiers all struggling to leave in an orderly fashion, and 19th Brigade was at the back of the queue. As they were finally preparing to leave the crowded square there was the sound of rifle fire only a few hundred yards away. Uhlans were already probing the town from the east, and pickets of the Cameronians, the nearest battalion, 'fixed swords'* and doubled to the sound of the guns. Meanwhile, the two Cameronian machine-guns were unlimbered and readied for action.

The 19th Brigade were the last troops to march out from Le Cateau, which was to lie forward of the British battle line. Covered by pickets of the Middlesex, they marched out along the St Quentin road. It was only then that they learnt that the retreat had for the present been abandoned and that II Corps would stand and fight. Captain Jack described the scene:

> As we passed through the infantry of the 5th Division, arranged in the usual firing line, supports and reserves, they were entrenching as well as they could with their wretched little tools, augmented with some village picks and spades; the field batteries were trotting to their stations, many of these only 200 to 400 yards behind the foremost infantry, and practically in the open as there had been no time to 'dig in'. . .The weather cleared after heavy rain and a hot sun tinted the large fields of cut corn to a golden hue. The remainder of the open rolling landscape was mostly covered with ripened grass, but patches of vegetable crops showed above the red brick villages, and greener grass beside the several small streams. Numerous roads and tracks intersected the countryside. . . By the time we had

*The Cameronians were a Rifle Regiment and swords was the terminology used for bayonets by riflemen.

reached our position at the wood, the bombardment seemed to be general along the front. . .[71]

On arrival the 93rd attempted to 'dig in' in a cornfield and were joined by two companies of the Royal Scots Fusiliers who had become separated from their unit. The Germans had learned the lesson of Mons and would no longer attack the British line without the benefit of artillery preparation, and this time the serried ranks of field-grey infantry were backed by intense artillery preparation and support. In response, the British Horse Artillery deployed their guns close behind the infantry to afford their comrades the maximum support. On the right of the British line heavy attacks developed, with enemy infantry advancing around and through Le Cateau to try and overwhelm the 5th Division. The fighting was hard and at about 1100 the 93rd and the Royal Scots were ordered forward in artillery formation to the 5th Division area, and were soon to be followed by the other elements of the brigade.

After their advance the 93rd quickly got their machine-guns into action at very long range onto the enemy to the east of Le Cateau, but this almost immediately drew down accurate artillery fire that soon put them out of action. Then two half companies of the 93rd under Major Maclean were ordered forward to support the hard-pressed Suffolks who were in danger of being overwhelmed. Major Maclean made contact with the Suffolks and found that they were occupying a salient overlooking Le Cateau and that their shallow trenches could be enfiladed from north-west, north, and north-east. The casualties were mounting steadily and Major Maclean led half his force in a gallant but futile attack towards the Cambrai – Le Cateau road in an effort to drive the enemy back. He and all his men were overwhelmed.

II Corps was now being heavily shelled by massed German guns and pressed by infantry assaults. Captain Jack summarised the position of the brigade:

> Up until 1 pm the positions of II Corps were nearly all intact in spite of the highest trials. In the early afternoon, however, the situation on the right of the Fifth Division became critical. Not only had the infantry and gunners there suffered fearful casualties which undeniably shook some units in their shallow trenches, but the German 7th Division was working up the Selle to turn the flank. The trickle of wounded who, carried on stretchers or sustained by damaged comrades, had since early morning hobbled south-west along the Roman Way now amounted to a stream. . .[72]

The situation was becoming increasingly desperate. In the early afternoon a long enemy column of reinforcements could be seen advancing across the railway line near Le Cateau. The *British Official History* records the fate of British in the little salient overlooking Le

Cateau as the Germans attacked with mass infantry supported by field guns firing over open sights:

The Suffolks and Argylls opened rapid fire to their front with terrific effect. Two officers of the Highlanders in particular bringing down man after man, and counting their score aloud as if in a competition. The Germans kept sounding the British 'Cease Fire' and gesticulating to persuade the men to surrender, but in vain. At length a rush of the enemy from the rear bore down all resistance and the Suffolks and their Highland comrades were overwhelmed. They had for nine hours been under an incessant bombardment, and they had fought to the very last, covering themselves with undying glory.[73]

The bloody little battle was also noted by the enemy. An officer wrote: 'I did not think it possible that flesh and blood could survive so great an onslaught. Our men attacked with the utmost determination, but again and again they were driven back by these incomparable soldiers.'[74]

By now the 93rd were scattered into a number of different groups, in what was becoming a very confused situation. The 5th Division was ordered to withdraw and Captain Jack was sent forward to organise a covering force. He found one battalion leisurely retiring in extended order and when he tried to persuade the CO to turn around and face the enemy, he was treated as if he had made 'a demand for a money subscription'. To his dismay the 'blankshires' simply continued to withdraw. But help was at hand:

Cautiously scouting around, we presently came on two companies of the Argyll and Sutherland marching quietly back in open order with tall, handsome Colonel Moulton-Barrett at their head. He answered the invitation to oppose the enemy a little longer by at once calling out '93rd about turn', the movement being executed on the spot with almost parade ground exactitude. His Highlanders were then again led forward to a suitable crest nearby.[75]

In the late afternoon Captain Jack came back to extricate the Argylls:

A fusillade of bullets was skimming the road bank and a wire fence stood between me and the Highlanders. Expecting to be hit at any moment, I called the men to tell their colonel to retire; then, to their kindly warnings 'Be careful, Sir', climbed the fence, slid down the track, and hastened crouching down to Moulton-Barrett. He said that he believed that all other units had already retired – none was to be seen or heard. We quickly divided those present into two parts, he taking the one and I the other, and doubling back alternatively to a hollow out of the enemy's view, reformed between 5.30 and 6 pm.[76]

The action at Le Cateau was all but over, and II Corps continued the retreat, having lost nearly 8000 men and thirty-eight guns. German casualties are estimated to have been between 15,000 and 30,000. II Corps had fought a coordinated rearguard action, delivered a checking blow and marched on in good order. Sir John French paid tribute to General Smith-Dorrien's achievement, writing in his Despatches:

I say without any hesitation that the saving of the left wing of the army under my command on 26th August could never have been accomplished unless a commander of rare and unusual coolness, intrepidity, and determination had been present to personally conduct the operation.[77]

But perhaps the last word on Le Cateau and the 93rd's first great action of the war should be left to Bugler Ditcham. He was still a boy soldier and should not officially have been at the front at all, although the 93rd had taken along the 'Boys' over sixteen. He was not though allowed to carry arms and had only his bugle. The battle made a lasting impression.

. . .you made a bit of a hole in the ground with your entrenching tool, and then you took up a position, and then the party started, and I mean the party started! The Hun came along in his hordes. This was what made me realise what war was about. . . we were just lined up in a cornfield, one company on the right one company on the left. Middlesex and other people, all mixed up, and this famous L battery behind, the one that got blasted to pieces. And to me – I shall never see a picture like this in my life again – these Germans literally came on in their hordes, and were just shot down, but they still kept coming. There were sufficient of them to shove us out of the field eventually. And then the realisation what war meant – when you see my Company Sergeant Major for instance, fellow called Sim, he was wounded in the mouth. He was going back dripping blood. And there were various other people getting killed and wounded. I can't remember how many in my platoon were killed or wounded. There was quite an amount. And then during the battle, what I shall never understand – what was I supposed to do with a bugle in the front line. . .[78]

The 93rd had suffered the heaviest casualties in the 19th Brigade with eleven officers missing, 150 Other Ranks killed or wounded, and 300 Other Ranks missing. Later it was found that of those eleven officers, six were killed, two died of wounds, and three were captured by the enemy. And after Le Cateau the retreat had to continue, although now in greater confusion than before. Separated by battle the 93rd left the field in three main groups and did not reform as a unit for several days. Captain Jack paints a vivid picture of the battered army painfully and slowly struggling on. Retreat after a fierce action was a distressing sight, which further depressed those taking part:

A large number of valises and entrenching tools were absent, having been lost in action or thrown away by order or otherwise: all troops however, had their arms, beside the residue of their ammunition. The officers were afoot, many of them carrying one or two of their men's rifles. The chargers bore equipment or exhausted soldiers, and towed a man hanging on the stirrup on either flank. Transport vehicles gave similar assistance. Frequently someone would fall or sit down for a rest, the first to be picked up by comrades and put on a wagon, and the second urged to his feet again. Here and there in this ghastly queue marched a fairly solid company, platoon or section.[79]

By a stroke of good fortune the Germans did not press their advantage and so slowly order was made out of the chaos. Conditions on the march gradually improved until on 5 September, 19th Brigade found themselves only fifteen miles south-east of Paris at Grisy. There, suddenly the fortunes of the BEF turned as Captain Jack excitedly reported from La Haute Maison on 7 September:

> A marvellous change has come over the situation. We have been chasing the Germans back for the past two days. Yesterday at Grisy when the brigade was formed up in columns of route at 5 am ready to march south as usual, an order arrived to say that a new French Sixth Army, north of Paris, had commenced an advance eastwards against the right flank of the German First Army, and that the BEF, French Fifth Army and Cavalry Corps were to move forward at once and attack the enemy on the Grand Morin. This totally unexpected news passed all belief after the long depressing retreat. . .[80]

New equipment and clothing also started to arrive and the first groups of replacements. On 6 September Captain Sandeman arrived with ninty-four Other Ranks for the 93rd, and the following day Aidan arrived at La Haute Maison with a further eighty-four. His journey from the Rest Camp at St Nazaire to the front had begun on 4 September when he had been placed in a detail of 19th Brigade reinforcements comprising Royal Welch Fusiliers and Middlesex, as well as his own Highlanders. There had been great confusion when they moved to the railhead, where they found no transport officer in charge and nothing to eat. Eventually rations arrived, which cheered them a little, and then 1200 troops were squeezed onto a very hot train, an exercise that was not completed until 1700.

Notwithstanding the crush, Aidan managed to secure a comfortable seat with only one other officer in the carriage. His remarkable instinct for self-preservation seemed to be developing well, although he jotted in his diary for 5 September: 'Awful lot of trouble keeping order among the troops. Very badly disciplined lot some of them. Reached Orleans via

Blois about 6.30.'[81] Arriving at Villeneuve the following day, the troops were split up into their respective Army Corps as soon as they detrained. They then started to march forward, Aidan's group spending the night in what he described as 'a very damp field'.

On the morning of 7 September Aidan's immediate concern was to find the exact location of the brigade and battalion, which were supposed to be close by. With the sound of artillery clear in the east, the draft marched as instructed to Villeneuve le Compte, only to discover that the brigade had moved the previous night to Villeneuve St Denis. But when they got there the camp was breaking up and in any case there was no 93rd. They marched on again, via Jossigny and Serries, to La Haute Maison, arriving at 1700 as firing started to their left. Here they bivouacked only four miles from the Germans and at 2000, to the undoubted relief of everyone, the 93rd came marching in.

Looking forward to cheerful friendly faces, Aidan must have been horrified to hear of the action at Le Cateau, and of the loss of so many of his comrades. It is interesting to note that, censorship aside, there is no mention of those losses in his letters home. Like so many British soldiers, his family correspondence tended to gloss over the awfulness of war and concentrate on little events rather than the great issues of life and death. He did not want to worry the family. This was, however, something that gradually changed as he, and presumably his family at home, became more battle hardened.

Chapter Nine

On the Marne and the Aisne

On 8 September, after two weeks of defensive actions and bitter retreat, the 19th Brigade was for the first time advancing to engage the enemy. The BEF had fortuitously found itself opposite a thirty-mile gap that had developed between the German First and Second Armies, and which was covered only by two weak cavalry corps and some Jaeger battalions. As the French counter-attacks began to achieve successes, the Germans felt perilously extended with an open flank to the north, and resistance still continuing to their rear in Belgium. Further British landings were reported on the coast, and there were even rumours of a substantial Russian expeditionary force that was expected by some to land soon in France. The prize of Paris now seemed out of reach, and the massive successes of August and early September could so easily be lost by a foolhardy gamble. So it was that caution prevailed, and when the Germans began to withdraw, the battered BEF was quickly hard on their heels.

British morale was suddenly high again as young Ditcham, the boy bugler with the 93rd explained in an interview recorded years later by an oral historian.

Well as long as you were going forward and pushing the German, you could go on for ever. To go the other way you were depressed for ever. I mean, that was my feeling. Your whole morale was down in your boots. But directly you went forward and were going forward – you talk about something lifting you up to the heavens – that was the difference between advance and retreat, to me, as a young man.[82]

The 19th Brigade was ordered forward towards the River Marne, as the leading brigade in the left hand column of the 4th Division. Moving in the direction of Pierre Levée with orders to attack the enemy to their front, they quickly found that the Germans had pulled back in the night. The advanced guard of 1st Middlesex then occupied a series of ridges, just to the south of the Marne. Aidan recorded his first day of action in his diary:

First troops started off about 2.45, and we left at 4.30. Firing commenced about 5.15. Lay in field in artillery formation for some time. Germans crossing the Marne at Le Ferté, and we are furnishing reserve to troops attempting to cut them off. Arrived too late apparently, and we occupied a ditch about 4 pm overlooking a wooded hill on the far side of the river, which was occupied by the German rearguard. Fired on until almost dark, when our gunners shelled them out of the wood. Were relieved about 10.30 am. Only one killed.[83]

The 93rd were fortunate with their single casualty, although somehow in the scramble Aidan lost his heavy broadsword, leaving it behind in some ditch or scrape. But there were more important matters to think about, for the Germans could now clearly be seen scaling the heights on the far bank, presenting a fine target for the British guns. Shells were soon bursting among them, but the German batteries were also firing shrapnel back, and it was the Middlesex, in their exposed forward position, that took most of the forty-one casualties in 19th Brigade, suffering three killed and thirty wounded. The River Marne appeared a formidable barrier, and no further advance was possible that day, as all the bridges had been blown, and there were no boats available. In addition, the north bank was strongly defended by infantry and machine-gunners, backed up by the artillery that had been causing such difficulty to the Middlesex.

It was a cold night in the open for the 93rd, although the Brigade HQ managed to do rather better than most, spending a comfortable night in a farm. However, the following morning, after they had enjoyed an excellent egg and bacon breakfast, the General and his staff were given an early morning call by the German guns. The farm was soon smashed and burning, albeit the startled occupants had already made a rapid exit with their maps, papers and other equipment, and a clear resolve that in future they would stay out of buildings close to the line. By now the enemy could once again be seen pulling back on the slopes above the river, with British shrapnel bursting amongst them to encourage their progress. For Captain Jack, one of the disturbed breakfast party, it was 'a gratifying sight'. That afternoon a heavy bombardment of the German riverside positions drove the defenders back from the bank and the Royal Engineers immediately rushed forward to begin work on a pontoon bridge.

Aidan's diary records his own experiences of 9 September:

Ready to move at 5.30. As picket was being withdrawn from the trench we had occupied, Germans opened on them with machine guns. Too high, no casualties. Welsh lost about 20 men during night. Column on our left shelled. We retired back about 2 miles and rested 1.30 pm. Battle still going on. Germans apparently hold the far bank in some force. Our guns still trying to shell them out. Later about 7.30 moved to Juarre, about 4 miles, for night. Lots of transport on the road, very slow moving. Arrived about 8 o'clock and were told we would move from our field at 12. At 12 told to stand-to till 3.30.[84]

Orders and counterorders, march and countermarch were commonplace, but during that night, six battalions of the 4th Division crossed the Marne under hostile fire, using boats or scrambling over damaged bridges. The news was similarly upbeat along the whole British line with major crossings taking place, so that suddenly the apparently formidable Marne barrier was broken. The following day British airmen reported that the roads to the north were packed with German troops and transport in full retreat. Aidan and the 93rd faced another early start and his diary graphically records the wanton damage left by the hastily withdrawing Germans. He crossed the Marne on the Sappers' pontoon bridge, with units breaking step in the approved manner to avoid rocking the boats with the pounding of their hobnailed boots. It was a wet miserable day and Aidan was to see for the first time the aftermath of battle.

Moved at 4.30 with large amount of artillery. Furnished left flank guard to 3rd Army. Germans have left La Ferté, and a pontoon bridge has been built during the night. Arrived at top of hill north of the river about 10 am. La Ferté badly sacked by Germans. Houses turned inside out, furniture broken, bedding in the streets. Shrapnel bullets all along the gutters up the hill, where our guns had shelled them as they retreated. 140 wounded Germans in the town. Bridge absolutely destroyed. Marched to Vendrest, arriving about 5.45. The whole road littered with bottles and dead horses. Stench appalling. Near Vendrest lots of shells thrown on the side of the road to lighten their limbers. Six dead horses on the hill.[85]

On 11 September the pursuit continued in the pouring rain, but the 93rd were in high spirits and were welcomed warmly by the French who told terrifying stories of the looting and drunkenness of the awful 'bosches'. But despite these excesses and the obvious overconsumption of alcohol, indicated by the large number of empty wine bottles by the roadside, the Germans were still fighting well. This was definitely a tactical withdrawal and not a rout. Aidan's diary records the warmth of the French hospitality for their liberators. He had slept well, which probably meant that he was billeted, for the weather had now turned so foul that urgent steps were taken to find shelter for the maximum number of soldiers.

Had an excellent rest. Reported that the French cavalry had taken 7 guns and 1000 men, numbers of machine guns and transport. Set off about 6.30. Very slow progress at first, then made a short cut and got on better. Rained in torrents during afternoon. Billeted at

Marisy St Geneviève and managed to get a capital house. The owner thought we were Prussians at first, as they had never seen British troops before. However, after explanations, were well looked after. Arrived about 6.30 and had boiled eggs and coffee. About 8, soup, omelette and sauté rabbit, and coffee and red wine. Battle meanwhile in progress about 4 miles away.[86]

The Battle of the Marne was over and the Battle of the Aisne was about to commence. Saturday 12 September was to be the last day of the pursuit, and that day the BEF engaged in a forced march of up to forty miles, which took almost twenty-four hours. The pace was punishing and large numbers of British infantry dropped out by the roadside and were unable to continue without rest. During the march Field Marshal Sir John French passed the 93rd on the road, and briefly stopped to deliver a short personal address to the Colonel and as many of the officers and men as could quickly be gathered round. The Field Marshal was brief, but the message was thoroughly appreciated:

I have not before had the opportunity of seeing the 93rd, and of thanking them for their work at Le Cateau. It was only by our troops holding on for so long, and I speak especially of the 93rd, that the French were saved from a very serious reverse. Please let your men know this![87]

For Aidan the march commenced at 0530 on the Saturday morning and finished at 1745. The 93rd then moved off again at 1230 on the Sunday, and bivouacked from 1630 until just after midnight. The battle could clearly be heard on the far side of river as the advance elements of the BEF attacked German positions on the heights to the north of the Aisne, crossing the river by pontoons and blown bridges that had been hastily repaired by the Sappers. The 93rd then marched on again from midnight until about 0500. All the while it continued to pour with rain, making the steep and twisting roads even more challenging for the exhausted soldiers. But at least the prolonged breaks from the march gave Aidan the opportunity to write his first rather damp letter home from the front. While being reasonably upbeat and matter of fact, he makes it clear how difficult the conditions had been, and how important creature comforts such as cigarettes and chocolate had become to the wet and utterly exhausted troops.

September 13th 1914

Dear Father and Mother,

There has been no opportunity of writing or at least of getting a letter posted up to now. I joined the battalion with my draft on the 7th. There was a small battle on the 8th. A fair amount of artillery fire, but very little rifle fire. We had only one man killed in the battalion. Since then we have marched every day. Starting generally about 4.30 or 5.00 am and getting in about 5 or 6 at night. The head of the Army has been in contact about every day practically, and today there is a very heavy artillery fire going on. We are standing by, ready to move. No-one seems to know what is exactly happening, but we seem to be pursuing the Germans with some vigour. The road most of the way along was littered with dead horses. The Germans are reported to be very done up. The last two days it has poured with rain, and has been very uncomfortable marching. I had no time when I left to make any arrangements about cigarettes or anything.

If you could send me some parcels of cigarettes, chocolates (Menier for preference), matches (those little boxes are most convenient), and any kind of sweets that are sufficiently durable to carry in one's haversack. Those seem to be the only things one wants out here. The mess manages to get us a meal of sorts every evening, but for other meals we only have rations, i.e. biscuits like dog biscuits, and salt corned beef, very monotonous. Postal arrangements seem very indifferent, especially as we are so much on the move, so it would be better to make up several small parcels, on the chance of one turning up. A weekly supply would be a God send. Any other little comforts would be very acceptable.

Things seem to be going quite well now. They are very reticent about telling us what is happening. This battle which is going on a mile or two away has been in progress for about three days. I just arrived in time to join in this driving of the Germans from Paris. They failed in their attempt to invest it, and are now on the run. No-one seems to know what the 15th[*] are doing. They are apparently not with the Army Corps we are in. I have met several people I knew at Oxford, two of them doing motorcycle orderlies.

One gets no opportunity for washing or any luxury like that. I haven't had my clothes off for exactly ten days now, and a week since my last wash. Not very comfortable, but I hope we get the opportunity of a wash and change of shirt soon. Have got quite a good start of a beard. In spite of all the wet during the last two days, and all the sleeping out we've done, am keeping very fit and well.

Another thing that would be very useful would be an envelope or two. One doesn't get much opportunity of writing, but there is a great scarcity of envelopes. However, cigarettes and chocolate seem to be the most important things. We get plenty of jam. But something to eat during the march and something to smoke is what is wanted.

[*] The 15th Hussars. Brother Bertie's regiment.

Hoping soon to be back, Love to you all from
Aidan.[88]

What followed on 14 September was really more of the same, although briefly the awful weather abated and the rain stopped. The BEF again attempted to carry the heights to the north of the Aisne, in the face of stubborn German resistance. The 19th Brigade were held in reserve at Venizel, occupying low ground to the south of the river that was dotted here and there with copses that screened them from the river and denied them a clear view of the battle going on to their front. British shells were passing overhead, and the 93rd also came under German bombardment, with shells bursting in the woods around them, although without causing casualties. Firing continued intermittently through the night. The next day the brigade remained in reserve to the 4th Division. However, its planned attack on the heights to the north of the Aisne did not proceed as other units to the flanks had failed to make the necessary progress. Aidan recorded the day in his diary:

Moved a little closer to enemy's line. Started at 1 am. Battle commenced again at 5.30. At intervals shells bursting all round us. In the morning two men struck by splinters. Reported that 12 guns and 300 prisoners were taken last night. Enormous gun-fire going on, and Bucy le Long, just about ³/₄ mile over North, heavily shelled. Venizel getting its share, and all the woods. Large French flank attack supposed to be going on in afternoon. Enemy must be retiring, as firing got more distant about 4 pm, but just as heavy. Turned out at 7.30 to dig trenches, about 10.30 recalled to be moved up immediately. Pouring in torrents the whole time. When ready to move off order cancelled. Endeavoured to sleep but got absolutely soaked. Pools of water where I was lying. Shelling continued.[89]

Indeed, all 19th Brigade units were still bivouacked in the woods in appalling conditions which their War Diary aptly described as 'very boggy and unhealthy'. It was also the day that, despite Aidan's optimistic pronouncements, the British and French decided it was too costly to continue the assaults on the heights. The following morning, Wednesday 16 September, the 93rd were awakened at about 0500 by four shrapnel shells bursting overhead. The only casualty was a Royal Army Medical Corps (RAMC) orderly hit by splinters. At 1000 the battalion marched off to Bucy le Long. Aidan watched two aircraft being shelled overhead, and noted that while shells were falling all around in the general vicinity, they were way off the mark, bursting at least 400 yards short of the target. As a pilot himself, he clearly took a keen interest in military aviation and frequently noted air activity in his diary. At Bucy le Long there were what he described as 'excellent straw shelters', and he was able to wash in a ditch. There followed three days of working parties, in which the 93rd attempted to clear up and make order of the aftermath of battle. On 17 September he recorded:

Battle still going on. Sent out at 10.15 with ten men to find some RFA (Royal Field Auxiliary) men who had to be buried. Found nine of them killed by a shell. Blown to pieces three days before. Unpleasant searching for identity discs. Had to collect bits in a waterproof sheet. While we were digging Germans commenced shelling the town, some of the shells coming short into the field we were digging in. Finished digging about 1.30. Returned and directly we got to the bivvy field the shelling commenced. Lay down behind a heap of earth and waited for 1½ hours, as the battalion had left. Shells going all over the place, town being blown to pieces. Several transport horses killed. A lot of shells burst quite close to us. Joined the Regiment about 3 o'clock, when shelling had practically finished. Only one of our men killed. Battle going on very noisily. Orders to join 2nd Army, but cancelled later. Moved near to St Marguerite.[90]

It was also the day on which the Commander-in-Chief issued a Special Order of the Day.

Once more I have to express my deep appreciation of the splendid behaviour of Officers, Non-Commissioned Officers and Men of the Army under my command throughout the great battle of the Aisne which has been in progress since the 12th instant. The Battle of the Marne, which lasted from the morning of 6th to the evening of the 10th, had hardly ended in the precipitate flight of the enemy when we were brought face to face with a position of extraordinary strength, carefully entrenched and prepared for defence by an Army and a Staff which are thorough adepts at such work.

Throughout the 13th and 14th that position was most gallantly attacked by the British Forces, and the passage of the Aisne effected. This is the third day the troops have been gallantly holding the position they have gained against the most desperate counter attacks and a hail of heavy artillery. I am unable to find adequate words in which to express the admiration I feel for their magnificent conduct.

The French Armies on our right and left are making good progress, and I feel sure, that we have only to hold on with tenacity to the ground we have won for a very short time longer, when the Allies will be again in full pursuit of a beaten enemy.

The self-sacrificing devotion and splendid spirit of the British Army in France will carry all before it.

J D P FRENCH, Field Marshal[91]

Despite the high praise, optimism and noble sentiments nothing changed for the 93rd. The following day Aidan was burying horses, not men, and generally tidying up St Marguerite, mending holes in the road and moving damaged telegraph wires. But the biggest challenge was the dead horses. The town was full of them. Seven were found in one yard. By 1330 they had buried twelve and dug pits for another thirteen. Then they were shelled for their trouble, with seven shrapnel bursts going off only 100 yards or so from where they were digging, forcing them to run to shelter behind a mound of earth as heavy shells burst all around them. To round off an eventful day Aidan watched two aircraft brought down, one by machine-gun fire and the other by a pom-pom.

The next day was Saturday the 19 September, but weekends make no difference in war, and the great clean-up continued. Aidan charted his platoon's grisly progress in his diary:

> Poured in torrents during night, soaked and very cold as my waterproof sheet has been purloined from my bivvy during shelling. Restful morning. Battle less vehement. In afternoon sent to bury four men who were buried in ruins on 17th. Buchanan had removed debris all morning. One foot visible. Two ? bodies burned in yard. We finished removing debris, and found only two legs and pieces of skull. Suppose the rest were blown into infinitesimal fragments. Big guns put two shells behind the town during afternoon and two during evening. Slept in hayloft, much more comfortable.[92]

The quiet morning also allowed for another letter home. In it he acknowledged a letter from his parents forwarded from Woolwich, and repeated his increasingly desperate need for the cigarettes, chocolate and matches that had evidently not arrived. He noted despondently 'postal arrangements are very vague, and it is not by any means certain that any letter from either end will reach its destination'. The letter eloquently summarised the events of the last few days, and graphically recounted his close encounter with the German guns. It had been much too close for comfort.

> There has been fighting ever since the 7th, while we have been on the move. Now (I am not allowed to say where we are), there is a big battle going on which started on the twelfth. The day before yesterday they shelled our bivouac. I was out with a party burying some dead gunners when they started. After an hour they stopped, and we returned. Just as myself and party were getting into the field, they commenced again. We lay down behind a little mound of earth about one foot high. The beastly things were flying all over the shop. Three burst in a triangle round our mound, two thirteen yards away, and one twelve. They were from a ten inch siege gun, and made holes in the ground where they struck, about four feet deep and eight across. Appallingly noisy, but they only killed one of our men

and several horses. The town was pretty badly knocked about. The battalion had of course left the bivouac field, and my waterproof sheet had disappeared in the excitement. As it rains in torrents every night, I would be glad if you would order another for me from Burberry's in London. Bigger than the ones they stock, 7'6" long and 5' broad, with little loops at each corner and half way along the sides. Ask them to pack it securely so it doesn't get damaged and send it at once to me. Otherwise I will perish of cold and wet. Last night it poured incessantly and I got no sleep. Just shivered in a pool of water.

There is no news here. We don't hear at all anything about what is happening. Nothing except noise and unpleasant smells and sights and jobs. However, I hope it will be over soon. By the way, a cake or two would be very acceptable now and then. The Germans have been through all the towns we have been through and there is nothing to buy at all of any kind.[93]

The following evening, after a wet Sunday, the 93rd marched out at 1930 and arrived shortly before midnight at Septmonts some four miles behind the front. After eight days in support on the Aisne in absolutely atrocious weather conditions, the Brigade was pulled back as Corps reserve. They were now behind the heights on the south side of the Aisne, and so sheltered from the German guns. There they found another draft of reinforcements waiting for them to replenish their still desperately depleted numbers. Best of all, they were to be in billets. The quality of life improved dramatically as Aidan recorded, although he was clearly a little uncertain about his French host:

Billeted chez M. Lafargue. Ruffian 1st water; slept in valise for first time since St. Nazaire. First decent wash, clean hose and socks etc. Very comfortable night and peaceful day. Sounds of firing still audible in north. They say there are some large guns now which have put the German 8 inch ones out of action. Mail.[94]

The next morning Aidan shaved for the first time since St Nazaire, and spent much of the day digging trenches. Soon a routine emerged, for the brigade was to remain out of contact with the enemy at Septmonts until 5 October. The Battalions paraded an hour before dawn, in full equipment, and stood to arms until daylight as was the prudent British requirement. Roll-call was then taken, and men and equipment inspected, after which the troops were dismissed and had breakfast. The mornings were generally taken up with military training, route marches to condition the men, or labour details to repair roads, dig trenches and erect barriers. The main meal was generally at mid-day and afterwards there were further work details or training, and sometimes games, which usually meant football. After tea, the guards were posted for the night, and the men finished the day with soup and bread or biscuits at about 2100, followed by roll-call and lights out.

During the day, General Gordon and his staff were much in evidence visiting the battalions in the brigade. The Brigadier was a lean spare individual with a strongly developed sense of duty who drove his staff and the brigade hard. He was a man of simple, even austere, tastes who worked with a bible at his desk and whose only relaxation was to read when work was eventually done. He firmly placed his mark on 19th Brigade and was greatly respected and well regarded as a soldier and commander.

But on Wednesday 23 September, the excitement for Aidan was the arrival of two machine-guns to replace those lost at Le Cateau. As a qualified machine-gun officer who had commanded the guns of the 3rd Battalion, he was the obvious man to take command of the newly arrived weapons. The full section establishment was a subaltern, two NCOs and twelve privates, with a further twelve men trained up to act as replacements. It was recognised that the machine-guns were a key component of an infantry battalion, but they were also heavy, mechanically complex and difficult to handle. Soldiers selected as machine-gunners needed special qualities, and were required to have 'good physique, good eyesight, calm temperament, fair education, and mechanical aptitude'.[95]

Within the section each man had specific tasks and responsibilities and they were asigned to work together as a team. The section officer commanded the guns in accordance with his orders and the developing tactical situation. He was responsible for selecting his gun positions, controlling fire and regulating the ammunition supply. He was also responsible for the dispositions and safety of his wagon, limber and horses. The sergeant was his deputy and understudy, and would take command if the officer was unable to continue. Similarly, the corporal had to be capable of deputising for the sergeant. There were then six private soldiers to each gun. No. 1 was the gunner, who also had particular responsibility for the working parts of the weapon, and keeping it clean and serviceable. He carried the heavy tripod into action. No. 2 assisted the gunner, and carried the actual weapon into action. No. 3 and No. 4 were ammunition carriers, while No. 5 was a scout, and No. 6 was the range taker. The men were also cross trained so as to be capable of filling each of the roles if it should be required. One of the other great advantages, from Aidan's point of view, was that as the guns and ammunition were conveyed by wagon and limber, he acquired a charger to go with his new responsibilities. He was also donated the riding breeks of the late Major McLean, who had fallen at Le Cateau. They fitted far better than he had dared hope.

His immediate task , however, was to take charge of the section, and to try to work it up to some semblance of efficiency. Although there is no record of how many of the 93rd's original Machine-Gun Section were still with the battalion, it seems many had been lost with their guns at Le Cateau. However, the wagon did survive and took part in the retreat. Aidan must have had a challenging task working up the section and training new men. They spent the Thursday stripping and cleaning the guns, and then filling the belts with ammunition, and on the Friday there was live firing. The section fired off 250 rounds to test the guns and familiarise themselves with the individual characteristics of each weapon. The French locals were absolutely terrified and thought the Germans had broken through! There was much to learn or remember: adjusting the tripod, mounting and demounting the gun, laying, ranging and firing. Ammunition belts had to be swiftly and correctly filled, the limbers packed and unpacked at the double, while the men had to learn range taking, the judging of distances and the correct use of field glasses. There were also horses to care for and the wagon and limber to be kept serviceable. On the Saturday Aidan had glad news about his broadsword as he recorded in his diary, although what use a machine-gun officer would find for a claymore is another matter.

Only incident, my sword which I lost on the 8th turned up, found by someone in the Middlesex on the field of Battle at Signy Signets I suppose. Several aeroplanes shelled quite close. Shells anything to 5.00 yards short of them![96]

On Sunday 27 September there was some brief excitement as the 93rd were called to arms at 0600. The brigade prepared to march to Serches, as the enemy was reported to be crossing the Aisne at Condé. The word was that the Germans had broken through, but in the event it turned out to be a small patrol that had got lost and blundered across to the British side of the line. Tranquillity was restored, the order to march rescinded and Aidan attended Church Parade at 0900. At 1100 General Gordon visited the 93rd and attended the Presbyterian service in an orchard at the east end of the village. The service was accompanied by the artillery, which continued to sound in the distance, as it did throughout the day.

The next morning, the 93rd route marched and in the afternoon Aidan rode his new charger to Soissons. Although the town was regularly shelled, he was surprised to find 'plenty of inhabitants knocking around' and some shops still open. His kilt though proved to be 'extraordinarily uncomfortable' on horseback! Perhaps the sovereigns were in part to blame! The next day there was another opportunity to watch a German aircraft flying across at only about 1500 feet, but no one seemed to take any notice of it. Aidan noted 'Sorry missed opportunity of using guns which were just outside. I think we would have had a chance of knocking it over'.[97]

By the end of September the Battle of the Aisne was all but over. The Germans had held the British and French on the river barrier, and both sides were now strongly entrenched 200 to 400 yards apart. Further attacks were judged too costly by the Allies, and in any case major changes to their dispositions were being planned. For the moment though, 19th Brigade were enjoying the rest, and were now largely re-equipped and replenished with stores and replacements, and morale was high. The mail, parcels and packages from home had also caught up with them. The Highlanders now had a surfeit of woolly waistcoats, mittens, food and post. On the last day of September Aidan noted yet another aerial sighting, enjoyed a stroll in the woods with Colonel Moulton-Barrett and recorded the latest rumours of the war:

Colder than ever at 5 o'clock. Watched one of our aeroplanes directing heavy gunfire with coloured stars. Walked through some woods with Colonel in afternoon. Very like home woods. Hazel undergrowth. Pheasants going to roost. Heard that the French have turned the German right so that it faces north now. Also that they are moving away from centre to their right flank. Heard in the morning that they had made a violent attack on 1st Army, and left 1500 dead in front of 2nd Division. Also that 2 battalions of their Guard are wiped out dead and captured.[98]

Unknown to the 93rd, plans were already well advanced to pull the BEF out of the line on the Aisne and replace them with French troops, in order to enable the British to redeploy to Flanders. There the BEF and the remnants of the Belgian Army would make up the left wing of the Allied armies.

Aidan's letter home of 3 October carried the sad news that despite the plentiful supplies enjoyed by 19th Brigade generally, his own eagerly awaited parcels of cigarettes, chocolate, matches and boiled sweets had still not appeared. His exasperation with the post was increasing.

I don't know what has happened to the mail, but I have only had one letter from each of you, and no parcel. I wonder if you have been getting my letters. The only thing I find I want is chocolate and cigarettes. Matches also are short. I detailed my needs in my first letter, but I don't know of course whether you got it.

It is getting very cold now, and the leaves are beginning to turn fast. There are lots of pheasants and partridges about here, and here and there an officer has managed to raise an antiquated shotgun, and annexes a few welcome changes in the ration line. You will have seen all about this big battle which has been going on for such a long time. We get the papers here generally about a week late, but now and then a messenger from England brings a new one. They give us really more news than we get here on the spot, as all we hear is an occasional official summary of the news, with nothing in it except that 'the situation remains unchanged and is satisfactory'. I see in a paper that arrived today that the Indian troops have started arriving now. Excellent fellows the Gurkhas will be for the Germans. The French have their Algerian troops (Turcos) fighting, and according to reports the Germans don't care for them at all. No-one seems able to form any opinion as to how long the war will last. Anything from a month to four years.

I see in the casualty lists that Maurice Dease* is killed. The 15th have suffered rather heavily too. However one can but hope that it won't last much longer. The unfortunate inhabitants of the country will be very badly off for the winter in most of the places the Germans have passed through. Such a lot of villages have been knocked about by being shelled by one side or the other, most of the unthrashed corn stacks have been pulled down to feed horses or to make beds for troops. Everything edible has of course been eaten and none except boys and old men in the villages. There are now ten 3rd battalion officers out with us. I was the first to arrive. I joined the Regiment on the 7th September and the next draft turned up on the 18th. Between those dates we had the hardest time I've had yet. On the move all hours of the day and night and lots of rain. In spite of the cold it keeps very fine now. I'm now in charge of the machine guns and have a horse to ride. A good deal more comfortable than walking.

Up to now letters seem to have taken about ten days to get home and to arrive from home. Today however some people had letters from England on the 28th, which is an improvement. The mail is all blocked by enormous parcels of shirts and socks for the troops, sent by well meaning souls at home. As GS** shirts and socks are arriving in hundreds by ordinary routine way from the transport people, it seems rather a pity and a waste of energy. I have been hoping to see something of Bertie, as we see people from lots of regiments at odd times, but I haven't come across anyone in his.[99]

Despite the obvious good intentions Aidan never did manage to link up with his brother Bertie who was still serving with the 15th Hussars. Later the Machine-Gun Section was inspected by General Gordon on one of his regular walkabouts. The next day, Sunday 4 October, marked something very special, for Aidan had his first hot bath, which he described as 'Quite an event!' Perhaps it was becoming too comfortable, for on the Monday came unexpected orders to leave Septmonts after a fortnight and march to the west. The great redeployment, which had actually started on 1 October, had reached 19th Brigade. Much of the move was to be conducted at night, with the

---

* See Appendix Two. Notes on Persons Mentioned in the text page 283.
** General Service.

troops lying up in woods during the day to escape German air observation. That day they trudged past a downed enemy aeroplane that had crash-landed. The pilot and observer, Aidan noted, had apparently broken their necks. The next day, despite the march, mail arrived at the column. With it Aidan's first parcel, and the eagerly awaited Menier chocolate and cigarettes. He must have been very pleased!

Chapter Ten

To Flanders and Le Maisnil

While 19th Brigade marched purposely towards the railhead, the brigade staff were battling with French bureaucracy and trying to make the necessary arrangements to transport what had become one of the largest British brigades on the Aisne. French military trains designated to carry an infantry brigade were simply not big enough, and for a while it seemed that men or equipment would have to be left behind. Five trains were allocated to the brigade, but the size was set and getting additional carriages seemed an impossible task. So while the exasperated staff officers planned, pleaded and argued, the brigade marched on, still by night, and with a wary eye on the sky above for German aircraft.

On Wednesday 7 October the 93rd moved off at about 1730 and arrived at Bethisy St Pierre around midnight. The 93rd's War Diary noted 'bivouacked under cover of trees. Freezing hard and bitterly cold'.[100] But Aidan did rather better than that, and the man who could assemble a telescope camera and strip down a motorcycle engine, had no difficulty in picking the lock of a motor works in the town. Before long they had a huge fire blazing in the fireplace, which kept them very snug, although Aidan later complained of a terrible draft on the back of his neck, and developed a nasty head cold.

Sitting in the flickering firelight, there was also perhaps time to contemplate the recent news from home. John and Emily Liddell had agreed that they wanted to make a direct and personal contribution to the war effort. They therefore decided, as did many others across Great Britain, to make their home available as a convalescent hospital for wounded soldiers. With three sons with the colours, their home a hospital, and their daughters preparing to lend a hand and serve as nurses, John and Emily were doing their very best for King and Country. Aidan wondered whether any of Bertie's Hussars or of the 93rd's Jocks would find their way to the Sherfield Manor Hospital, and one imagines that strings were pulled to ensure that they did.

Next morning, they were to lead the brigade to the railhead at Pont-St-Maxence. The 93rd were ready to move at 1100, then again at 1300, and eventually moved off at 1400! They arrived at the Pont-St-Maxence at about 0530, and bivouacked on the ground to the south west of the railway station, where they waited to entrain. They were readied to move at 2100, then 2300 and again at 0100, after which the entraining orders were cancelled. Clearly the brigade staff had more work to do with the French! Meanwhile, the 93rd spent a dreadfully cold night on the ground next to the railway, and moved off at 0715 to Estrées St Denis, arriving at 1100. Once again they bivouacked in the open close by the station, but this time progress was being made. The first of the brigade trains had left the previous evening with the Brigadier on board. There were none the less a further series of false starts for the 93rd, and they had to be divided between the 2nd and 3rd brigade trains.

Brigade HQ, and B and C Companies went in the first train of the day, boarding at 2200 and departing at 2300, and Aidan and his Machine-Gun Section went with them. Troop trains enjoyed a frightful reputation, with space always at a premium, and French trains were judged the worst of all. However, Aidan managed to find a place in a First Class carriage, which after the rigours of the field he found 'very comfortable'. The route was Amiens, Etaples and finally Blendecques, where they arrived at 1300 on 10 October. As Aidan's diary records, the young subalterns of the 93rd were soon doing their best to make life more tolerable.

Arrived Etaples about 7, then to Blendecques about 1, marched to St Omer, arriving about 3.30. Battalion billeted in cavalry barracks. Henderson, self and Aitken off to Hotel de Commerce, and had eggs and coffee. Rooms for night. Did some shopping and then excellent hot bath. All the officers messed at the hotel, where we had an excellent dinner. Turned in about 10 o'clock, slept in sheets.[101]

On that pleasant and convivial evening he must have reflected that he was now at St Omer, where his old school had for so long been established. He had also travelled through Blendecques, where the boys of long ago had gone on school outings. At Stonyhurst College 'Blandyke' was still the popular name for a holiday. But while the 93rd messed and slept, the Cameronians, occupants of the first 19th Brigade train, were sent to establish outposts in the region of Renescure. Henderson, Liddell and Aitken would have little time to enjoy the warmth of the Hôtel de Commerce.

Captain Jack economically described the situation in his diary.

It seems that the BEF is to advance eastwards against the right flank of the German Northern Army, in the hope of driving it (in conjunction with our Allies) out of Belgium, and anyhow of making secure the Channel Ports still in our hands. [102]

In fact, this was what has become known as 'the Race to the Sea', in which both sides had the intention of turning the other's flank and rolling up the line. Armies from both sides moved into the dull, flat and featureless Flanders countryside, which now had the potential to become the decisive point on the Western Front. It was a time of considerable confusion as the opposing forces tried to locate each other and seize the initiative before the lines were set. For the 93rd it meant probing and blocking, marching and countermarching, and never really understanding where they fitted into the unfolding battle plan.

The following day the 93rd marched to Renescure where 19th Brigade was attached to the 6th Division and had the 4th Division on its left. Cavalry scouts reported Germans in the area. Aidan was billeted in a château near the church, and once again there was the sound of guns firing in the east. The following morning the 93rd paraded at 0545 and marched at 0600, via Ebblingham, passing Hazebrouck on the right. It was a very cold and misty morning, and they passed French infantry digging trenches along the road. They were billeted at Eecke, which already contained six battalions of French Territorial infantry and the Field Ambulance of the British 5th Cavalry Division, which had a brigade in the vicinity. The French Brigadier indicated that his troops would soon be moving out to the nort-west, and the 93rd took up outpost positions with A, B and D Companies holding the line and digging in, with C Company in reserve. German cavalry were reported to be close by, and the Middlesex were in touch with the enemy. Aidan and the officers not on picket were billeted in an estaminet.

The next morning, Tuesday 13 October, the brigade concentrated at Rouge Croix, forming the III Corps Reserve, while the 5th and 6th Divisions attacked the enemy along the line Vieux Berquin – Meteren – Berthen. The 93rd moved into position by 1130 and the action commenced at 1200, with III Corps eventually turning the enemy flanks and forcing their centre to retire. It rained heavily throughout the attack, and the 93rd were permitted to move into billets while remaining at ten minutes' readiness to move. They were not called forward and at noon the next day the brigade set off, with an RFA battery attached, as one of several British columns advancing eastwards. Moving along the road towards Bailleul, the advance guard of the RWF found German outposts in the town, but they quickly melted away, causing three casualties among the Welsh, and leaving quantities of their own wounded behind.

Entering the town, 19th Brigade was greeted by cheering French civilians who were lining the streets and hanging from the windows. The cries were 'Vive L'Angleterre 'and 'Vive Les Ecossais', and the Highlanders had bread and chocolate pressed upon them by the excited people. Taking the Steenwerck road, the brigade was ordered into defensive positions around Mont deVille, a few bare knolls rising out of flat fields full of root vegetables. It was another cold, wet and uncomfortable night, with the sound of a major engagement being heard at dusk from the direction of the River Lys. There was also the periodic crackle of musketry sounding out much closer from British patrols and outposts. Farms and villages smoked and burned in the gloom of what was a very grim night.

Thursday 15th October was little better, with the 93rd rising from their beet field at 0530. They then waited until 1500 before marching back to billets at Bailleul, ariving at 1730. They were just allocating billets to the tired men when word came to be ready to move in an hour. Aidan, however, somehow found time to take a meal.

> Dined at 47 Rue de Lille, French Vet officer's house. He had a motor in his garage, and as the Germans could not take it away they smashed it to atoms. Prince Oscar has been in the town and only left there before our first troops arrived. Terrible tales from inhabitants of Germans' behaviour. [103]

At 1930 they paraded again and marched off towards Steenwerck in the south-east. Although the country was flat and open, the brigade used the roads unless actually in action, for the many wide and wet ditches made cross-country progress painfully slow. The roads were by now full of French and Belgian refugees and this added greatly to the confusion, and increased the fear of spies or German trickery. The Welsh led the columns, and with them lumbered a pair of RFA guns, ready to unlimber and fire instantly at any target that presented. Steenwerck was reached without serious incident and there the RWF advanced guard pushed forward against the German garrison which hastily withdrew before the advancing British. They left behind some barricades, improvised booby traps and a great deal of damage and confusion. The 93rd arrived at about 2200 in drizzling rain and bivouacked in another wet field to the west of the village. The brigade was generally in poor humour, after a long day, marked first by damp inactivity and then by some eleven miles of hard marching. The conditions were miserable, although Aidan recorded that the 93rd's officers somehow managed to acquire a barn and cottage for their accommodation. That night he wrote to his father:

> I received your letter of the 4th this morning. For some days we got letters from home about six days after they were sent, but we are on the move again and haven't had any for a week. I got the first of cigarettes and chocolate then (on the 7th) and the Burberry sheet yesterday. I hear that the first army (in which Bertie is) is coming up behind us, so I may see him with a bit of luck. I caught a bit of a cold the other night; very cold and damp and we slept in a wood; but it has gone now. I still keep very fit, though I could do with a wash occasionally. . .

> Apropos of letters, I have just heard that there are still 30 bags of mail for the battalion in the supply wagons. So there is probably a large supply of cigarettes there. I meant to ask before whether my

car was at home yet, as I had to arrange about having it repaired, and notice sent to you by letter, and was uncertain whether all would go right. I am glad it is finished.

The fine weather seems to have finished. It has rained both the last days and during the nights too. Not very comfortable.

The Germans are on the move again now, and we after them. Far more tiring than sitting still. We were to attack a town they held yesterday, and had just got near enough to start getting into proper formation when a message came that they had gone, so we were able to walk in without having to fight for it. I hope they'll do the same at all the towns we come to. Makes it a much quicker business getting them out of France. That we are on their track again is obvious from two things, the dead horses by the roadside and the hundreds of empty bottles. It was the same on the way up to the Aisne. Every house or cottage had all the bedding pulled out into the fields, and bottles, bottles everywhere. I believe we took quite a number or prisoners, men lying drunk in the wood. There were also a terrible number of dead horses, sometimes ten or a dozen on one hill. Not very savoury as some had been there some time. Mail is just going out, so

Love to all

Aidan[104]

The following morning the rumour was that the 93rd would be moving from their damp field into billets at around midday, but it was just that, a rumour. Instead, at 1230 they marched off through Steenwerck to Neuvéglise, crossing the Belgian frontier at 1330, with the 93rd leading the brigade. They were now acting as reserve to the newly formed British IV Corps. It must have been a special feeling for the veterans of Mons to be back on Belgian soil, this time with the Germans retreating in front of them. Reaching Neuvéglise at around 1400, they were ordered on to Vlamertinge, via Kemmel. Here the countryside became hilly, with wooded spurs and streams winding slowly through the areas of low ground. The dominating feature was the imposing Kemmel Hill and beyond was the flat Belgian plain. The 93rd had marched fourteen miles on the tiring *pavé* roads all the way. A and B Companies then took up outpost positions to screen the town, and the remainder of the men moved into billets. Aidan found himself in a school that had been equipped as a military hospital. He acquired a comfortable bed, again with the luxury of laundered sheets.

Saturday was a peaceful and uneventful day, and there was even time for shopping, the town surprisingly having been left largely unscathed by the Germans. After another comfortable night he attended Church

Parade at 0845. The troops made the most of the quiet time, resting, cutting their hair, and cleaning weapons and equipment. Aidan's diary records the remainder of the day:

Saw a demonstration of 'embussing' the Cameronians into 40 motor buses. London advertisements still all over them, and destination boards on a few. In the afternoon visited Château belonging to Marquis de Parc whose wife is English and has a house near Ashford, Kent. Slept in an armchair over some old *Punch*es.˙ They gave us coffee (the domestics) before we returned to our billets. Heard a lot of rumours about Antwerp.˙˙ Our guns arrived, but the Belgians had made no platform for them. Too many German officers in the Belgian Army! They are asking for English officers. All these motor buses had come from there.

There was also time to pen a swift letter to his mother, although news was scarce and creature comforts seemed to be the main preoccupation. However, brother Bertie attracted admiring comments after a close encounter with the enemy. In mid-September, while commanding a patrol of B Squadron of the 15th Hussars, he had been sent to search the forest of Pont Arcy. His patrol had noticed wisps of fresh straw hanging on the branches of the trees, and following the trail they came across a small tent carefully concealed deep in the wood. Inside were four or five terrified Germans who gave up without a fight, for they had been told it was the British custom to lop off the right hand of all German prisoners!

Dear Mother,

Matches arrived alright, the same day as your letter of the 8th (arrived yesterday). . .

Could you send me a change of clothes too? Those blue drawers and vests I have. One of each, a khaki shirt and collar and tie, and some coloured hankies. It is next to impossible to get things washed, and the simplest thing is to throw one's changed things away. Extravagant, but they aren't worth washing once they've been 'well' worn. I still have some socks. Those tartan ones I have, though expensive, are extraordinary, as they simply won't go into holes, and I've never met any before that I could keep my feet inside for more than a few days. . .

In my address there is no need to put Special Reserve in, just Second Argyll and Suth Hrs. Expedit Force, or 93rd if you like. We are never in the same division for any length of time. The 19th Brigade has been in every army corps except the first so far. Just doing bottle washer when wanted, and being rushed from one place where someone was wanted to another.

The helmets and second batch of chocolate haven't arrived yet. I

˙ The humorous British magazine.
˙˙ The city had been evacuated by the Belgian Army and the supporting British contingent on 7 October and was occupied by the Germans on 9 October.

have only a very indifferent woolly waistcoat with no sleeves, it is gradually dissolving into its original condition of strands of wool, and another would be very grateful and comforting if you could manage it. I brought a very nice soft khaki one from Wings with me, but it was stolen with my waterproof sheet. Excellent effort of Bert's with the four Germans.

Aidan's suggestion in his letter home that 19th Brigade were the gap fillers rushed here and there at the whim of the generals was borne out by their newly acquired nickname, 'French's Flying Brigade'. True to this soubriquet, on 19 October they were posted to III Corps. The 93rd paraded at 1315 and moved off at about 1340 to march back to Steenwerck, and then on to Estaires and Laventie. Aidan did not arrive until 0230 and during the twenty-two-mile march south had a single stop of an hour and a half. The Cameronians, on the other hand, did the journey in some style atop their London buses, the advertisements, including those for Pear's Soap and Dewar's Whisky, attracting ribald abuse from the marchers. Large formations of French cavalry were present in the area, and the troops heard that II Corps was heavily engaged to the south near La Bassée. The Germans had been strongly reinforced, and were now fighting hard to the east of Ypres. At Laventie Aidan was billeted in a house that had been previously occupied by the enemy. He noted 'Everything smashed, all the clothing pulled out of the drawers, and scattered about the floors and stairs.'[105]

By the morning of the 20 October it was clear that something significant was about to happen. It was the start of the First Battle of Ypres and the Germans now launched a prolonged series of attacks along the Allied line from the La Bassée canal in the south to the Yser estuary on the coast. French and Belgian forces were involved, but the critical point of the battle was to be between fourteen German infantry divisions, and seven British infantry divisions, supported by three much smaller cavalry divisions who were dismounted and fought as infantry. It was to be another great test for the BEF.

Despite the tension Aidan had slept well, although he still felt very tired when woken. The 19th Brigade War Diary succinctly explained the events of the day as the Brigadier made his dispositions, and moved forward to face the enemy.

7 am Cameronians and Welch Fusiliers commence to entrench on the line Fauquissart – Croix Blanche. At 12 noon the whole brigade ordered to move on Fromelles which place was reached at 3 pm. The situation at this time was as follows. The right of the 3rd Corps was at Radinghem: the left of the 2nd Corps was about Aubers. The space between these two points being held by French cavalry. Two battalions, the Welch Fusiliers and the Middlesex were pushed

forward to the line Fromelles – Pont de Pierre to hold a line slightly to the rear of the French cavalry. The enemy were in touch with the French cavalry along our front and were engaged with 6th Division at Radinghem during the afternoon. The two battalions in reserve were bivouacked about a mile NW of Fromelles for the night.[106]

Captain Jack provided further commentary in his personal diary on the local topography, and on the developing situation.

About one mile in front of Vert-Touquet, in the direction of Lille which is about 8 miles away, a low distinct ridge runs via Aubers, Fromelles, Le Maisnil and Radinghem. The country is open except at the villages and farms where there are orchards and other trees. The ditches on the low ground are lined with willows, most of them 'topped', while three quarters of a mile to our rear the sluggish Layes brook flows parallel to the ridge. The Germans, who all the time have been trying to drive back the French cavalry, commence attacking the 6th Division in the early afternoon; and from this hour fighting is in progress everywhere along the ridge where we see shells bursting incessantly.[107]

When the 93rd arrived at Fromelles at about 1630 Aidan noted 'Heavy fighting just outside the village. French cavalry in action, lots of artillery'.[108] Fromelles itself had been all but deserted by its inhabitants, although there were still quantities of livestock roaming the village. There was already serious damage to buildings. Many were on fire, including the church. The steeple hung suspended at a crazy angle and looked as if it was about to crash to earth, although it actually remained in this precarious state throughout the war. The people had clearly removed themselves in some haste when the shelling started, leaving their animals and poultry behind. Many of these became a helpful supplement to the British rations. During the night orders were received from III Corps that 19th Infantry Brigade should occupy Fromelles and Le Maisnil and fill the gap between II and III Corps. To carry out this objective the 93rd marched at 0400 to Le Maisnil, which was held by some French cavalry and cyclists, while the RWF deployed to their right to hold a line from Fromelles to Pont de Pierre. Again, French cavalry were in evidence, and one of the Fusiliers described the scene that awaited them:

A trench relief by our Ally's cavalry was a most interesting sight. As the French had no field-service uniform until 'horizon blue' was issued in 1915, they were in their full Cuirassier dress: enormous white metal helmet with horsehair hangings; breastplate, covered with cloth, over a dark blue tunic: red breeches and black leggings. They advanced to the line in single file carrying a carbine, like a popgun, in the left hand, and a lance in the right, and an enormous sabre was hooked up on the left hip. When asked why they carried lances, they said that their popguns were no use, and, having no bayonets they wanted something to deal with the enemy if he came to close quarters.[109]

With two battalions forward, the Brigadier ordered the Cameronians and the Middlesex to a central position around Bas Maisnil. The 93rd arrived at Le Maisnil at 0415, and immediately established contact with the French who were deployed to the south and east of the village. They set outposts and began to dig in on the outskirts of the village behind the French. D Company deployed to the south where they were in contact with the RWF on their right. B Company deployed to the east towards Radinghem, which had fallen to the Germans in the night. A and C Companies and Brigade HQ were in reserve in a field just west of the church with four Small Arms Ammunition (SAA) carts and other elements of the battalion transport.

Aidan arrived at about 0430 with his transport, and later noted 'We had not much time to dig trenches before it was light'.[110] He set up his guns to the south-east of Le Maisnil close to where B and D Company positions converged. His friends Blacklock and Max Aitken were close by with their platoons; the former on his left and the latter some 300 yards to his right. Patrols were being fired on from the south, and an attack was anticipated from the direction of Radinghem. What they did not realise was that the Germans had begun a series of coordinated attacks all along the front that were a determined effort to break the Allied line in Flanders.

The usual precursor to a major assault was an artillery bombardment and, as Aidan, explained, it was not long in coming. 'The Germans started to shell about 5.30 am with all kinds of guns, Black Marias*, and high explosive beasts with green, pink, white, black and yellow smoke. Heaven only knows why there were so many colours.' Then at 0600 the French cavalry began to withdraw, which came as a great surprise to the 93rd. The French did, however, leave behind four squadrons to screen Radinghem, and reported that the village was now clear of the enemy. The British were now beginning to take casualties from the shelling, with two men from A Company wounded by shrapnel. At around 0630 the Germans started to press forward with infantry, advancing from south and north-east. Soon strong rifle attacks developed that were at their height at about 0700. The strong attacks from the south came as something of a surprise, and Colonel Moulton-Barrett ordered A Company forward from his reserve to reinforce the southern perimeter and fill the gap between D Company and the RWF. It was also around this time that the Middlesex and the Cameronians arrived at Bas Maisnil,

---

* 'Black Maria' was a term used to describe a heavy German shell that exploded with a lot of black smoke. 'Jack Johnsons', named after the black heavyweight world boxing champion, were similar.

so at least the brigade was concentrated again with strong reserves in place. These initial German infantry attacks were soon driven off, and at 0745 Colonel Moulton-Barrett sent a message to Brigade HQ, summarising his position.

Whole of French Cavalry from La Voire and Bas Flandre have been withdrawn and are concentrating on La Boutillerie. They report 4 squadrons remaining on line Le Maisnil en Vespres and pt 27 just N of the 2nd S in Vespres.* This will necessitate my placing ½ Company on the Fromelles Road. The village is now being shelled from the south.[111]

The German artillery was indeed a problem, for 19th Brigade had no RFA units attached and so was without direct gunfire support. The Brigadier determined to do something about this and dispatched Captain Jack, who described his personal intervention with the French.

During the morning the action becomes very hot. I am sent by car to the commander of some French batteries, supporting us from three-quarters of a mile in rear, with a message giving our positions and asking him to open fire on the enemy's concentration in front of them. The French guns are not 'dug in', but concealed from the ridge by hedges and the trees of orchards. The commander of the batteries, a fiery little man, shouts out orders and is quickly surrounded by the necessary subordinates. In a few moments the 'soixante-quinze' field guns are blazing away by map direction at targets out of their view but described on the written messages delivered by me.[112]

45. *French field artillery supporting the 19th Infantry Brigade at Le Maisnil.*

But while Jack was seeking artillery support the position for the 93rd continued to get more difficult. The French reported that their remaining cavalry had now been driven out of Radinghem by the enemy who were now advancing on Le Maisnil. The cavalry fell back to La Boutillerie, leaving 100 cyclists to cover the two Le Maisnil – Radinghem roads. Meanwhile C Company,

* British troops often used the individual letters of place names on maps to indicate exacly where particular activity was taking place.

the 93rd's only reserve, was moved 300 yards to the west to try to find some relief from the shell fire, and the battalion horses were moved back to a farm a quarter of a mile to the north-west. Another infantry attack was mounted from the south-east and for the first time Aidan brought his machine-guns into action, helping to drive back the Germans before a serious threat developed.

Shortly afterwards Brigade HQ received a message from 19th Brigade timed at 0920.

Le Maisnil is to be held as long as at all possible, but if obliged to retire by superior force the British Infantry under command of senior officer will fall back in the direction of La Boutillerie, but retirement is only to be carried out in case of absolute necessity, of which the senior officer on the spot will be the judge. Similar instructions have been given to the Royal Welch Fusiliers and their direction of retreat is similar to yours. Please acknowledge in writing.[113]

General Gordon also ordered Colonel Ward and two companies of the Middlesex to move forward from Bas Maisnil and reinforce the 93rd. His arrival at around 1000 was preceded by another message from the Brigadier, which commented on the news of the French withdrawal and the reported German advance.

Your ASH 6 received. I do not always credit French reports and hope they may be wrong in this case. On hearing musketry fire in your direction ½ an hour ago I ordered Col Ward to take his battalion, less two companies, to reinforce Le Maisnil. As Senior Officer he will, on arrival, of course assume command. Show him this message at once. Also I have informed commandant of French artillery (ten guns) at Fromelles that you are being shelled from Bas Flandres or vicinity and asked him to shell the neighbourhood.[114]

At 1100 the church steeple close to Brigade HQ was battered by the German guns and thereafter Aidan reported a brief lull in the enemy shell fire. The remaining French troops, the cyclists, requested permission to withdraw through the British lines, but eventually agreed to stay in position screening the roads from Radinghem to the front of B Company. At noon the remaining two companies of the Middlesex moved forward to be closer to Le Maisnil, as the enemy shell fire resumed with increased intensity. After it had been going on for about fifteen minutes Aidan watched two Germans climb onto a haystack about 1100 yards away and ordered one of his guns to engage. 'Opened on them and saw one roll off, the other jumped off. Ten minutes after the same stack was again mounted by one, whom we dislodged immediately. Did not appear again'.[115]

Shortly afterwards, a German salvo burst around the house behind his position where he had concealed his section transport. The horses of the limber wagon bolted and careered off down the road and through Le Maisnil for half a mile, eventually overturning the wagon and smashing the rear portion. Most of the ammunition was in the limber and this was to cause substantial difficulties during the remainder of the action, although Aidan did manage to organise the recovery of a certain amount of it by hand.

The 93rd was now facing heavy German attacks from the south and the east and there were concerns that the Germans would exploit a gap that had developed between A Company and the RWF. A company consequently extended their line to regain contact with the Welsh. But the most serious threat was from Radinghem, where at around 1500, in the face of a heavy German attack, the French cyclists suddenly pulled back without warning, dangerously exposing the British flank. C Company and a company of the Middlesex were ordered forward to strengthen the threatened flank.

Lieutenant Blacklock, who was dug in close to Aidan's machine-gun positions, left his trenches which were facing south and dashed back with one section under heavy fire to meet the new threat that had suddenly appeared over the left shoulders of the defenders. Blacklock's intention was to form a new line facing east that could cover the positions vacated by the French and meet the new German assault, but almost immediately he fell to the ground mortally wounded. Realising the seriousness of the situation, Aidan also left his prepared positions and moved his guns forward after Blacklock's men to counter the developing attack. As he put it 'I moved the guns up to the corner of the field and tried to help'.[116]

This was the critical point of the battle. The enemy had a strong infantry force supported by at least one machine-gun in the wood and farm buildings adjacent to the road and only about 100 yards from Aidan's new position. Only moments before the Highlanders had believed the area was safely covered by the French, and now the Germans were attacking in strength. The Machine-Gun Section immediately started to suffer casualties, with Fulton being hit in the chest while carrying one of the guns forward. But the section quickly deployed the guns and kept them both in action until about 1545 when the Middlesex and some of C Company under Captain Sandeman arrived to reinforce the threatened flank. Aidan later recalled the action: 'Guns steaming like chimneys, ammunition short, and impossible to get up enough. McLellan hit while firing gun.'[117]

At about this point in the battle for Le Maisnil, Captain Jack was ordered to ride forward from Brigade HQ to assess what had now become a very confused situation. He found the Defence HQ in ditches just behind the ridge line which was under very heavy shell fire.

Some machine gun bullets are whistling past; bursts of rapid rifle fire are continually breaking out from the front companies; and the German infantry are pressing gradually nearer, particularly on Le Maisnil. The situation is growing acute. Colonel Ward says that he thinks that the Middlesex can hold on, although his only reserves have been taken away to help the Argylls; Colonel Moulton-Barrett is more doubtful.[118]

With casualties mounting and no more ammunition to service his guns, Aidan and his Machine-Gun Section retired at about 1600 and carried the heavy weapons and tripods back more than half a mile to the upturned limber. Here they collected the salvageable equipment, and packed it into the front half of the wagon. Aidan, having replenished his ammunition supplies from the limber, managed to get one gun into a nearby trench. He was soon firing on the enemy although not with great effect. 'Gun worked wretchedly, but had to stay with it as firing became very heavy.'[119]

The shelling continued too and also at around 1600 Defence HQ was hit, with OC Middlesex narrowly escaping injury. Casualties were now becoming a major problem for the 93rd and the Middlesex. At around 1630 C Company, holding off the main German assault, were enfiladed by machine-gun and rifle fire, resulting in Captain Sandeman, and Lieutenants Campbell, Fairlie and Lothian being wounded. The situation was growing increasingly desperate as the Germans continued to press, and the last reserve company of the Middlesex was ordered forward. Shortly thereafter, Colonel Ward was severely wounded, shot in the neck by a sniper. Command of Defence HQ therefore reverted to Lieutenant-Colonel Moulton-Barrett. Captain Moorhouse managed to extricate the survivors of C Company and they fell back to the crossroads. Elements of the Cameronians were also ordered forward from Bas Maisnil by the Brigadier to support the defence. Meanwhile at around 1715 Lieutenant-Colonel Moulton-Barrett, realising that the defence was collapsing, ordered a general retirement towards Bas Maisnil. Captain Thorpe, who had taken over as Adjutant that day, set about informing the battalion but the situation became increasingly confused. Moulton-Barrett then informed OC 2RWF, on his right flank, of his intention and requested that the Cameronians should cover the withdrawal. Captain Jack was moving up with the advancing Cameronians, and described the desperate situation that confronted him.

Le Maisnil is burning. . . I am horrified to meet two companies of Argylls retiring down the slope, their position having become untenable – especially through French cyclists on their left having been forced to give way – and their advanced companies decimated. I am informed that Colonel Ward, always so kind to me has been killed. . .[120]

Jack then galloped the news back to Brigade HQ, and General Gordon, accepting that the situation could not be reversed, ordered 19th Brigade to withdraw.

Aidan was still in his trench trying to nurse along the badly functioning machine-gun when the order to retire was received. Returning to the site of the crashed wagon with his gun, he found the limber gone, and one more of his men, McLean, lying dead on the ground. He also heard that another, Patrick, had been wounded. The withdrawal continued and without the horse-drawn limber, Corporal Campbell carried the gun and Lieutenant Goldie the tripod, all the way back to La Boutillerie. Later Aidan wrote of the action to his mother:

> The Germans had a machine gun in the wood, but I got that, and pretty well stopped their rifle fire until I ran out of ammunition. My limber had bolted down the road some time before, and smashed, and I had to try and get ammunition from the wreckage about 1/2 a mile away. So the guns had to be retired, and the Germans then got their gun into the farm on the far side of the road, and the net result was that everyone had to retire. We lost 200 odd men and five officers in that little corner. The distance between the hedge and wood was only about 80 yards![121]

He was a little more graphic in a later letter to an old school friend:

> The first nasty show I encountered was on October 21st. We were suddenly dashed down from near Ypres to a village called Le Maisnil which had to be held. Unfortunately the middle of our line was held by 150 French cyclists, who decamped in the middle of the afternoon without anyone knowing. We had been unmercifully shelled from about 6 am until 4 pm when the Germans suddenly started firing from a farm house and wood about 50 yards from the left of our line. I am machine gun officer, and moved my guns up within 100 yards of the edge of the wood. Two companies of ours were also brought up, and we held on until I only had three men actually left with the two guns and no ammunition. (The limber had been bolted about 1/2 a mile down the road by a shell.) The two companies lost 230 men and 5 officers, and a company of the Middlesex lost 100 men; all of this in the end of a small field not 100 yards broad. I was just behind and to the flank of all these poor devils, and it was a regular shambles.
>
> There's no doubt we did a lot of harm, as I had both guns going hard for 1/2 an hour on the wood and house, and practically silenced the fire there.

2nd Lieutenant James Cunningham also had particularly vivid memories of the withdrawal.

> I had my first experience of what real discipline meant. We

149

withdrew down a narrow lane with a rank marching on either side of the road and diving into the ditch as each salvo of German shells arrived. During one of these episodes, Captain Hyslop continued to march down the middle of the track, looking neither right nor left. After that we too withdrew in proper order. A short while later one of our men was wounded and we carried him to an empty cottage we were passing. Putting him on a bed we saw a round black hole just above his kilt, virtually no blood, and obviously very serious. At that moment Hyslop entered, took one look at the wound, and in an almost peremptory voice said 'Get out.' I thought it awful to leave the poor man but the tone of the order brooked no delay and we went. I do not think we were fifty yards down the road when a large German shell took the house at its foundations, and put it right across the road. Not one of us would have survived had Hyslop's order not been obeyed instantly.[122]

Later he recalled the Company roll-call beside a blacksmith's shop. They had gone into Le Maisnil at full strength with 230 effectives. Now only thirty-two answered their names. But perhaps the last sombre word on the action at Le Maisnil should rest with the Field Ambulance. Recovering the wounded had proved particularly difficult as their War Diary indicates.

Mid/late afternoon. Received the information that Brigade had been thrown forward to cover the village of Le Maisnil which was now under heavy shrapnel fire. The AS Highlanders and the Middlesex Regt was partially entrenched on the S and E side of the village, and had had a few casualties. The GOC ordered me to send up ambulance wagons to get the wounded. Lt Greaves proceeded in charge, but on getting near the village church, he had to return with the wagons owing to considerable danger both to men and horses from the shell fire. As dusk came on, B Bearer Sub Division with Major Rattray and Lt Williamson proceeded out to Le Maisnil to collect wounded at the same time as a message was sent for A Bearer Sub Division to immediately come forward to help, but such a rapid retirement was carried out, they were unable to get up to where B Bearer Sub Division was working in collecting wounded behind the only available cover – a straw stack. B Bearer Sub Division had managed to collect from the outskirts of the village under severe artillery and rifle fire, a good number of wounded behind the straw stacks, and on the general retirement taking place were able to render assistance to those wounded on that occasion on their way back to Bas Maisnil.

It is believed that many wounded were left behind in the darkness as some 56 men only were finally brought into the Field Ambulance.

The Brigade retired to the village of La Boutillerie and entrenched a line covering this village.[123]

Chapter Eleven

First Ypres

Le Maisnil had been Aidan's first direct encounter with the enemy and he and the battered remnants of his Machine-Gun Section had acquitted themselves extraordinarily well. Indeed, it was subsequently said that he and Cpl Campbell had saved the 93rd. However, it had been a torrid baptism of fire and Aidan described the battlefield as 'a shambles'. Lieutenant-Colonel Moulton-Barrett's decision to withdraw the 93rd was taken in the face of unrelenting German attacks, and he feared that after taking very heavy casualties his outposts were being overrun and that the Battalion would be lost. His snap decision in turn forced the withdrawal of 19th Brigade, and was made so swiftly that many wounded could not be evacuated. In addition elements of the 93rd did not receive the orders to retire and fought on or were overwhelmed. It was not just men that were lost but much equipment and regimental transport too, and this included the Regimental War Diaries, which had to be painstakingly reconstructed by the surviving participants later in the war.

The RWF, to the right of the 93rd's position, were astounded to get the order to pull back, but they had enjoyed a quiet day and despite the sounds of battle had not appreciated the success of the German assault on Le Maisnil. A serious hole had been driven into the III Corps line at Radinghem; 19th Brigade was unsupported on the left, and had only three remaining companies of Cameronians in reserve. This was clearly insufficient to restore the situation. Unaware of this, the CO of the RWF sent a message back to brigade asking if it were really necessary to retire as they were well entrenched and in touch with the French. *The War the Infantry Knew* records how he received 'a snorter in reply from the Brigadier',[124] after which the Welsh rapidly withdrew their line as ordered.

Later the RWF noted 'Two companies of Argylls at Maisnil, who did not get the order to withdraw, stood fast. They got away in the morning without trouble, but there was a to-do about it'. In the immediate aftermath of the battle, there was much discussion as to what had happened and why. The truth was that the Germans did not realise that the British had abandoned Le Maisnil for several hours and only realised that most of the British had gone in the morning.

Aidan wrote in his diary on 22 October 'Announced that 230 are unaccounted for' and later '198 men, 5 officers, is latest and most accurate account. Ure apparently walked out of his trench into the Germans arms, not having received the word to retire.'[125] The next day he described a slightly different version:

Another story about Ure is that he never got the message to retire, and long after we left, saw lights burning on front, went forward and was captured. His sergeant and a LC followed, the latter returning under an escort of Germans who made a section prisoners. Another section in a trench a few yards away lay doggo, and were able to withdraw later.[126]

Whatever the truth, it had been an awful day for the 93rd, but for the present the immediate task was to complete the withdrawal and re-establish the line. Moving back with the guns, Aidan came across a badly wounded NCO of the 93rd. Sergeant Conroy was lying down cold and disorientated on the freezing ground and without assistance would probably have died. Aidan's clear duty was to preserve his guns and recover them to safety with the few men he had left. Despite this he encouraged Conroy to get up, tended him as best as he could and then helped him to the road where there were other soldiers. There he left Conroy crawling painfully but positively in the direction of the nearest Field Dressing Station, while he ran back after his guns. Conroy did reach the Field Dressing Station and always maintained that Aidan's intervention saved his life, although militarily it was probably the wrong thing to have done.

Captain Jack described the situation in the immediate aftermath of the withdrawal and explained how the brigade 'rather mixed up and in little more than one single extended rank, lies lining the road and buildings, rifles ready and bayonets fixed, expecting the Germans at any minute'.[127] But things got better quickly. Screened by covering parties, and with the added encouragement of enemy shells bursting around them, the brigade began to dig defensive positions on the line La Boutillerie – Rouges Bancs. They also established contact with 16th Infantry Brigade on their left and with French cavalry on the right, and so the fractured line was restored. The Germans continued to probe the defences, but the covering British companies although hard-pressed, were able to drive them off, before retiring on their units as planned at dusk. The battered 93rd were in brigade reserve with A and D Companies forward and B and C Companies in the second line.

It was flat agricultural land that gently sloped down from the Fromelles Ridge. The roads and many of the fields were bordered by deep, dry ditches. The front was broken up by numerous hedges that divided the fields, many of which were ploughed, or still contained root crops. There were also numerous farms and agricultural buildings that would be ideal vantage points for artillery observers and snipers. The

93rd's appreciation of the terrain is not recorded, but it was almost certainly exactly the same as that of their comrades in the RWF, who were scathing in their analysis.

Company officers had a great deal to say about the site. A withdrawal and a straightening of the BEF line was an accepted necessity; but it was agreed that a worse position could hardly have been chosen, whatever the Higher Command responsible for choosing it may have thought. The Germans could look right down into it and see our every movement from the dominating Fromelles ridge which had perforce been abandoned to them: the ridge rises about 90 feet above the position. Higher Command in those days didn't leave their offices to go and look at the ground over which they drew lines on maps. The local view was that another mile would obviate the serious disadvantages of the new line without endangering the railway communications or the Channel Ports![128]

But like it or not, the orders were that the line must hold and there could be no more going back.

Aidan reported that there were further probing enemy attacks during the night and although they were not pressed home the battle recommenced at dawn. This time, however, there was much more British artillery, and he had heard that they were now attached to the 6th Division, and so had the support of their guns. There was also the additional comfort of knowing that the newly arrived Lahore Division was behind them at Estaires together with a brigade from II Corps, and so fresh units were available to give support if necessary. But it was still a grim situation and he wrote in his diary 'Several houses burned in the village during the day. While having lunch, a shrapnel bullet struck the ground about a foot from my elbow, entered about 2 inches into the ground.'[129] During the day the brigade suffered another sixteen dead, forty wounded and twenty were reported missing.

The following morning, Friday 23 October, German shelling commenced at dawn and Aidan wrote of shrapnel bursting all round their positions. The mess cart arrived about 0800, and Aidan testily noted that it had arrived two hours late. When it did pull up outside the cottage that was RHQ, the Highlanders immediately started unloading the provisions. A shell burst close by, spooking the horse, and a soldier stepped forward and seized the halter to calm the animal. He was immediately struck in the temple by a shrapnel bullet. There were six 93rd casualties altogether that morning, and another in the evening. In fact it was the beginning of what became an epic fortnight in which the brigade was subjected to constant harassment from shelling and sniping during daylight, with repeated infantry attacks each night.

But for the present Aidan and his much-reduced section worked on the

Maxims. He had cleaned the bad gun and discovered that the side plate spring was defective, although he was not sure whether this was the sole reason that the gun had functioned so poorly during the action. Then he found a spring for the defective belt-filling machine, and after a struggle managed to insert it, so easing the laborious task of filling the ammunition belts by hand. After the shrapnel bursts earlier in the day their cottage was again spattered by a shell, and had a window broken. It was of no consequence, however, for that evening they moved their headquarters across the road into a more spacious house. The 93rd were getting organised again, and there was even time for a brief note home:

> Dear Father,
>
> Just a line to let you know that I am still flourishing. We were in a bit of a battle two days ago and got rather a hot time of it. We were defending a village and there were more Germans than we expected. We had 198 men and 5 officers casualties. It is still going on, heavy shelling at this very minute.
>
> I hope this letter will go this evening. I got one from you last night, but no parcels for some time. However, they will no doubt roll up before long.
>
> Love from Aidan

Saturday 24 October began fine and cold. Aidan had had a much quieter night, and it had been confirmed that the 4/7th Sikhs were now in position behind the brigade. However, the Germans were soon active again as the RWF reported:

> In the morning, when we were all digging, the Germans were seen coming over Fromelles Ridge and down its slope. I counted eleven lines in open order. We lost them when they got to the bottom of the ridge because of the high hedges. We were digging again when, suddenly, they appeared from behind the hedge lining the Ver Touquet road. They deployed smartly and came on across the beet fields. At once our men began to fire rapid, and our machine guns opened. Failing to advance in line they tried to come on by short rushes of sections. Our fire stopped them. Where a platoon of A downed two or three they swung off. Everywhere they fell back and started to dig in, with snipers in all the houses to cover them. This then was not the real effort so we got on with our digging.[130]

The 93rd were still in the second line, but Aidan was anxious to test his recently adjusted 'bad gun', and so took it forward to the Middlesex trenches to try it out. It was, he wrote, 'working quite decently'. That evening the Germans made what the RWF judged 'the real effort' and continued to attack at intervals throughout the night as Aidan noted in his diary:

At 4.50 a vigorous attack began all along the line, lasted about ½ hour. At 6.15 they began again, and there was a terrific noise. All our guns going as hard as they could. Died out about 7.30. At 8.10 started again, stopped about 10 minutes later. 10.45 recommenced, did not last long. Other furious fusillades at 1 o'clock and 3.30 approximately.[131]

But the 93rd, less one Company, had moved out of their trenches at dusk and bivouacked in a field to the rear, returning to the line at 0500. This offered the brigade reserve some protection from the probing German guns, already ranged on the static defensive lines, and was to become the practice of units in the second line over the coming nights.

The pattern of artillery exchanges was also being set, as Captain Jack explained:

The Germans pound our trenches daily for about three hours in the mornings and three in the evenings with heavy howitzers. Our artillery reply is relatively feeble since we have few howitzers and not enough shells for them. Field gun shrapnel and high explosive shells, while effective against troops in the open, are useless for dealing with men in good trenches.[132]

The Germans, inevitably, had been entrenching hard on the higher ground some 500 to 700 yards distant, and their earthworks could clearly be seen in some places. The brigade front was stretched out for about two miles and was thinly held with the advanced battalions forming only a single line, with gaps between the individual companies. During the day these could be swept by defensive fire, and at night they were covered by outposts and patrolling. The infantry units established their battalion headquarters in houses or farms along the La Boutillerie Road, some 300 to 400 yards to the rear of the fighting companies.

The best possible use was made of the natural features, and the deep willow-lined ditches that were suitably placed were quickly pressed into service and improved. Barbed wire, made up on wooden reels and suitable for carrying by a single man, was starting to arrive from the rear, although still in limited quantity. It was pegged out after dark 30 yards or so ahead of the trenches in order to trip up an oncoming enemy. It was a far cry from the deep revetted trench lines and thickets of defensive wire that would come later in the war. The Germans probed under cover of darkness, sending out small patrols to crawl down ditches, and get as near as possible to the British line to test the defences. It was all very unsettling for the Tommies and Jocks, leading to frequent and prolonged outbreaks of musketry as straining eyes saw movement and blazed away at the real or imagined intruders. Ammunition was therefore another concern. For example, on the night of 25 October a series of attacks were made on the RWF and a platoon on their left officially fired off 780 rounds, although it was suggested that the true number was even greater. The techniques of night defence had to be quickly learned. As well as patrols and listening-posts, tripwires were rigged to rattle tins or even, more ambitiously, to fire a rifle set up to cover the line of the tripwire. Of course, as well as Germans, wandering livestock, made homeless by the war, foraged the battlefield to add to the confusion. There were even occasions when a bullet-riddled farm animal was to be found beside a tripwire in the morning, but then fresh meat was always a welcome addition to the rations.

Resupply was another challenge for the British. Ammunition was replenished by the two-horsed Small Arms Ammunition carts (SAA), which would trot briskly up the road from the rear echelon to their battalion headquarters around midday. The theory was that the German gunners were at dinner, and that the SAA carts were swift enough and lucky enough to avoid the few shells that came their way. Rations and other less critical stores were moved up by wagon at night, or even manhandled across the fields by infantry carrying parties if the German artillery was particularly active.

On Sunday 25 October Aidan wrote 'Only 12 casualties last night in our brigade. Shelled again most of the day, quite near headquarters in the afternoon. Quieter than last night, although there was a certain amount of firing'.[133] During the night the French troops on the right were relieved by the 8th Indian Brigade, with two battalions of British and two of Native troops. At dawn a heavy attack was made on the RWF and on the Indian troops. The latter took heavy casualties and were forced to give up some important ground on the right.* In the afternoon though, the RWF reported 'our shrapnel was bursting well and doing damage'.[134] That night the Germans attacked the Welsh again, opening the attack with very heavy rifle fire and then firing star shells 'which lit up everything as bright as day'.[135] This was judged a most unusual occurrence at this period and was specifically remarked upon. But even with the illuminating rounds, the Germans made no progress.

For Aidan, the high spot of the day was the arrival of a parcel containing woolly helmets, chocolate, and, most important of all, a tin of cigarettes. It had been posted on 17 October, and so had found its way to the front in a little over a week. Acknowledging the parcel, he also remarked enviously in a postscript:

Bertie was lucky getting some pheasant shooting. I've been in some parts of the country where there have been thousands of pheasants, but no opportunity of shooting them. The inhabitants have buried their guns so as not to be caught with firearms** I suppose.[136]

---

* The Indian troops were not a success on the Western Front. They were trained for a different type of colonial warfare and found the winter conditions particularly testing. They were soon to be redeployed to the Middle Eastern theatre of War.
** Local people later were forbidden to have firearms as a precaution against enemy saboteurs.

The following day, despite an awful night of pouring rain, Aidan's brief diary entries were again very positive. He was still snug in his house, although in the trenches the muddy conditions were becoming increasingly trying. He was no doubt also buoyed up by the double blessing of chocolate and cigarettes.

> A few shells not very far from our house in the morning. A certain amount of fire all day. Good news from other parts of the line. I Corps pushing on well. Say they haven't had such artillery targets even on manoeuvres before. Russians also reported again victorious. Moving our sleeping quarters nearer Bde headquarters.[137]

The 19th Brigade staff reported that there was no serious attack from the Germans, but a good deal of shelling and sniping, and it was sniping that was beginning to cause a particular problem for the British. Like most things military, the Germans were very good at it, and had specialist soldiers trained in the art, who enjoyed extra privileges and wore distinguishing green lanyards. The enemy also had the advantage of holding the higher ground, and made the best use of buildings, concealing their marksmen under the eaves, where it was extremely difficult to locate them. Proper communications trenches were still lacking in much of the British line, and the snipers were quick to exploit this. They systematically covered the areas where trench systems had still not been connected, and men had to dash across open ground in the daily course of their duties. This was becoming a serious cause of British casualties and the Germans were quick to seize any opportunity. The snipers also protected their own working parties, and were active during Germans attacks, which made it very dangerous for the British to employ the standard defensive tactic of lining the parapet until the enemy was almost upon them.

The RWF noticed that some of their casualties were apparently being sniped from behind, and so became convinced that an enemy patrol had somehow penetrated their line, and was now firing at them from the rear. They organised a search party, led by an officer who had already accounted for a number snipers. Eventually, they came across a large straw rick to the rear of their positions. One of the men noticed some empty German cartridges lying on the straw-covered ground and some vigorous bayonet thrusts into the rick resulted in a yelp and a frightened German came tumbling out. He had constructed a comfortable den with a number of different firing positions all carefully screened by the straw, and had enough food for a week so that he only needed to come out at night to stretch his legs and find water. A Welch Fusilier explained the grim outcome '. . . his carelessness with his used cartridge cases cost him his life, for he was finished there and then'.[138]

The rain continued to pour overnight, and the muddy conditions were not only very unpleasant but began to have an impact on the operational effectiveness of the soldiers. It was proving almost impossible for them to keep their rifles clean. The mud gummed up the working parts, plugged barrels, and risked a bulged or burst barrel if a shot was fired. There was simply nowhere to put a weapon down and keep it clean. The RWF passed forward the rifles of their reserve company to those in the front line, and some even made use of captured German weapons. Everywhere the cry was for ramrods to clear the plugged muzzles. Aidan's much more complicated machine-guns must have also presented problems in the all-pervading mud of the trenches, but at least they had a tripod and a team to carry them and keep them clean and dry.

Tuesday 27 October proved relatively uneventful, although the RWF noted that 'There was the usual Hun attack in the evening'. Aidan's diary was rather more upbeat than that, and it seems that friends and acquaintances were talking positively about the news, albeit the reality in Flanders was that the BEF was being sorely tested. He wrote:

Quiet except for our guns going last night. Saw Bourdillon* last night. Says Russians advance about 80 miles. French advanced near Verdun. Germans also supposed to be retiring in front of us. Some of our heavy guns retiring. About 9 pm heavy rifle fire broke out along the line. Stood to arms, and soon a message came from Thorpe, who is on left of brigade, that an excited officer has arrived saying that Le Touquet was captured (centre of 17 Bde) and that the Bde Headquarters were surrounded. Henderson dispatched in support. Everybody on the run. Patrol sent out and eventually reported everything normal!! All hot air. Didn't turn in until 1 am. Everyone was annoyed. Two German prisoners of 12th Bavarian Corps taken by Welsh, after having sat within ten yards or so of our trenches all yesterday and night before. Gave themselves up. One had Iron Cross.[139]

Despite the night time panic, the prisoners were clearly a great encouragement, and Aidan found the Iron Cross of interest. During the night the RWF searched the enemy dead on ground to the front of their positions and collected 438 identity discs or 'meat tags' as the Tommies called them, with typical gallows humour. There were even more dead Germans further out, that could not be reached. Over the same period the Welsh had lost thirty-four dead, but German morale and their will for victory seemed unabated as one Welshman noted:

Can't say I notice any loss of morale among the Germans, and their shooting is damned good. The most awful twaddle is written in the papers. These cocks in front of us are as bold as anything, and don't give a damn; they push through the line at night, and snipe us during the day from all sorts of places.[140]

---

* 2nd Lieutenant Rober Bourdillon was a friend from Balliol who was serving with the Intelligence Corps.

On Wednesday night, after a quiet day, the Germans attacked again with even more determination. An RWF officer described it: '11.30 pm. The Hun attacks: the hardest I have yet encountered. It was all we could do to beat them off. My servant badly wounded. There were dead Germans on our parapet and in our trench.'[141] There were Black Marias flying about over the 93rd, and Aidan stood-to several times in the night. He noted in his diary. 'Heavy rifle fire and gun fire. Our big howitzers working and making a tremendous noise when they burst'. He also explained the riddle of the misleading messages of the previous night, which had caused the 93rd to dispatch troops under Captain Henderson. 'Last night's rumour due to a Territorial Major (or Spec Reserve) in the Y and L* having nightmare! Woke up thinking he couldn't get back to his trenches. Everyone was very jumpy.'[142]

The following day, Thursday 29 October, was strangely quiet and Aidan reported only 'fitful shell fire and occasional bursts of rifle fire'. It was also noticeable that there were more hostile aeroplanes than usual flying over the lines. They flew high enough to avoid small arms fire, but were harassed by anti-aircraft shells that burst in white puffs around them, although these seldom seemed to find their targets. Over the previous week, despite the constant attention of the enemy, the battalions had worked hard to refine their defences, digging communication trenches to the fire trenches, linking up the line, and improving their shelters with timber salvaged from the damaged buildings to the rear. They also continued to lay wire, although snipers were still causing casualties. That evening the 93rd deployed a platoon to the rear of the firing line, under 2nd Lieutenant James Cunningham, to conduct a sniper watch and harass the harassers and try to hunt them down. Perhaps they had heard of the Welsh success.

Another enemy attack was expected, and it began shortly after midnight on 30 October with an intense artillery and machine-gun barrage. The British infantry immediately returned fire and the British guns were also quick to respond as Captain Jack described:

> In two minutes, or less, from the commencement of the bombardment the couple of 18-pounder batteries supporting the brigade are hard in action: a few seconds later these are joined by the 4.5 howitzer battery and the two 6-inch howitzers further away. Their shells whistle over the trees by our headquarters, the flash of their explosions fitfully lighting up the front; the clamour of all arms is deafening.[143]

This was clearly no local demonstration, but the prelude to a major infantry assault. General Gordon immediately informed HQ 6th Division of the attack by telephone and motorcycle dispatch rider. The 93rd, in reserve near Croix-Marechal, were ordered forward to the

*Yorkshire and Lancashire Regiment.

second line of defence. Captain Jack noted that 'The Argylls, a mere handful, 200 to 300 men, are soon on their way to their position of readiness'.[144]

After two hours of heavy bombardment the German guns fired at the British second line at around 0200. The machine-guns increased their volume of fire, sweeping the British lines for several minutes before suddenly stopping. This was the signal for the infantry assault to begin, and the Germans rose out of their trenches and surged forward with great courage, blowing bugles, and cheering loudly.

The 93rd were soon called to support the forward positions, with A Company being the first to move. They supported the Cameronians against a strongly delivered attack, and forced an enemy machine-gun out of action. Here the enemy was finally driven back at about 0400, leaving behind about sixty dead and eight wounded. But the most dangerous enemy penetration was on the Middlesex front, where the Germans had found a gap and were pressing forward. The remainder of the 93rd were ordered forward to turn them out, and 6th Division sent forward 200 men of the 1st Liecesters to act as the new brigade reserve. D Company, under Captain Henderson, located the Germans in a small nullah, and after heavy firing 1st Platoon cleared the enemy position after a bayonet charge, leaving fifty-eight Germans dead and twelve wounded or captured.

Aidan was stood-to for four hours during the night. He then moved forward with his guns at about 0430 am to strengthen the RWF line, by way of Brigade HQ and RWF HQ, eventually arriving in the trenches at 0700. Black Marias were bursting in great quantity, and on his way forward he had passed about fifty German prisoners, some of them wounded. The attacks had ceased at dawn, and had failed to break the British line. Three hundred or so German dead, mostly soldiers of the 223rd and 224th Reserve Regiments, were found lying in front of the defensive line. In contrast 19th Brigade casualties were four officers and seventy other ranks.

In the morning the Germans were seen to be making some efforts to reach their dead on the ground near their trenches, and so the Welsh did their best to stop them. They felt it was 'good for him to see how many there are',[145] and so at 0800 the RWF machine-guns traversed the front to discourage further activity. Aidan was more concerned to find that no gun emplacements had been prepared for him, but in their defence, the RWF had been rather busy. However, he soon got one gun set up in a firing position, although it quickly attracted the attention of the snipers, which he found 'most disturbing'.[146] Two German machine-guns were also active and that night the British line was shelled. It was wet again and another attack was anticipated, although there was some comfort to be derived from a message of congratulation from the Commander-in-Chief that had been telegrammed to the Brigade.

The next morning, Saturday 31 October, Aidan reported to RWF HQ and was ordered to stay on for the day and withdraw his guns at dusk. But when he returned to the Machine-Gun Section he found an instruction awaiting him, ordering a move to join the Middlesex by 0800. This time when he arrived there were gun emplacements ready, and he was impressed by the quality of the trenches. There was the usual shelling and it was very cold, but otherwise he spent an uneventful day with his men.

Sunday 1 November brought the news that the 93rd had marched off to Armentières, leaving Aidan feeling rather uncomfortable. He was still in the front line and with his second strange battalion in two days, although the Middlesex did make him a present of some additional belts for his guns. The shelling continued, and the latest rumour was that the Kaiser had arrived at the front to personally direct operations.

Someone else who was not at his best on 1 November was the energetic and courageous Captain Jack of the Cameronians, whose graphic diary entries have informed this story. The 19th Brigade Staff Captain wrote 'I feel about at the end of my tether and must have a rest'.[147] He was very unwell and at the point of complete collapse.

The physical stress of combat was severe and was compounded by the awful living conditions and the terrible weather. The health and well-being of the combatants, quite apart from the obvious dangers of enemy activity, was starting to become an issue. The tough professional Captain Jack lay on the floor of Brigade HQ trying to shake off whatever it was that afflicted him, while the Germans shelled the building. On 4 November he was sent back up the line to No. 7 Stationary Hospital Boulogne, where he was found to be suffering from an acute feverish chill. Shortly thereafter he was admitted to a hospital in London.

Meanwhile, the Middlesex were dealing with the aftermath of battle. One pressing task was the burying of enemy dead, in this case large numbers of very young soldiers. The Germans had begun to feed in new Reserve formations, made up of men who had not previously been called to the colours. These included university students, and those awaiting university, who had volunteered en masse at the beginning of the war and formed a new Volunteer Reserve Corps. Young, eager and intensely patriotic, many of them were under military age, but like many young men in England, they joined up anyway. These youngsters were supplemented by a cadre of experienced reservists whose ages were at the other extreme, and their junior officers were provided by cadets from the academies. They were commanded by more senior officers from the retired list. After only eight weeks of basic training, these new units were judged by some to be ready for combat and ten new Reserve Divisions were added to the German order of battle in Flanders. It was a gamble that might have won Germany the war. In fact they were slaughtered in their thousands, marching bravely forward, singing patriotic songs and cheering, and employing the old-fashioned close order formations of their pensioned-off instructors. It was dubbed the 'Massacre of the Innocents'.

Certainly, the Germans captured by the 93rd and the Middlesex were very young, and had been primed with drink before the assault. It was said that their officers only came halfway across with them, and left them to continue by themselves. Whether true or not, they had penetrated the British line, and now the company Aidan was with was burying a hundred of them, and held another fifty prisoner. He wrote to his mother, 'They are a Bavarian reserve regiment. Poor little lads, not one seemed to be more than 20 years old. One whose papers I had to take to headquarters was only 17'.[148] But the attack and the aftermath made a lasting impression, for he wrote of it again in more detail almost a month afterwards.

I suppose you saw about the Germans getting through the Middlesex trenches and the A&SH bayoneting them. It reads as a much more thrilling story than it was. The attack was made by the 224th Reserve Bavarian regiment who I think I told you were all lads from 17 to 20 and thereabouts. They seem to have primed them up with rum and sent them off to attack. There was a gap between two of the Middlesex trenches, and as there was no fire from there a few of the Germans got shepherded through; they disappeared into the darkness and went on until they got to a ditch about 50 yds behind the line of the trenches. No one knew where they were, and a platoon of ours was sent to find them. They suddenly commenced to sing and shout and loose off their rifles, and as they wouldn't stop firing had to be bayoneted. An astounding show altogether. I went into their trenches the day following and we buried about 200 all along the brigade line. I only heard of one officer being buried, and one of the prisoners they took said that their officers came halfway with them and then went back! One couldn't help being very sorry for them. All their kit and everything brand new. I believe they had only left Metz five days before, and had been told that they were going to attack the French. All such boys, judging by photos of their families etc which they had among their papers, were of very good class. However, we got a little of our own back for the episode of 21st Oct where we got rather a gruelling.[149]

But the Germans remained a formidable foe, and although they did not attack again, they continued to snipe and shell, making good use of their advantage in artillery. The 19th Brigade assessed that the artillery opposing them included a battery of heavy howitzers, a battery of 4.5-inch howitzers, and at least one horse artillery battery that had dispersed and deployed right forward in order to operate at very close range. The Germans also continued to develop their trench line and were constantly sapping forward, so that in most places their positions were only 200 to 400 yards away. On 3 November, after a quiet night, the Germans put down a heavy barrage, presumably to give some cover to their infantry. Aidan was watching them and wrote in his diary 'enemy advanced a bit during night and digging like rabbits about 400 yards in front. Got gun on to some of them with effect'.[150]

The news from the 93rd was that Lieutenant-Colonel Moulton-Barrett had relinquished command to Captain Hyslop, and was returning to England. Major Kirk, who commanded the 3rd Battalion at Woolwich, would be coming out to assume permanent command. The reasons are not stated, but the man with whom Aidan had strolled through the woods and hazel undergrowth on 30 September and watched the pheasants roosting, had fought at Mons and Le Cateau, participated in the retreat, and fought through the Battles of the Marne and the Aisne and now First Ypres. He had lost friends and seen his cherished battalion reduced to only a few hundred men. Under his leadership the 93rd had fought magnificently and now he would return to England with his memories. But for Aidan it was another grim night with the Middlesex, as he recorded on 4 November:

> Very misty indeed last night. Impossible to see more than 50 yards in front. However, apart from three 'stand to arms' and a dozen shells or so, mixed with some very high rifle fire, nothing happened. Shelling didn't begin until about 1030. Suppose 50 shells burst just along trench that I am in, during 1½ hours. Not much reply from our guns. Kaiser stated to have ordered Ypres to be taken by 30th ult. . . Heard yesterday that 91st were somewhere behind.* Bombardment again in afternoon. Poured with rain from 3 pm onwards. Trenches a quagmire. Very dark night.[151]

The next day one of his emplacements was badly damaged, and he withdrew the gun and in the evening dug another. On 6 November he wrote home:

> Dear Mother,
> We're still in the trenches, so as I told you in my last letter, my guns and self are attached to another regiment. Just a week since I wormed my way in. The German trenches are only about 400 yds

---

* Aidan was wrong about the 91st, or more accurately the 1st Battalion the Argyll and Sutherland Highlanders, who were *en route* home from Dinapore in India. They were actually somewhere between Port Said and Gibraltar at this time, and were to arrive at Plymouth on 17 November. They landed in France at Le Havre on 20 December.

away, so one can't show one's head much. We have very deep, narrow trenches, only about 18 inches wide, with wider places here and there. They shell us regularly, but have only made one attack, 50 prisoners and over 100 dead, buried all by the one company I am with. . .

I have a little snuggery to sleep in, about 4 ft long, 3 wide, and 3 high, burrowed out in the side of the trench, and with a waterproof sheet over the opening. I can have a candle burning, which makes it feel quite cheerful.

I was disturbed during the last paragraph by a violent burst of rifle fire on our right, but it died out very quickly. The nights are very misty now, and it is impossible to see more than 30 yds or so in front. So on the least alarm one has to be jumping up and standing to arms. Some nights are much quieter than others, but there is generally a vigorous fusillade for ten minutes or so twice or three times a night. Being separated *pro tem* from the battalion I don't get any letters or parcels, but I hope to rejoin soon.

I had my boots off and changed my socks today, the first time since 18th September!!! Been kept pretty busy since then. Everybody, including the Germans I imagine, is longing for the war to finish. It is fearfully tiring and monotonous (if that can be applied to a day of heavy shelling) but everybody keeps very cheerful. The Regiment I am with has been in these trenches since Sept 22nd, the day after the battle I told you about. You will see in the papers we lost five officers that day. Had to retire and were unable to move the wounded. Left them in a house (one of the sole standing ones) with a Red Cross flag, so I suppose and hope that the Germans are looking after them. Two were killed, I believe, but no-one was quite sure.

The Kaiser has been over here. Thank heavens; he ordered Calais to be taken against the will of his generals, and has apparently failed. Bungled it as usual.

Well, goodbye,

Love to all,

From Aidan[152]

A few days later he wrote another informative letter, this time to his father, and as well as imparting news and information, he dwelt on the vital necessities of cigarettes and chocolate.

November 8th

Dear Father,

I have got your letter of the 31st ult. Please don't stop sending the cigarettes. When I said that they didn't arrive regularly I meant that I didn't get them at weekly intervals, but they all seem to turn up eventually. I got two boxes within two days of each other about a week ago. I really couldn't exist without cigarettes. The shirts, vests, drawers, arrived two days ago, and also a newsy letter from Dolly.

I am sorry to hear that I missed Bertie. I know we were within six miles or so of each other.

I am still in the trenches. Very dirty, as it is all clay, and every night it is so damp and misty that the clay just rubs off on one's clothing in sheets. Of course it is quite impossible to wash or anything like that, and sleep is not a very restful performance. I've had a little hole cut out for myself, where I get a certain amount of shelter. It is extraordinary the number of shells and the variety that the Germans throw about. It is only 3 in the afternoon and it has been going on since about 8 this morning. We estimate that about 350 shells have burst along and behind one bit of trench about 700 yds long. I'm becoming quite deaf with the noise. However, apart from throwing a little dirty mud on one, they do surprisingly little harm. We've got some siege guns up here now though of our own, that make more noise, and have apparently infinitely more effect than the German Jack Johnsons.

You might tell mother that I have seen an excellent little box of sweets called 'Pascall's Expeditionary Chocolate and Confectionary Ration.' It includes a packet of throat lozenges which are useful these cold nights.

Love from Aidan[153]

His descriptions of the shelling accords with the Brigade War Diary, which noted that on 7 and 8 November the Middlesex positions were heavily shelled. But while Aidan makes light of it, the recorded result was 'heavy casualties'. What is more, the hostile guns that were doing such damage could not be located. The only reply that could be made by the British gunners was to bombard the enemy's trenches, rather than getting to the heart of the matter and the source of the Jack Johnsons.

Chapter Twelve

'Plugstreet' and the Middlesex

While Aidan remained with the Middlesex under the German guns, his comrades in the 93rd marched off to the rear and the prospect of some hard digging. Major Kirk had joined them on 6 November to command. On 7 November they bivouacked at Pont de Nieppe, where the orders had at first been 'Do no work today as you will be required to work elsewhere tonight.'[154] Two officers were at once sent to reconnoitre the position to be entrenched, but this was to prove a wasted journey for at noon a General Staff Officer from the 4th Division called at Battalion HQ, and warned Major Kirk that the 93rd should ready itself to move at short notice to support the Division if required. They were indeed required, and the word was not long in coming. Only an hour and a half later they were ordered to march to Le Bizet and were placed under the orders of Brigadier General Hunter-Weston commanding the 11th Infantry Brigade. Shortly afterwards they moved forward to Ploegsteert, and bivouacked to the north of the village. That night Lieutenant Rose was wounded.

The following morning, Sunday 8 November, the 93rd moved into billets in Ploegsteert at 0500 and in the afternoon were warned for the trenches in Ploegsteert Wood. It was a place that was to become a famous battleground for most of the war.* The 93rd's relief was completed by 2300 after a very muddy march in. The rest of that night and the Monday morning were quiet in the front-line trenches. However, at noon there was a problem with British lyddite shells dropping short onto the Highlanders, and Captain Sotheby was wounded by British shrapnel. B Company complained bitterly, and shortly afterwards they were shelled again, this time by German howitzers, which wounded Lieutenant Macpherson, and a soldier. They also learnt that the 93rd were to make an attack on the German trenches that night.

A conference was held during the afternoon to plan the attack, attended by the COs of the participating units. These were Lieutenant-Colonel Butler commanding Ploegsteert Wood Section; Major Kirk commanding the 93rd; Major Prowse commanding the Somerset Light Infantry; a Lieutenant-Colonel commanding the East Lancs; and Captain Woodman commanding the Lancashire Fusiliers. The 93rd had

* Lieutenant-Colonel Winston Churchill commanded the 6th Royal Scots Fusiliers at 'Plugstreet' in 1916, when he briefly left Westminster to return to soldiering.

already sent a party to carry out a reconnaissance of the ground to be taken, and so were able to contribute positively to the planning process.

The enemy were holding a trench line at right angles to the edge of the wood which was protected by a deep wet ditch, which would delay any advance against their flank from the wood. It was a strong position and the unburied British dead from two previously failed attacks covered the ground in front of the German line. The enemy trenches were being shelled during the day and it was agreed that the attack should take place at 2330 and would be preceded by half an hour's intense bombardment. Three salvos by the guns would mark the beginning and end of the bombardment. The infantry were to move forward under cover of the artillery barrage and take up assault positions. The East Lancs would attack the German positions furthest from the wood on the right, while the 93rd would advance from the Lancashire Fusiliers' trenches against the two sections of enemy trench on the left. It was important that the enemy were attacked in a coordinated way, so that all were engaged simultaneously and could not enfilade the attackers. The plan was that the Germans' defenses would be suppressed by the bombardment, and that they would also be distracted in advance of the main assault by half a company of Highlanders. These would make a noisy demonstration on their right flank from the edge of the wood.

During the evening, as the troops moved to their start points, the British artillery kept up desultory fire. At 2300, as planned, the heavy artillery bombardment commenced, setting fire to a house that blazed merrily in the area that the Highlanders were due to attack. When the guns ceased at 2330, half of B Company, under the newly arrived Major Maxwell Rouse, moved to the edge of the wood, which they had reached without coming under fire, and made their demonstration. The two assault companies now advanced towards their designated areas of the enemy trench line, and after arriving at the burning house Captain Henderson gave D Company the order to charge. Lit up by the blazing building the Highlanders were easily seen and fired on by the enemy and almost at once Henderson fell wounded. Without his direction his men lost their way in the noise and confusion of battle and moved on the section of trenches that were already being assaulted by A Company. Part of the German line was thus not under direct attack and was able to enfilade the attackers, who although they cut the wire to the front of the German trenches, were not able to penetrate the position. Major Rouse was watching the deteriorating situation from the edge of the wood with his half company. Seeing that the barrage had broken down the hedge in front of the German trenches and realising that the plan was going wrong, Maxwell Rouse moved his men forward from the wood and tried to charge. This attack was at once met by very heavy fire and he found that, despite the shell damage, his men could not get past the still formidable hedge barrier. At this point the enemy twice tried to counterattack from their trenches, but were driven back by Major Rouse and his Highlanders.

One young man involved that night was the boy bugler Ditcham, now pressed into service as a Company Runner. It had been recognised that the bugles and drums had become redundant, and in any case only five of the original sixteen boys were left. Carrying messages was a vital task that need not involve carrying arms, and conveniently the five youngsters made for one per Company and a spare. They were attached to Regimental HQ and carried sealed messages, or anything else that might be required to their respective companies. Ditcham serviced Maxwell Rouse's B Company, and that night, having delivered a message and obtained the required signature, he was hit as he dashed back to HQ.

> . . . what saved me from getting injured was the bullet hit me in the pack, went through my haversack, my emergency ration, not my haversack ration, my tin of bully, my biscuits and my clothing. And fortunately enough that was sufficient to stop it going into me. But what it did do was knock me straight on my face.[155]

But despite their casualties the 93rd were still not finished. Lieutenant Clark who commanded the battalion reserve, the other half of Major Rouse's B Company, now collected together the survivors of the two failed company attacks and led them back around the burning house to try again. But the enemy had now brought up reinforcements, were firing with machine guns, and were able to threaten the rear of the brave new assault. Captain Hyslop was sent forward to lead them back, and under his direction the 93rd withdrew to the support trenches in the wood. The attack had been a costly failure. Captain Henderson, Aidan's dining companion at the Hotel de Commence in St Omer, and the leader of the bayonet charge in the nullah was dead. The battalion, that would normally number around 1000 men had entered the battle with 330, and had now lost another 130 killed, wounded or missing.

The next day, 10 November, congratulations were received from GOC 19th Brigade, 6th Division and III Corps and from the Commander in Chief, but it had been another severe test for the battered 93rd. The Official History spared the action just two sentences:

> In the 4th Division area, the group of houses held by the enemy in front of Ploegsteert Wood was shelled all day by three field batteries, and a field and siege howitzer; and at 11.30pm, an attack was made on it by the1/East Lancashire, 2/Argyll and Sutherland Highlanders and 2/Lancashire Fusiliers, each battalion putting in two companies. Success was gained on the right, but as no progress was made elsewhere the trenches regained were abandoned before daylight.[156]

Lieutenant Cunningham wrote later of the failed attack:

The position was afterwards called 'The Bird Cage' and I think was not captured until much later in the war. I was wounded in this action, being hit in the eyes and forehead and a bullet going through my cheek and out of my mouth – fortunately my mouth was generally open.[157]

Back with the Middlesex, things had been much quieter, but Aidan's thoughts had been with his comrades. He noted in his diary:

Several alarms as the night was dark, but never fired gun. Star shells very comforting. Shelled D Coy in morning. 58 shells in about 5 minutes. Heard last night that 93rd are with 4th Division and were going to make a surprise attack. Dreadfully cold, very little sleep.[158]

By this time of course the surprise attack had taken place, but it is interesting to reflect on how quickly the 'secret' news had spread. Security was an issue and the fear of spies already an abiding fear along the front. Only recently a Belgian farmer had come under suspicion, and was tried and convicted by the French of collaborating with the enemy. He had owned a white horse and was alleged to have used it in sight of the enemy in accordance with some prearranged code in order to signal vital information. It might sound unlikely today, but he was found guilty, and the mayors of the local communes were obliged to attend his execution. Smoking chimneys and the manipulation of the hands of church clocks were other suggested methods of communicating with the enemy in the paranoia that prevailed.

The next day Aidan heard of the outcome of the night attack, noting very briefly: 'Heard 93rd lost 90 and 5 officers. Quieter day, not much shelling except far back.'[159] He must have felt desperately concerned about his friends, but there was still a job to be done with the Middlesex. Although enemy activity was now much reduced, the weather was getting steadily worse and making living conditions increasingly difficult. Extracts from his diaries begin to have a trying monotony. 'Rained in torrents during night, gale of wind at times and sleet. Trenches a quagmire. Impossible to get any sleep.'[160] 'Heavy rain at nightfall, trenches in an awful state. Rifle fire on left about midnight, didn't come to anything.'[161] He was also missing his comrades in the 93rd.

Saturday 14 November was a particularly bad day for Aidan. First of all, a Middlesex officer that had befriended him, Captain Evatt, was killed by a sniper in the morning. Then came the seemingly excellent news that 19th Brigade was to be relieved by the 20th Brigade, and that the Middlesex would be moving out of the line, to be replaced by the Border Regiment. Unfortunately, the news carried an unpleasant rider, for Aidan and the Machine-Gun Section would have to stay behind. The next day, there was another more personal disaster. It had snowed overnight and poured with rain during the day. Determined to make the best of things, Aidan had made his way to see friends in a nearby RFA battery HQ, where he had a wash and a 'very comfortable sleep.' However, on returning to his 'bivvy' in the trenches, he found that all his gear had been stolen, presumably by the light-fingered Cumbrians of the Border Regiment.

When I returned, found that all my stuff, waterproof sheets, haversack, water bottle, cigarettes, everything had been taken from my dugout. People on right kicked up an awful hullabaloo during night. Trenches in an awful muck. No mess or seeming possibility of getting any food. [162]

The next day it poured with rain. Cold, wet, hungry and thoroughly fed up he wrote a disconsolate letter home:

November 16th

Dear Mother,

Still in the trenches. The regiment I was attached to has gone away and been relieved by another one, but I remain. It has rained almost continuously now for about five days, and the whole place is a sea of mud. I have had everything I had with me taken by some ruffian, so feel rather at a loose end. I'm afraid there's no chance of seeing any of it back. My haversack with all my possessions which I could possibly cram into it has gone with the rest. All taken out of my dugout while my back was turned. Most annoying! Getting rather tired of this underground existence, especially with the weather as it is. Trenches are dug in clay too. My battalion went away about a fortnight ago, but I have heard nothing of them since. Very lonely without them and hoping to rejoin soon. This seems a never ending business, no-one getting any forrarder.

Love to all of you,

Aidan[163]

But in the evening the news was much better and he was told to withdraw his guns and rejoin the 93rd. He found them two miles back, and very bucked to see him and to have just received a new draft of 97 men under Lieutenant Purvis who was also rejoining them. However, there was to be no rest or respite for Aidan. The following day the 93rd moved off at 1430, passing through Armentières to trenches near Houplines, which they took over from the Royal Warwickshire Regiment and the Royal Dublin Fusiliers. It had rained for most of the day and the trenches were a sea of mud. Somehow, Aidan managed to find a snug dugout. The new brigade line ran from L'Epinette to La Ruage just east of Houplines, with the Cameronians on the left, the RWF in the centre and the 93rd on the right. The Middlesex were behind in brigade Reserve.

The defenses here were a single trench, really little more than a ditch about five feet deep, and ankle-deep in water and slimy mud. There were no proper fire-steps in most places, but these were gradually added. They were carved into the front wall of the trench, to make a ledge a foot or so above the bottom of the trench that enabled the soldier to step up and handle his rifle more easily over the parapet. Dugouts were very rare at this time, and most soldiers had to settle for crude 'bivvys'. These were ledges or recesses cut in the back wall, or parados, of the trench, in which the Highlanders lived when not actually on guard, dredging the mud from the bottom of the trench, cleaning their weapons or carrying out any one of a dozen or so other repetitive tasks that filled their days and nights.

Often the 'bivvys' were roofed with old doors or other timber, salvaged from bombed and abandoned houses. A ground sheet or some other material would be draped across the entrance as a makeshift curtain to keep the cold and damp out and the light and warmth in. But the reality was that these niches were neither dry nor comfortable and they certainly offered very limited protection from the enemy. The floors were wet and slippery, the mud walls constantly oozed water, and the wooden roofs and fabric fronts offered little protection against flying metal.

The other great difficulty at this time was that the trench lines were still not properly linked up, either laterally or to the rear. This meant that men had to scramble out to deliver messages or when casualties had to be evacuated, or even to relieve themselves. Any exit from the trenches in daylight involved either a breathless dash to the nearest cover or a lengthy crawl on the belly through the turnip tops. The German snipers knew this and watched carefully, so that any exit from the trench was at considerable risk to life and limb. It made life extremely difficult and the death toll slowly mounted, even as the trenches were gradually extended and communication trenches dug to the rear.

One young man who was only too well aware of the danger from snipers was the B Company Runner, Ditcham, who reflected on the improvement slowly being made, but still acknowledged the dangers:

Well life became easy to a degree because you didn't expose yourself, because you had a communication trench back. Of course in some cases you couldn't use the communication trench because it was so flooded with water. And you had to use your own means of getting there. You used to know the good sort of spots and the bad spots. Either to walk or where you would expose yourself too much. I mean, if you exposed yourself of course, you were lucky to get away with it because the snipers would come on.[164]

But 17 November was remarkable for another reason too, for it was chosen to mark the official end of the Firest Battle of Ypres. The so-called 'Race to the Sea' was over, and neither side had managed to find their way around an exposed flank and turn the line. Germany had made a last great effort to try finally to secure the quick victory in the west that she had so long planned. The Allies, and particularly the BEF, had held the line, although the Germans clearly now had the tactical advantage in terms of the higher ground that they occupied. Both sides were now physically exhausted. For a few months there was to be a generally quieter period while the combatants recovered their breath, restocked their supplies, and continued the lengthy process of making their positions habitable and trench life sustainable.

On a personal level, Aidan started on the replacement process immediately. He wrote a lengthy letter home, giving the good news that he was back with the 93rd, and setting out his extensive requirements to replace his stolen equipment.

November 17th

Dear Mother.

I am afraid my last PC* was not very cheerful in tone. I was rather fed up at not being relieved with the Middlesex. However, I only stayed in those trenches two days longer when I got an order to rejoin the A&SH. I fully expected a rest, but we marched straight to some other trenches the day after I rejoined (which I did in the dead of night). So here I am again having been in contact with the enemy since the 30th of last month. It freezes hard at night now, and for the last five days (today was fine), has rained heavily. Makes this life rather uncomfortable. This part of the line has been very busy, but both sides seem rather fought to a standstill.

My Burberry is just about done. All this pushing along trenches has worn it round the sides, and at the elbows and higgin. Could you order me another from the London people who have my measurements? Made of stout gabardine, cavalry pattern, and lined with heavy fleece. Not detachable lining like the last one I got from them, but with the fleece firmly stitched in.

Boots too are done. Bartlay in Piccadilly has my measurements, but they must be ever so much larger than the last pair of shoes he made for me. They were small even with thin socks, and I like wearing two pairs of very thick ones.

Clasp knife with tin opener also disappeared with my haversack. I can get the latter replaced locally. Woolly gloves would be nice also. The cardigan and the humbugs and chocolate I got yesterday when

* PC - Postal Communication.

I joined the Battalion again. Waistcoat very comfy indeed, and the hankies were much needed. I devoured Ivelcon soups with much relish this morning, very good indeed. Other food stuffs, such as anchovy paste, *paté de foie gras*, the St Ivel veal and ham pie with eggs mentioned in the Ivelcon box, mixed biscuits, cakes (in tins) especially the latter, would make a very welcome change in the rations, which is practically all we are able to get in this trenched existence.

We mess by companies nowadays, and little comforts such as the above are always very acceptable. There are three of us only messing together at present.

Most important of all, which I nearly forgot, my air pillow was alas stolen, I am desolate at night without it. It must be a thin one which one can fold up into one's pocket.

Gaiters, black Stohwasser pattern, are also going to pieces. Below are the approximate dimensions of my leg over breeches. Length along side of gaiters 13 inches.

Also a pair of military spurs, chains straps and instep protectors. Last but not least my wrist watch strap broke and the watch is lost. If you could get me one of those luminous ones I would be very grateful.

I am afraid this letter is full of wants, but what with thefts, losses, wear and tear, I am becoming less well equipped than I was at the beginning.

Just remembered, collapsible knife, fork and spoon.

I just missed seeing the Northumberland Hussars. They were billeted in the same village as the A&SH when I rejoined. One of our subalterns, Anderson, lives near Hexham and told me they were there. I went along next morning, but they had gone at daybreak. Alec Leith, Stobart, Savill Clayton, are I believe with them. The battalion had another engagement while I was away and lost fairly heavily again, you will have seen that though by the casualty lists. So I didn't miss much by staying in the trenches, though my trials were more extended. It was very trying for the men for there was a certainty of there being casualties every day, and the uncertainty as to whose turn it would be next. One saw a lot in the papers at the beginning of the war about the Germans' rotten rifle fire. Well, they have some extraordinary good shots. There were always a few on the lookout all day, and woe betide anyone who happened to show the least bit of his head above the parapet. They didn't miss very often if time was given them to get an aim. There was a high brick wall behind part of the trenches, which they shelled to pieces. There was a communication trench behind this, where the men used to cook by day. If anyone showed up against one of the holes in the wall, he was sure to be fired at.

Altogether their snipers were extraordinarily good. Of course our men played the same game, and as the Germans seemed very careless about walking about behind their trenches we more than got our own back. One of the prisoners we got said they had 800 dead in their lines. That I suppose was during a length of time our brigade had lost about 150 or so altogether, so they didn't do so well.

I've just wrapped up in my blanket, 3 waterproof sheets and a German bivouac cover I found, and am feeling tolerably warm, and quite ready for a sleep. Three German machine guns are firing on our left, at what I can't make out, as there is no rifle fire either from their side or from ours. However, I hope it doesn't mean I have to turn out as I am feeling quite snug. Also my feet feel almost warm. As they have been wet now for some ten days or so, I don't know whether they are there or not sometimes, they get so cold and numb. I am hoping we don't have to spend Christmas in these trenches, but I suppose it's quite on the cards.

I wrote to Uncle Matt, congratulating him, a week or two ago, and heard from him about three days ago.[*]

Time for a little shut eye.

Lots of love to all

from Aidan[165]

The next few days were particularly cold with snow and hard frosts and Aidan was anxiously awaiting the arrival of his parcels from home. The Germans were not nearly as active at Houplines as they had been at La Boutillerie. There was some sniping but much less hostile artillery fire against the line. Only about 100 yards separated the combatants on the left of the brigade line, but opposite the centre and the right they were between 500 and 800 yards apart. For the 93rd the distance was about 500 yards.

On 19 November the brigade was strengthened by the arrival of the 5th (Territorial) Battalion of the Scottish Rifles who moved into billets in Armentières. On 21 November a further draft of 150 men arrived for the 93rd, under Captain Kennedy and Lieutenant Hutchison, although for the present they remained behind the lines. The previous night the draft had been billeted in Bailleul when it was bombed by German aircraft. Hutchison was another diarist and machine-gunner, who had attended the same Machine-Gun Course as Aidan at the School of Musketry at Hythe in 1913.[**] For the moment though, the prime task of the 93rd was to make the trenches as habitable as possible, and to extend

---

[*] Aidan's Uncle Matt had just got married.
[**] Hutchison was to write a number of memoirs of this period which have served to inform this account.

and improve them so as to withstand the ravages of both the winter and the Germans.

On Sunday 22 November, another date sometimes associated with the end of First Ypres, Aidan wrote another lengthy letter home. Writing to his middle sister, Mary Monica or 'the Toad', now nursing at Sherfield Manor, he was rather more forthcoming about the realities of life than was his habit with his parents. Accompanying the letter was a leaflet entitled 'HOW THE SOLDIER MAY GUARD HIMSELF AGAINST INFESTATION WITH LICE'.

November 22

My Dear Toad,

Hope you are keeping fit and managing to nurse the *blessés* Belges without squalor. Talk of dirt and unshaveness. It's now one month and twelve days since I had a bath and have been in the trenches now for 24 days with one solitary attempt to wash about ten days ago. The major RAMC sent down to the medical officer of the Middlesex (to whom I was attached for a fortnight while the battalion took things more or less restfully behind) to know if any of the men were getting infected with insects. The MO's (Medical Officer's) reply was to the effect that all the men and most of the officers were hopping with them.

The only reply was a hundred or so pamphlets similar to the enclosed. But of course no Xpol, Benzene, flat irons, boilers or even fine combs were provided, so until that welcome parcel of change of clothing came I suffered in silence. Pleasant thought isn't it.

I rejoined the battalion about five days ago only to go straight into more trenches with every prospect of staying in them for months. Thank heaven the Allebosches leave us quite in peace at present except for an occasional shot every ten minutes or so which never goes near anyone.

The cold is awful. They do say that there were 22 degrees of frost last night. I don't know whether its true, but I can quite believe it. It's almost intolerable, snow too. However it's better than rain of which I endured ten days or so. Mud a foot deep in parts of the trench and no way of dealing with it. Caked in mud from toe to summit of the cranium. However one exists and almost grows fat. If you are at any time feeling indolent and wanting something to do, and are also feeling affluent you can purchase any little luxuries such as chocolates of rich assortment, or even *marrons glacés*. Things get here in under the week now that we are glued to one spot.

There is talk of allowing officers eight days' leave in France or ten if they want to go to England. Hardly seems worth while though because it would be so horrible having to start off for here again: worse than going back to school. I believe if one could get a motor to give one a lift to the coast it would be an easy matter to get home. Only five or six hours to Boulogne. But trains are not very well organized at present.

I wonder when people at home will realise what it is like out here, how urgently more men are wanted. It makes one sick, to see the *Daily Mirror* and *Sketch* treating the whole thing as a huge joke arranged for their benefit. Perhaps the fact that 57,000 casualties to men and 2000 officers up to the end of last month, and the fact that there have been bigger casualty lists so far this month than ever previously will begin to wake them up. Rather sickening all the fuss about the London Scottish.* There isn't a regiment out here that hasn't bayonet charged probably dozens of times and lost far more than the London Scots. Yet the censor allows their name to be known and all the regiments who have done far, far more heroic things never get heard of.

Well goodbye Toadmine,

Love to all from Aidan[166]

The following day, Monday 23 November, the new draft arrived in the trenches, and the battalion remained very worried by the snipers who harassed constantly. There was also some shelling, and the Germans managed to set fire to a farm and haystacks behind the lines where the 93rd's rations were stored. The British guns shelled the farms in the German rear areas in retaliation. A new scheme was also introduced to allow one platoon per company out of the line for a couple of days at a time to give them a rest. It was, of course, a good idea, and appreciated by the men. However, it was of little consolation to the 93rd's little band of machine-gunners, who had been continuously in action since 30 October and could not be spared to rest.

The newly arrived Lieutenant Hutchison quickly appreciated just how deadly the snipers were, writing later:

On my first day in the trench I witnessed my first casualty, an elderly man who, coming from his bivvy, for an instant raised himself to stretch in the morning air. The warning cry was too late. His cap tumbled off and he sagged at the knee, as little bits of bone and blood spots spattered his comrades and the trench side. Then he collapsed in a heap, a neat hole drilled in the forehead and a gaping

---

* The London Scottish were a Territorial Force Battalion involved in heavy fighting on 31 October 1914. They attacked up the slope of the Messines Range on Halloween night and were involved in fierce hand-to-hand fighting, taking many casualties. This action was widely reported in the press.

wound at the back of the skull. Almost every day one or two men, for a moment unwary, were hit in like fashion.[167]

British snipers were similarly active against the enemy, but the Germans dismissed their efforts with light-hearted disdain, signalling the fall of their shots with pointer sticks as magpies and misses in the manner of the butt parties on the ranges at home. Hutchison's other contrasting memory of those first days in the line was the incongruous sight of a stout-hearted Flemish farmer who, despite the spy mania, continued to plough his fields immediately behind the British line, just as his family had done for generations. The old man walked slowly behind the plough pulled by a great white percheron draft horse, totally oblivious to the danger both to him and his precious beast, as his small world was changed for ever by the war.

News spread down the line that a huge British gun, a high-calibre howitzer, had been brought up to support the brigade. A gunner subaltern then appeared in the line, touting for business and anxious to ensure that the arrival of his new weapon would quickly make its presence felt. He asked for any particular targets to the front of the 93rd, and a trench periscope was used to point out a farm with a window covered by a green shutter. It was an active nest of snipers and also housed a machine-gun. To prove the point, the periscope immediately attracted the attention of an attentive sniper with a loud crack sounding close by as the marksman spotted the movement on the parapet. But the gunner officer had the position noted. 'Mother' will soon take care of that he told them and went off to pass the coordinates to his comrades at the gun. Later there was a loud thud and the hiss of a shell overhead and then the house disappeared in a cloud of smoke and pink brick dust. Mother had done her work and was soon to be joined by a second gun of naval 4.7 type, which was christened 'Baby'. Mother and Baby were to become stalwart supporters of the 93rd and served them well.

Aidan was feeling much better now that he was back with his friends and was keen to explain what life was actually like to his elder sister Dorothy:

Everyone has a dugout shelter, and a coke fire in some utensil or other. One can be very snug and get up an immense frowst in one's rabbit hole. Also as meals are practically the only distraction, housekeeping becomes quite interesting. The little fires make excellent toast, and as we quite often get an issue of ration butter (very good in tins) piles of hot buttered toast can be consumed. Of course just when one has the opportunity of cooking most luxurious stews they cease to issue fresh meat. However, a large field of leeks is cut in half by our bit of trench, and Ivelcon-cum-leek soup and bully-beef-cum leek stew are very good.[168]

He had been given news of the hospital at Sherfield, where Dorothy was now the commandant, and the Toad and Figs were nursing. He was delighted that it seemed to be doing so well:

> The hospital must be a great distraction and also a very useful way of helping. Really much more so than knitting socks and shirts (not that many of the latter get knitted). The people who send them mean very well, but apart from the fact that these huge bales stop everything else coming through the post, the government ones are much more appreciated by the men, and with reason as they really are tophole garments, and some of the efforts that arrive are very thin and shoddy. Especially do I condemn the atrocity known as the heelless sock. [169]

Aidan had previously entertained a hope that it might have been possible for some of Bertie's wounded Hussars or his own soldiers to find their way to Sherfield and convalesce there with his family. However, now he felt that in respect of the 93rd this seemed most unlikely.

47. *Monica Mary Liddell, the Toad, as a nurse at the Sherfield Manor Military Hospital. Photo Mark Liddell.*

> I am afraid there is not much chance of getting many of our wounded at Sherfield. All our shows have been in the nature of a hot twelve hours or so filling in a gap, and our casualty lists are terribly full

of missing, meaning that it has been impossible to get the wounded back. It is the worst part of all having to leave them. Altogether our

46. *Staff and patients at the Sherfield Manor Military Hospital which closed in November 1915. Photo Mark Liddell.*

casualties have been about 800 men and 25 officers: pretty heavy isn't it? And a huge percentage missing.[170]

He also seized the opportunity to put a word in for his machine-gunners. Having previously submitted his own extensive and expensive shopping list for personal equipment, he now sought to get the women of Sherfield-on-Loddon knitting on behalf of his men. Being the young squire did have some advantages:

If you have any spare mufflers or helmets or woolly gloves at home, remember that I have a gallant little band of, at present only eight survivors, but full strength sixteen men, who are really nobody's children, and don't really get their fair share of things sent to various companies by the relations and friends of the officers belonging to the said companies, in spite of my efforts and freebooting excursions.

There was also an exciting rumour doing the rounds that the 19th Brigade was going to Egypt after returning home first for an extensive refit. Aidan said it was 'rather too good to be true', but there was a kernel of truth in it, for plans were being hatched to withdraw the Indian troops, and redeploy them to the Middle East.

It was also about this time that a benevolent Edinburgh gunsmith donated two sets of telescopic sights to the Battalion. Lieutenant Hutchison was a good shot, an instructor in musketry, and having been brought up in Rhodesia had hunted game in Africa. All of this he felt, made him particularly well qualified to tackle the German snipers who continued to make life such a misery. Selecting as an assistant a young soldier who had been a gillie in civilian life, he carefully prepared his weapons and with the help of his sporting assistant searched out a suitable building as his den. They selected a farmhouse that stood about 150 yards behind the 93rd's line and there they built a carefully concealed sniper's post in the eaves. Then Leiutenant Hutchison painstakingly began a lengthy process of observation. He watched the enemy through powerful field glasses day after day, spotting the patterns of German trench life and the places where heads momentarily showed, or soldiers were gathered believing themselves far removed from danger. Even when the Middlesex rotated with the 93rd, he stayed behind and watched from his post until his preparations were complete.

His first day of shooting was grimly satisfying: 'I fixed my rifle and looked along its sight, my finger upon the trigger. During my first memorable day I bagged seven heads; and from what I observed I believe one to have been a senior officer.'[171] However, the Germans were quick to appreciate that a new force was set against them. A few days later, as he was striding out towards his farm, with his trusty gillie by his side, a salvo of shells ripped overhead. The farm, roof, eaves and sniper post

48. *Officers of the 93rd in the trenches near Houplines (Aidan third from left).*
Photo Mark Liddell.

disappeared in a high-explosive roar and a cloud of pink and black smoke.

On Wednesday 25 November, after another very wet and miserable night, Aidan managed to arrange a trip to Houplines for himself, leaving at 6 am and stopping off for breakfast at RHQ on the way. It was an opportunity for a proper bath, his first since St Omer, and a shave and change of clothing. Most of the 93rd were now not only lousy, but ragged, stinking and sporting beards, for water was far too precious to waste on washing or shaving. He noted in his diary:

49. *Aidan and Lt Max Aitken at Houplines near Armentières.*
Photo taken with Brownie Kodak by Lt Hutchison, and sent to Mrs Liddell by Colonel Maxwell Rouse after the war.
Photo Mark Liddell.

Excellent lunch, and walked into Armentières with Aitkin. Very little left in shops. Civies repairing their houses. News of further Russian victories. Back at 6 or so, freezing again. Boyd arrived yesterday evening.[172]

Despite the pain and rigours of modern warfare, and the daily challenge of the winter weather,

Aidan continued to keep amazingly cheerful, and discharged his military duties with great professionalism. He also worked hard to keep body and soul together in a way, at least from time to time, that resembled the manner to which he had become accustomed. He was after all, an officer and a gentleman.

Chapter Thirteen

Trench Warfare

It was a cleaner, fresher and happier Aidan that returned to the 93rd after his brief respite in Houplines. Hutchison did not have such a good day. He had to take the 'dog watch' that night and his platoon finished the construction of a new fire-trench. He then crawled out to inspect the wire in front of the line with two men. A sniper got one of them, which was hardly the best introduction to patrolling. However, Hutchison was not discouraged and the following night he led another party into No Man's Land. It was particularly dark, although the British guns were shelling farmhouses opposite D Company's positions and the Germans retaliated with Black Marias. A little further back, behind their right, Armentières was being shelled by German guns. This time he investigated a farm that had recently been occupied by the enemy but was now believed to be empty. The patrol came back loaded with potatoes and enemy entrenching tools. Food and the ability to dig deep were both vital, so Hutchison must have been very pleased with their little haul, particularly as the enemy had trained a large searchlight across the lines at various times during the night. It would appear very suddenly from a flank, brilliantly lighting up the ground. Anyone unlucky enough to be caught out in the open was instantly subject to rifle and machine-gun fire.

The next day, Thursday 26 November, Aidan noted 'Still rather slushy, though a bit of wind drying things. Snipers rather active though very inaccurate. Guns rather busy on left in afternoon'.[173] The officers and section commanders of one of the companies of the brigade's new battalion, the 5th Scottish Rifles, visited the 93rd that day to start to learn the realities of trench life. The Middlesex took over from the RWF, who in turn moved into brigade reserve. The rain was once again beginning to cause problems, and the Highlanders were again finding it difficult to keep their weapons clean. Rifle bolts became impossible to open and rounds were simply too muddy to risk placing in the weapons.

For Aidan, there was also time for a lengthy letter home.

November 26th

My dear Father,

I was so glad to hear that you had had such good days shooting, and very sorry to have missed them.

There seems to be a chance of getting leave for a week at home. One might get a chance at a pheasant time. I don't know whether it will materialize, but I have put my name in for it. They motor bus one up to Boulogne, and thence all is simple. It would give one a chance of refitting. It's extraordinary how one's clothes fall to pieces. Wet and mud and wear seem to finish them in a remarkably short time.

The post is very good now. Letters only take four or five days. I managed to get back to Headquarters yesterday for a shave, bath, change of clothes, which were sadly needed. There is a shortage of water even for drinking purposes, so one gets no opportunity for washing. We are still in the same trenches and have been very peaceable for a week. Except for half a dozen shells and a continual steady sniping, nothing else has happened. We hear a lot of transport moving about, at night time, so the Germans are moving to some other part of the line apparently, to try and get through somewhere else, or at least that's what it leads one to think.

French sent round a very cheering special order the other day to the effect that he hoped that now most of our trials were over. The Russians seem to be getting on well, so everyone hopes that the show will be finished soon.

I have heard that General Headquarters are betting 5 to 1 on its being over by the end of January, 7 to 1 by the end of February. Two rumours from different sources.

It's a war with no glamour or glory, such as one expects in a huge world-wide show like this. Modern weapons are too deadly, and the whole art of war, and all tactics as laid down in our books, and in the German dittoes, has been quite altered. No advancing across the open by short rushes. Now it's all digging new lines of trenches by night until one is within a couple of hundred yards of the enemy. Then a bombardment with enormous shells for a couple or more of days, until trenches and men's nerves are smashed to ribbons, and a surprise rush in the middle of the night. Then more digging. Each side is left therefore with row upon row of trenches behind them at short intervals, and a successful attack only means that the enemy are pushed back to their next line, not very far.

So it's a very slow and tedious and also gruelling business.

The Boer War, according to everyone I've spoken to who has seen both, was a picnic compared to this. However, if we can only keep the supply of men up from home, it oughtn't to last so long as the Boer War, but if we get progressively weaker at the same rate as the Germans, it would seem that it would be an interminable business.

Yesterday it thawed and rained, but there has been a good wind and it has dried up a lot. The frost was infinitely preferable to the wet. It looks very much as if it would snow this evening. Even that helps as it makes things so much easier to see at night.

While I've been writing, a tremendous gunfire has commenced on our left. Some three miles away perhaps, but there is a lot of artillery taking part.

We get mail every evening nowadays and I have been very well off for letters. It gives one something to look forward to all day.

I believe they are issuing fur coats to all the troops, with long goatskin hair all over them. The battalion will look very funny then with these on. I don't know whether it's colder here than it is at this time of year at home, but I suppose it's the impossibility of taking any exercise that makes it feel so bad. There have been quite a number of cases of men getting their feet frost-bitten. We had one a day or two ago, quite a bad bite too.

Well, I'll let you know the result of my enquiries in the matter of the week's leave, and if there seems any likelihood of its coming off. It would be a great change, but a still greater one coming back here again.

Goodbye, love to all of you,

From Aidan[174]

Aidan messed with B Company, and the officers under Major Maxwell Rouse had set about arranging some rather more suitable living accommodation. It was comparatively large and elaborate and Hutchison described its evolution:

By great labour, too, keeping us both warm and provoking an appetite for eternal stew and tea, we dug out a kind of mausoleum, and in this laid doors from the village which served as beds. After a few raids on those houses which had been hit by shell-fire, we had as our headquarters a large and comfortable dwelling room, something like the basement of a suburban house, with a glazed window that looked towards the Battalion Headquarters across the turnip-tops, fitted with lace curtains, and the whole well carpentered and finished.[175]

Perhaps he made it sound grander than the reality. It was roofed with barn doors, with mud settees and some old chairs rescued from the village, but luxury is relative. Bedstead frames and mattresses were acquired, indeed anything to improve the comfort of the place.

The next morning, Friday 27 November, the newly arrived Colin Boyd had a bullet through his Glengarry, which bent his cap badge. It must have dented his confidence, but it did him no permanent damage. Aidan described the day:

A dozen or so indifferent shells during morning. Theory that new gunners taking over trying ranges. Snipers very busy, Boyd getting one through his Glengarry. News of another great Russian victory. Dug new gun pit at night, cracked a bottle of Dom with Sammy.[176]

His machine-guns were in action again against an enemy trench, and later he went out after dark with Anderson and two other men to investigate suspected snipers between the lines. They crawled forward for 250 yards but 'drew a blank'. Whether this particular excursion was wise after the bottle of champagne is another matter.

On the following morning another of the mess members was victim to the German sniper. Major Maxwell Rouse was a thoroughly professional and serious-minded officer, and was peeved when his young friends, who were also his subordinates, failed to treat him with what he regarded as appropriate respect. With an exasperated snort, he picked up his tin plate of eggs and bacon, stomped out through the dugout entrance and placed his breakfast on the parapet. A moment later he returned to his friends with a pained look on his face. The laughter ceased when they saw the blood and realised that a sniper had neatly drilled a bullet through his arm. Refusing immediate assistance and still quite mobile, Rouse decided to make his own way to the aid-post. The shock of the wound made him act irrationally, and before his comrades could assist he was gone. Ignoring the new communication trench, he climbed directly out of the trench and was striding smartly to the rear when he was again fired at. The sniper appeared to be operating from a small house about 250 yards in front of their trench and only 150 yards or so from A Company's picket. Rouse ended up crawling on all fours through the crops for half a mile to reach headquarters and the aid-post. Aidan later recalled:

> Maxwell Rouse was hit in the arm the other day. He had only been out here about a fortnight. It must have been a stray bullet, but it went through his upper arm, only a slight wound though. Our trenches are such a wiggly line that bullets come smacking in from all sorts of unexpected angles. We're facing exactly the opposite way to that the Middlesex trenches faced.[177]

It rained again, particularly during the evening and the 93rd rotated their companies through the positions and the battalion was reinforced by a company of the Scottish Rifles. The Germans again played a searchlight along the front and fired on working parties. The next day, Sunday 29 November, the Germans displayed a yellow flag with a black eagle in the centre over their trenches. Aidan noted the event and the musketry competition that resulted:

> Dull weather. Germans hoisted a little yellow flag in front of Sammy's company, so we hoisted a Union Jack. They removed theirs then, and sniped furiously at ours. Only one bullet through it

by the time I left. Later they put two through the stick and sixteen through the flag.[178]

This sort of dangerous tomfoolery was not unusual. On one occasion when a mud effigy of the Kaiser was made during the night and placed on the British parapet, the Germans later replied in kind with a model of John Bull, resplendent in top hat. The Highlanders decided to knock it down with rifle fire, shooting through loopholes. The enemy again demonstrated their familiarity with the British method of target practice, and signalling the bulls, centres, magpies and misses, exactly as at a range day at home.

That evening there was more serious work to be done. A Company sent out a covering party with a Royal Engineers demolition team to eliminate the snipers in the farm. The mess members may in retrospect have laughed at Rouse's bloody and undignified retreat, which made an amusing anecdote, but they were none the less determined to nail the sniper. The raiding party moved forward under cover of darkness. They found the ground floor of the farm fortified with barricades built of coal, and the floor littered with cartridge cases; but of the enemy there was no sign. The Sappers quickly laid their explosives and then the raiders withdrew. At 1900 they fired the charges and with a roar the snipers' lair was blown to pieces. Honour was restored for the disrupted breakfast.

Monday 30 November was St Andrew's day, and therefore special for the 93rd. There was haggis for breakfast, the weather was warm and sunny, and there was a large and very welcome mail. There was also

celebratory rum punch for the soldiers. Fortunately, the Germans were very quiet, and Aidan's section made the most of the opportunity to build another machine-gun emplacement on the Pont Ballot road. It was also the day that Aidan and his friends finally occupied their splendid new accommodation.

Hutchison described the inhabitants:

In this new house were

50. Highlanders in the trenches.
Photo Argyll and Sutherland
Highlanders.

gathered a country gentleman with parochial affairs as the urge to a useful existence: a professor of biology at Oxford: a stripling from Sandhurst: a lad who had not yet thought beyond house parties; a law student of brilliant academic attainment, and myself who had footslogged in India and Africa. We filled in the hours of boredom with debate upon the widest of subjects. And sometimes, as they do in the House of Commons, one or another would fall asleep.[179]

Maxwell Rouse was the 'country gentleman', but there was clearly some poetic licence with Aidan. His third class honours degree hardly warranted a professorship, but then he always had a studious air about him. Unfortunately the lice gathered with them, for it was not just the Middlesex that were so afflicted. Soldiers wore wool for warmth and comfort, and hardly ever removed their clothes. The men and the dugouts were infested, and although every effort was made to destroy the little parasites this was one battle that it proved almost impossible to win. Bayonets were deployed, heated in the coke braziers and drawn across a vest or inserted up the pleat of kilts. This resulted in a most satisfying popping sound and the slaughter of hundreds. One soldier told Aidan that he'd like to put his kilt and shirt on the Kaiser and handcuff his hands behind him for a week! But the men could tolerate the lice, and the coke fumes and the smoking guttering candles in order to be warm. At times they experienced an odd sense of peace and tranquillity that both sides were reluctant to break. Hutchison described those odd November nights:

> Except for mounting the parapets and improving the forward defences, which could not be done by day, we sat at night like night watchmen around coke braziers warming our hands, and smoking endless cigarettes. And as we sat in the stillness we could hear with great distinctness the sound of transport on the Radinghem road bringing up German rations, in the same way as they must have heard the wheels of our wagons rumbling through the streets of Houplines and down the dog-leg road. But there seems to have been some unwritten law of 'live and let live', for the ration parties of either side were never 'strafed'.[180]

Aidan had now been in the trenches continually for a month and the following day wrote to Miss Finnegan, his old governess.

Dec 1

Dear Figs,

So many thanks for your letter. As the official information says, there is no change in the situation. We are still in the trenches, and I have been in them since Oct 30th, with 24 hours off when I changed into another lot, and twelve hours at headquarters for a bath and a change. Getting rather tired of them, and my tummy more so. No exercise, the damp and cold and perpetual overeating with nothing but extremely strong tea to drink, makes one very uncomfy. I got your letter and mother's yesterday evening. Will you tell mother that the Ivelcon tablets are excellent. I wrote and said so in a long letter of wants which ought to have arrived by now. We moved into a new and very elaborate dugout yesterday, which is much more comfortable than the first one we had here.

The trouble is that we can't get candles, only two a day and have to economise terribly. It's just four and I can hardly see the paper, so if the writing is all over the place you know what that is due to. It must have been a surprise Bertie's turning up like that. I have put in for leave, but the officers who have been out for longest go first. As it is I am the seventh on the list, i.e., that only six of the officers who came out with the regiment survive.

The candle has just arrived, as I've just been out for a quarter of an hour firing at two carts and a ruined farm which the Germans are supposed to occupy with snipers at dusk. We manage to get a large quantity of tinned foods from a large town just near our trenches. Lobster, mackerel, herring, all vin blanc, tinned fruit etc etc but drinks are not to be come by, and we're left pretty well alone here, and have had very few men hit. The line of trenches here is so woggly that bullets come at you from every direction in the most surprising way. There is a deep ditch near our trenches and we always imagine ourselves very safe in that. However two people were hit even in there.

Hope to see you all before long, love to all

From Aidan[181]

There was also a thaw after the hard frost, and the wet caused ever more damage to the trenches, necessitating constant repair and attention. It was a taster of what was to come, but for the moment the attention of the battalion was on the visit by His Majesty the King. Just as the Kaiser had visited the front to raise German morale, now his cousin King George V was in France and anxious to see and be seen by as many British and Imperial troops as possible. A special 6th Division Operation Order was received by the 93rd on 1 December, detailing that each battalion in the trenches was to send one officer and eight other ranks to attend on the King. The following day, Aidan's friend Max Aitken led the little party from the 93rd who paraded smartly dressed in marching order. The RWF briefly recalled the event. 'Rather a unique occasion with guns firing half a mile away. The Prince of Wales, who was with the King, was observed to have grown. The parade was spick and span without, but most verminous underneath.'[182]   The 93rd War Diary recorded that 'After the inspection His Majesty presented the Distinguished Conduct Medal to Sergt R Ross for gallant conduct during the action at Le Maisnil'.[183] There were to be other awards for that action later.

It was a good day and that evening Aidan wrote 'Had an excellent dinner, which I enjoyed in spite of feeling seedy for a week or more. Haggis, mashed spuds, peaches, and a bottle of fizz: coffee with Sammy afterwards'.[184]   Despite the good cheer, Aidan was starting to get very tired as he hinted in a letter to his mother on 4 December. 'I believe we get relieved for a rest in about ten days. I will be more glad of it than the rest, or at least I think I have more reason. I've already been in the trenches for more than five weeks now, with only the move from one set to another for a change.'[185]

Aidan's parcel of new kit from home had just arrived, which must have lifted his spirits. He and his friends had been trying very hard to keep cheerful, as this extract of a letter to his mother suggests.

The parcels and your letter arrived this evening, everything quite safe and very acceptable indeed. The Ivelcon tabloids had just been finished the day before for lunch, and we had a tremendous dinner in the evening. A haggis, peaches, anchovies on toast and champagne to drink. A very special effort with no special reason. The only result (besides making me feel a little sicker than usual) was to cause one of our company commanders to walk in his sleep. He woke to find his best fur lined greatcoat torn to ribbons this morning, and on making enquiries found from his sentries that he had left his trench and crossed a deep ditch in front, and proceeded towards the German lines, until brought to a standstill by our wire entanglements, into which he plunged to the detriment of his coat. He returned to his dug-out and knew nothing about it this morning.[186]

The Battalion Headquarters were now situated in 'Ration Farm' about a mile behind the line, and this had so far been left untroubled by the enemy. It had deep cellars, a large courtyard and other outbuildings and was also used as the resupply point for the brigade. At night the quartermasters brought up the rations and stores in wagons for distribution to the battalions. There was also a cemetery, dug in the farm garden, for use by the brigade. Other nearby houses were used as billets for the platoons being rested from the line, under the new rotation arrangement designed to give one company at a time a break from the trenches.

But about this time it was also noted that air observation had begun to increase, although it was still unusual if more than one aeroplane was seen to circle over the line. There was still much confusion over aircraft recognition, and the soldiers gathered in the vicinity of Ration Farm for working parties did not know whether to take cover out of sight, open fire, or ignore them.

It was soon evident that the Germans felt that they had located a worthwhile target, for on 4 December the area was heavily shelled, wounding three soldiers and causing the billets to be evacuated. In the middle of that move, at 3 pm, the 93rd War Diary noted: 'High-explosive shells were turned onto the neighbourhood of the farm, but the company was moved without further casualties.'

Five civilians were killed in another attack around the same time and it was apparent that German activity was increasing. Hutchison suggested that the reason might be spies, but the circling aeroplanes appear to be the more likely culprits. British Farman biplanes were also seen overhead, adding to the confusion of the soldiers on the ground. The Brigade Diary summarised the position thus: 'A good deal of rain fell during this period, and much work required in trenches to keep them in order. Enemy's infantry and artillery active – hostile snipers active.'[187]

As an antidote to collapsing dugouts and falling traverses, new games had been invented in order to raise the spirits. Hutchinson wrote:

Our utensils now have names - 'Bertie' the breadknife: 'Oliver' the opener: 'Thomas' the tea-strainer: and 'Horace-Rumbold' - he is Falstaffian like his name - the rum jar: 'Martha' the milk-bottle. L. has become Count Slabonga', and I the 'Super-Man' (I know not why); B continues to smoke hundreds of cigarettes.[188]

That night though, Aidan, aka Count Slabonga, slept with a new air pillow instead of the straw-filled sandbag of the last ten days, and was comforted by a woolly muffler knitted for him by Miss Finnegan.

On the following day, Saturday 5 December, it continued to pour with rain and Aidan described the trenches as being in a fearful state. That evening he wrote a brief and rather tense letter to his father, expressing his hopes for leave, and giving the good news that two officers had been granted passes so the process of granting leave was beginning. It was not a communication to inspire confidence at home.

Dec 5th

Dear Father,

Just a note to let you know that I received your letters of 26 Nov and 29th. I haven't read the whole of Kitchener's speech before. I must say that from what one had heard and read in the papers, I would never have thought we were getting as many as 30,000 recruits a week.

Our first two officers went on leave for 10 days this evening, and the Commanding Officer says he is going to recommend me for next turn. That depends of course on lots of things, such as whether things are still quiet in this district, and also if the General commanding the Division thinks fit. However, I have hopes, and if I am lucky will leave here somewhere about the 17th. I only hope I'm able to go as I could do with the rest. I'm feeling pretty done now. It's not a picnic, and I never thought a fortnight ago that I would be able to hold out much longer. However, we're having a quiet and comparatively restful time now. Thanks so much for ordering the Burberry and boots etc. I hope they arrive soon in time for me to wear on my journey, as I look like a scarecrow now.

Love to all

From Aidan

PS We're not in 2nd Division. 2nd Bn A'SH is sufficient address.[189]

Sunday was not a day of rest either. Houplines was shelled in the morning, and then the Germans turned their attention to Ration Farm again. Three platoons billeted in a school close by had to be moved to a safer location while about thirty shells fell in the area. There were no British casualties, but eight civilians were killed in one house. Aidan was interested in several RFC machines operating overhead. 'Three just over us at one time. Germans fired furiously with rifles and shelled one, but with no result. Fine morning, rained in evening.'[190] Monday dawned very wet again, but two new officers and a draft of 204 men marched in. On Tuesday, after a quiet day, Aidan had some action with his guns.

After dark the German searchlight began working and I got heavily sniped as I was going through Pont Ballot farm as they switched the searchlight suddenly on to me. At about 10 o'clock they started firing heavy volleys along the trench and behind, which they lit up with the light, so at 12 midnight I turned the MG on to it. Fired about 150 rounds, searching up from 400 (where the gun was laid) to about 2000. Light swung round rapidly and went out. Waited for it to reappear until 2.30, but it and the snipers were quite quelled.[191]

On Wednesday 9 December there was some more serious activity from the enemy, although the day began quietly enough. It had started to rain in the middle of the night, and the state of the trenches got progressively worse as the rain continued to fall throughout the day. The Germans

51. Jocks in their goatskins. Photo Argyll and Sutherland Highlanders.

were now aware that in some places the 93rd's parapet was no longer bullet-proof, which made the snipers even more deadly. However, at about 1100 A Company spotted a white flag being waved from a bombed-out cottage to their front. A sergeant went carefully forward to investigate and came back with three soldiers of the 39th Regiment of the German XIXth Corps. They were fed up, and explained that they were hungry and were only getting a single meal a day. They also indicated that the Germans had a great deal of artillery dispersed along the front, and that their own trenches were more strongly held than the British ones in which they were now sitting.

That afternoon Aidan went to Armentières for a bath, and returned to the lines in time for dinner. 'Just as we were dining and before our plum pudding arrived, heavy rifle fire commenced.' Machine-gun fire opened up as well, and it was apparent that an attack was taking place, perhaps explaining the motivation behind the surrender of the three Saxons. The enemy had pushed forward with infantry and about fifty men got to within 150 yards of the centre of the 93rd's line and then opened fire. There was also an advance towards the centre and right of the Middlesex. Aidan doubled to his gun, which had already opened fire and expended the first belt by the time he arrived. Hutchison had some difficulty getting his men into firing position, owing to a platoon working on

193

entrenchments in the rear who returned to respond to the alarm without arms. He recalled seeing rifle flashes coming from 50 yards in front, although other reports indicate that the enemy did not get that close. In a throwback to colonial days, he organised volley fire, although there was some trouble with dirty weapons. Shells then started to fall on the 93rd's positions, although Aidan was disparaging about their effectiveness.

I should think half of the German shells were dud. Some 200 yds short, most miles behind. Pathetic exhibition of gunnery. However they burst some quite close and I got a splinter on the little finger.[192]

The British guns then opened and the attack petered out at around 2030. The 19th Brigade Diary's summation was that 'the general impression was that enemy intended to make an attack, but failed to push it home'.[193] Much later in the small hours Hutchison spotted the Germans trying to recover their dead and wounded on a stretcher.

The next morning the news on casulties was good. Brigade losses during the previous day had been six killed and thirteen wounded, including three Scottish Rifles' men killed by a single shell. The 93rd had five wounded, but they were only 'scratched' as Aidan put it. His No. 1 gun had fired 1000 rounds and the Germans were said to have got as far as the British wire in places. Later he wrote:

Last Wednesday the Germans attacked us. I had my guns separated, and it was the left hand gun that got most of the shooting. I was with the right hand one. They fired about 20 shells quite close to the emplacement, and I don't think more than five burst. I believe they were using the 75mm guns captured from the French, which has a fuse setting machine, and which the Germans seem unable to work. I got hit on the little finger of the left hand by a piece but it only made a tiny cut. I also got a bullet through my Glengarry. We never saw more than the flashes of their rifles in front of us (the attack was at 8 pm until 8.45) but they were reported to have got up to the barbed wire entanglements near the other gun. However, though both sides shelled hard and the rifles were firing as hard as they could for about ³/₄ of an hour, we only had 5 men very slightly wounded.[194]

There is no indication of the German casualties but they were probably substantial. The 93rd heard later that morning that the Cameronians were to relieve them the following evening, and so Aidan spent his last night in the trenches, where he had served since 30 October. His diary entry for Friday 11 December was brief: 'Relieved by Cameronians. Poured with rain, trenches like a river. Horrible business handing over. Marched into Armentières, where we billeted in the lunatic asylum.' He had served in the trenches continuously for forty-three days.

Chapter Fourteen

To Christmas and Beyond

There was a certain grim irony to living in an asylum, which was not lost on the Highlanders. But in the event it proved very satisfactory for the 93rd and they were not expected to share it with the previous occupants, of whom there was no sign. However, the Germans quickly made their presence felt. The buildings were large enough to house the whole battalion in some degree of comfort and it had the great advantage of proper beds. The asylum at this time was hardly damaged, except for a great hole blown in the eastern wing. Broken furniture dangled dangerously through the smashed masonry of the upper floor, providing a tangible reminder of the effectiveness of the enemy artillery. The shops in Armentières were open though, and doing a brisk trade. True to the song, *Mademoiselles* of every age were much in evidence.*

While the soldiers were keen to seize every opportunity to relax after the rigours of trench life, the battalion was still in brigade reserve and might be needed at any time. Indeed, even as the 93rd left the battle line the 19th Brigade had been ordered to show increased activity to hold the Germans to the ground and prevent them from withdrawing units to the north where a French attack was in progress. Sappers commenced their work, sniping became more active, and British artillery bombarded the hostile trenches daily. The warlike activities of their comrades did not restrict the activities of the 93rd. Indeed, it probably made the men all the more determined to enjoy themselves out of the line as Hutchison described:

> Soldiers sampled 'vin rouge' and 'vin blank' in all the estaminets. Since the lawful occupations of men and women had ceased, every house became a wine shop labelled 'Estaminet', and vending, besides beverages, eggs at famine prices. The wines were of some parentless vintage, and often presented men with the belly-ache, such gripes as curled them up in an agony of torture. Then, unwary fellow, he would sometimes mix his drinks, pouring a portion of cognac into his innards to cure the pain. Perhaps such drastic treatment eased the stomach, but it set the brain on fire.[195]

Failure to parade was a chargeable offence with potentially disastrous

---

* 'Mademoiselles from Armentières' was a popular song that was a favourite among the BEF, and had the chorus Inky Pinky Parlez Vous. There were numerous verses, mostly unprintable, and various versions of the chorus, including Hinky Dinky Parlez Vous.

consequences for the individual. The death penalty was available and sometimes used at this time, but the 93rd dealt with its soldiers with some sympathy and tolerance, and the knowledge that some excess and its muddle-headed consequences was inevitable. It was not just the drink, it was that it was unfamiliar French or Belgian stuff of uncertain strength and quality, although by now 'vin blank' was becoming all too familiar to the Highlanders. Officers who cracked the odd bottle of 'Dom' with chums were thus not inclined to be too hard on their erring charges, who could not afford the luxury and certainty of a known vintage.

That first day out of the line Aidan and his team stripped, cleaned and overhauled the guns. The troops were then marched by companies to the 6th Division baths at Erquinghem. It was an oddly impressive operation run by the Royal Engineers and organised like a factory production line. First the Highlanders bathed naked in the warm soapy water in the enormous vats of an abandoned brewery. A dozen out and another dozen in, and then they dashed shivering under a makeshift shower that dribbled water onto them from a punctured two-inch pipe to wash away the soap. But it was not only the men that were so treated, for their filthy clothing was taken and they were issued with clean replacements. A special service was provided for the kilts, as Hutchison explained.

The Sappers ushered along the protesting men to another department of this laundry improvised to meet the exigencies of war. Here behind trestle tables stood stout-armed Belgian girls, hot iron in one hand, a skewer in the other. No Institute of Industrial Psychology was needed to train the girls in their duties. Two Sappers organized and directed the workshop practice. Like lightning a hot skewer sped up the kilted pleats searing its farthest recesses: then out again carrying its load of dead and wounded lice. Wielded over arm the iron came down like a sledge-hammer upon the remains. Thus twenty women with the precision of machines, thrust and slammed kilt after kilt. And Jock got his own back, even with a fleeting smile, as the worker for an instant lifted an eye and handed back so strange a nether garment.[196]

On Sunday 13 December the 93rd held a Presbyterian church service. There is no mention by Aidan of a Roman Catholic mass, and it is interesting to note that throughout the extensive personal papers that Aidan compiled during his active service, he makes no mention of any personal religious activity. His life before and after this period give testimony to the strength of his religious convictions, and so perhaps it was simply not remarkable enough to get a mention.

In a letter home written later in the day, he acknowledged the arrival of the woollies for his men, which he said 'are very much appreciated'.

However, because his section numbers had now swollen to twenty, he was four sets short and so in his customary manner asked for more. His new Burberry had also arrived and was 'topping', but his arm was not. 'I have been inoculated against typhoid today, and am just beginning to feel rotten, and not a bit inclined to write.'[197] His arm soon became very stiff. However, he did derive some amusement from a press clipping he was shown from the *Cambeltown Courier* which contained a letter from a soldier of the 93rd. He enclosed a copy with the tongue-in-check note 'Wow wow'. It read:

> We have a splendid officer in charge of the guns, one of those men who would give the faintest-hearted confidence. May he be spared to see us all safely through the lot, for you have no idea what it means to lose confidence in your superior.[198]

The next day the Germans fired about a thousand shells into Armentières, creating a huge commotion among the townspeople, five of whom were wounded and one woman was killed. The shelling began at about 2030 and went on until 0730, The 93rd took shelter in the downstairs rooms of the asylum as shells burst around them in the grounds. It was all very alarming, although no damage was actually caused. Aidan wrote in his diary: 'Armentières lit up by an enormous blaze. Stood to in case it became too hot, but got to bed at 3.30 only to stand to again immediately. Got to bed again 5.30, but unable to sleep much owing to the noise.'[199] The following day was even worse:

> Shelling was directed indiscriminately against all parts of town and continued 'til 7 am ending with a large number falling in the asylum. About half the shells failed to burst. Although over 700 shells were fired over the asylum and many into it, there were no casualties.[200]

On Friday 18 December General Gordon inspected the 93rd and expressed his satisfaction with their turnout and bearing. Minds were already turning towards Christmas and bales of presents were starting to arrive at the front. That evening Aidan wrote a Christmas greeting to his father:

> Dear Father,
>
> This ought to arrive in time to wish you all a very happy Xmas. I got your letter of the 11th last night.
>
> At present leave seems to be in abeyance, but I hope it will get started again soon. We have just heard that Scarborough and Hartlepool were bombarded by the Germans. That ought to wake recruiting up a bit, if it does nothing else. I enclose a copy of the weekly *Scotsman* which may amuse you. Needless to say there is not

a word of truth in it, and the same can be said for a very great number of 'stirring stories' told by soldiers at home. The only incident with regard to rations and the A&SH which is rather amusing is that one night one of the men bringing a basket of 40 loaves to our trench missed his way, and went on straight past the trench. Lots of people shouted 'This way Jock' to him, but I suppose he thought he knew better, and continued on towards the German trenches until he was swallowed up by the darkness. Not a sound was heard so I suppose the Germans let him walk right into their trenches with his 40 loaves. He must have got rather a surprise when he found where he was.

We are still having our rest, and everyone feels much better for it. We have had several drafts now, and are practically at full strength again. My gun team is 22 strong now: an improvement on 8!

Well, I only wish my leave would come on now, so that I could be at home for Xmas, but it can't be helped.

Love to all of you from

Aidan[201]

The next morning, Aidan heard that the 93rd would relieve the Middlesex Regiment in the trenches the following evening and that their brief but noisy sojourn in Armentières was almost over. That night the Germans shelled the lunatic asylum with shrapnel and high-explosives, although with little effect, and they did so again the following morning during church service. This time they were rather more successful. One round entered the cookhouse wounding three men, and another went into B Company's Barrack Room, which was full at the time. Amazingly, only a single man was wounded, although several were badly shaken up by bricks and flying bedsteads. Then, to add to the mounting misery of the local inhabitants, a German aircraft bombed Armentières.

After the excitement of the bombardment Aidan, now familiar with the problems of night time trench reliefs, went up to the front line to survey the positions he would be taking over so that he could see them in daylight. He found that his friends in the Middlesex had their machine-guns emplaced on a salient that stuck right out towards the German lines, which were only about 300 yards away. That evening the 93rd marched out to relieve the Middlesex with the unattractive prospect of Christmas in the front line to look forward to. Aidan's promised and much anticipated leave now must have seemed a distant prospect, although his chum Aitken departed for home that very day, clutching a bundle packed up by Aidan for delivery to Sherfield Manor.

The 93rd were not impressed with what they found when they arrived at the front line. It was wetter than ever and Hutchison called them 'the worst trenches on earth'. Aidan though soon made himself comfortable, and they set up their mess in a sort of cellar. It was clearly light enough and dry enough for him to write an extended letter home to his mother.

Dec 21

Dear Mother,

I sent a small parcel off to you by one of our officers who is going on leave, so I hope you will get it. It contained a fuse from a German shell that burst just in front of me at the trenches I was in with the Middlesex. It is practically unscratched as it landed in a heap of beetroots. It isn't often one finds one so perfect. I thought it would make a good inkstand, fixed on a plinth and hinged just above or just below the fuse ring. You will notice the ring is set at 38, i.e. 3800 metres. Also the bright blue paint with which all the German shells are covered. The other trophy is a medal I found at a place the French had been fighting. A Legion of Honour I think. We are back in the trenches again. Got in last night and are swimming in mud. The Germans are varying distances away along our line, 80 yards to 500 yards, and I've got the machine guns on a salient i.e., a place where the trenches run out towards the German lines.

We have a farmhouse just behind the trench, where the officers of the company nearest take meals, an excellent cellar vaulted over, and the officer commanding the company and myself sleep in a cow byre, plenty of straw and no mud. It is very handy, as it would take only about a quarter of a minute to get into the trench on the darkest night.

We hear most gruesome stories (a little tall I think) of some of the trenches where both sides have sapped forward until the trenches are about 20 yards from each other. All the ground is full of dead bodies, and when the wall of a dug-out or part of the trench falls in, there is generally a body exposed. One man wanted to cut some ends of roots that were sticking out of his dug-out wall, and discovered they were a corpse's fingers!

In another place our officers were reported to have made a practice of going over to the Germans' lines by day for a chat with the men, the latter warning them when one of their officers was approaching, and helping them over the parapet so that they could get back.

They shelled our billets and the town behind the other night from about 9 pm until 7 am. Every shell that went into the town went over our billets, so one heard the whistle and curled up very small in one's bed for every one. Altogether they sent about 700 shells during those ten hours. (estimated or counted by our own artillery). We didn't have anyone hit, but it was not a very pleasant night. They shelled the billets again on Sunday while the Presbyterian service was going on. We only had four men hit, although one shell went right into a room that a company was occupying.

The Scarborough show seems to have jogged the British public a bit. It's a pity the papers forgot to mention that every town near the firing line gets that much or more most days of the week. The universal opinion here is that it will do a lot of good to recruiting. One hears more 'That ought to wake them up' than expressions of sympathy. The news made the Germans cheer like anything, or at least I suppose that is what it was. Last night they made a tremendous hurroosh, and I suppose it would take about that long to get as far as their advanced trenches.

Everyone seems to think there is some move in the wind. Possibly the French may get busy. We don't hear any definite news about any movements here, but it seems certain that the French are massing somewhere on the line. Well, I hope something does occur and we do some good. This trench squatting is an interminable game. Lately our side have been attacking, and gained quite a number of trenches, only to be driven out again in the majority of cases. The Germans have just the same luck when they attack, except that they don't get into our trenches as often as we get into theirs. However, the result is a heavy casualty list, and the positions as they were in the beginning. Seems pretty hopeless, doesn't it?

I wonder if you could send another box of tinned foods and Ivelcon tabloids, etc. The last were much appreciated in the trenches, where tinned fruits or potted meats are a very welcome change.

It's getting near Xmas now. I must say nothing would have made me believe last Xmas that I would be spending this one in trenches opposite the Germans. Someone on our left shouted to the Germans opposite them, asking them to come over and spend Xmas with them. The answer was that they wouldn't be there at Xmas (meaning they would be relieved by then). 'We know you won't', was the answer to that (meaning we would push them out by then), a retort they answered with a shower of bullets.

Goodbye,

Love to all

Aidan[202]

The reports of fraternisation had also been heard and noted by the

Corps Commander Sir Horace Smith-Dorrien, who at the beginning of December was pondering the problem and recording his thoughts in his diary. A student of military history, he knew of the dangers from the Peninsular War and determined to issue clear instructions in a directive to his commanders. His Chief of Staff penned an appropriate document, as the following unequivocal extracts indicate:

Experience of this and every other war proves undoubtedly that troops in trenches in close proximity to the enemy slide very easily, if permitted to do so, into a 'live and let live' theory of life. . .

The attitude of our troops can be readily understood and to a certain extent commands sympathy. So long as they know that no general advance is intended, they fail to see any object in undertaking small enterprises of no permanent utility, certain to result in some loss of life, and likely to provoke reprisals. Such an attitude is, however, most dangerous, for it discourages initiative in commanders, and destroys the offensive spirit in all ranks. . .

The Corps Commander, therefore, directs Divisional Commanders to impress on all subordinate commanders the absolute necessity of encouraging the offensive spirit of the troops, while on the defensive, by every means in their power.

Friendly intercourse with the enemy, unofficial armistices (eg 'we won't fire on you if you don't' etc) and the exchange of tobacco and other comforts, however tempting and occasionally amusing they might be, are absolutely prohibited.[203]

For the moment though food was the general preoccupation in the 93rd. The rations were stodgy and monotonous, and were carried up to the forward positions nightly from the transport unloading area a half mile or so behind the forward trenches. Six men per company was the usual number detailed to make the collection, under the watchful eye of an NCO. There was usually tinned bully-beef and Maconachie stew, Quaker oats and bacon, and bread, cheese and jam; and to drink, tea, cocoa and tinned milk. Best of all was the rum, half a gill per man, poured from great stone jars and issued under a strict regime that meant it had to be consumed at once and witnessed by an officer to prevent hoarding. Hutchison recalled 'that the rum issue throughout those winter months became for all men the high peak of happiness'.[204] Aidan and the other officers had long made their own particular additional arrangements, but now the usual meagre fare of the soldiers was being supplemented by the fulsome Christmas gifts of a grateful nation that for the most part could be eaten, smoked or worn. Presents were beginning to pour into the front line and military activity seemed to dwindle, suppressed by both the growing Christmas spirit, and the continuing rain. Hutchison complained 'My dugout is a quagmire. Baled for hours, men wonderfully cheerful'.[205] The war news seemed good too, with successes reported again on the Eastern front. He was also heartened to record the surrender of the German garrison in Tsingtau to the Japanese.

However, not everyone approved of the excessive Christmas spirit. Some officers felt that the decision of the High Command to suspend the delivery of war stores for twenty-four hours to ensure the timely arrival of wagon loads of personal presents to the troops and gifts from the royal family was little short of madness. Major 'Ma' Jeffries of the 2nd Grenadier Guards called it 'a positive nuisance' and noted in his diary that 'Our enemy thinks of war while we must mix it up with plum pudding'.[206] But the mass of festive messages and material had to be dealt with somehow, so the staff were simply facing up to the inevitable and introducing a degree of military organisation and efficiency to the haphazard giving of the nation. Saturday 12 December was the target date for the Christmas preparations to be in place. The newspapers reported 250,000 parcels addressed to the troops in the preceding week, and another 200,000 parcels, together with 2,500,000 letters, the next! Firms such as Callard and Bowser and Cadbury sent their famous butterscotch and chocolates, the *Daily Mail* donated countless crates of Christmas puddings, and the newspapers advertised gift hampers and special offers on tobacco products. Nine bob was all it took to send a thousand Woodbines and a Christmas card to a Tommy at the front.

On 22 December, although Christmas was only days away, the 19th Brigade turned its attention to the planning of an attack on the German line, which was discussed at an early morning conference. The Brigadier had clearly taken the Corps Commander's directive to heart, but in the end his plan was turned down by the 4th Division. Warlike preparations subsequently diminished with the coming of Christmas, although they did not stop altogether. Aidan and his men sited and constructed a new gun emplacement in support of B Company, and that night Boyd led a patrol through the German advanced wire and lay with his men watching the enemy working parties constructing wire entanglements. The next morning, 23 December, the rain had turned to snow. However, the 93rd were cheered by another draft of reinforcements, and the arrival of an especially large mail delivery.

Hutchison received a bag of mufflers knitted by friends in Surrey for distribution to his Company. There were also gifts for the officers from Queen Alexandra, consisting of gauntlet gloves, a pipe and chocolate. There was also the gift for the soldiers from Princess Mary's Sailors' and Soldiers' Fund which was made in the style of Queen Victoria's commemorative chocolate box presented to the troops in 1899 during the Boer War. The small brass gift box, embossed with a likeness of King George V's seventeen-year-old daughter Mary, contained cigarettes and pipe tobacco, and a photograph of the princess. There were alternative versions issued for non-smokers, which held sweets and a pencil case, and another for the Indian troops with candy and spices. With the boxes came a Christmas card from the King, with the message 'May God protect you and bring you safe home. Mary R. George R.I'. The creation and delivery of these little presents was actually a colossal undertaking. By Christmas, 355,500 had been delivered to the soldiers and sailors of the Empire. The gesture was appreciated for it proved a very popular gift and many were sent home as souvenirs. Afterwards, Lieutenant-Colonel Wilfred Smith, commanding the 2nd Grenadiers noted: 'Having to dish out all these things has been a great burden, and came at a somewhat harassing time.'[207] But he still found the time to parcel up his festive gifts, noting 'I am sending home my Christmas card, and shall send my Christmas present from Princess Mary. Bless her – she has been a nuisance.'[208]

That night German transport could be heard moving from west to east. In the morning Aidan was summoned to Battalion Headquarters and then sent on to the Middlesex to take part in a Field General Court Martial. It was Christmas Eve, and General Headquarters (GHQ) in St Omer issued an ominous warning to the BEF, suggesting it was possible that the enemy were planning an attack over Christmas and New Year. The British and Indian divisions were exhorted to maintain special vigilance throughout the period. But the reality was rather different, for the enemy were generally just as full of the Christmas spirit as the British. The Germans had also been swamped by presents and provisions from well-wishers at home and they too had received royal gifts. The *Kaiserliche* for enlisted men was a box of cigars inscribed *Weihnacht im Feld, 1914,* and Crown Prince Frederick William issued a meerschaum pipe with his likeness engraved on the bowl for the soldiers of his Army. His grandfather had presented similar Christmas gifts to his soldiers in France during the Franco-Prussian War. The Germans also brought to the front their tradition of decorating fir trees. Along the front-line in many German trenches lighted Christmas trees were symbolically lifted onto the parapets on Christmas night, to the initial consternation and then delight of the sentries opposite. The RFC too were in high spirits and on Christmas Eve with typical exuberance and some style dropped a plum pudding onto the German airfield at Lille. Not to be outdone, the German airmen responded by delivering a much padded bottle of rum to the RFC on Christmas morning!

On 24 December the 93rd continued to strengthen the line with work on their communication trenches, and there was also a visit from Brigadier-General Congreve whose 18th Infantry Brigade would be taking over the line on Boxing Day. That night the Germans held a concert with a band and joyful singing. It was a beautiful starlit night and was freezing hard. Before long the Highlanders began to call for encores and sing their own songs in return, accompanied by a deal of good-natured banter. Then, in response to a shouted invitation, a sergeant went forward to meet the Germans and talked to a Saxon soldier who knew Glasgow well. The Christmas truce of 1914 had begun for the 93rd.

On Christmas Day the 93rd's War Diary recorded 'Very quiet day. Germans came out of their trenches unarmed in afternoon, and were seen to belong to 133rd and 134th Regiments. The position was reconnoitred by Lieut Anderson. The Germans asked for leave to bury ten dead. This was granted'.* This official notice, recorded for posterity and consumption by the chain of command, was accurate as far as it went, but was also economical with that truth. Aidan's private diary was more explicit:

Xmas day. Rather foggy, still freezing. In the afternoon the Germans brought two barrels of beer over to the Welsh Fusiliers. Our men and theirs walked over to the halfway fence and had a chat. Astonishing sight. Walked over, Kennedy, Thomson, and all of us, and had a long chat. Met the man from Glasgow, and gave him tobacco in exchange for cigars. Also newspapers. Talked to a lot of them in English, and promised to send more papers over each night so far as the halfway fence. They are all confident that the Russians

52. *The trenches near Houplines, with Saxons visible on the sky line.* (Christmas 1914) *Photo Mark Liddell.*

* Pro 93rd WW Diary, 25 Dec 1914.

53. *The trenches near Houplines, with Saxons visible on the sky line. (Christmas 1914) Photo Mark Liddell.*

are beaten, and that the Austrians are in Belgrade. Victory for them in 6 months. They all seemed very friendly, lots of handshaking, and '*Auf wiedersehen*' on parting, which took place just before dusk, owing to their officers recalling them.[209]

Hutchison's diary was very similar:

A great rum issue. Many expressions of goodwill. In the afternoon war ceased and we advanced across our trenches and chatted with the Germans. Most amusing. Can this be war? Some had played football against Glasgow Celtic. All were certain of victory in about six months, for Germany, and the end of the war. They gave us cigars and cap badges. They were men of the 133rd and 139th of the XIXth Saxon Corps. We parted saying, 'Tomorrow it is war.'[210]

Up and down the lines in France and Belgian similar scenes were being acted out between the British and Germans, and to a lesser extent the French and Belgians and the Germans. It was entirely spontaneous, and had no sanction from above. Indeed, it happened despite the positive steps that had been taken to discourage it, including the Christmas Eve warning from GHQ of an imminent attack. But the truce was certainly not universal either, for in many places soldiers did not come together and Christmas was just another day. Captain Jack, now back from sick leave and serving with his original battalion the 1st Cameronians in 19th Brigade, enjoyed a rather more restrained banter with the enemy on Christmas night.

We are astonished to hear from them the strains of our National Anthem played on a cornet and accompanied by a chorus. (A German hymn has the same air.) C Company gives three hearty cheers on hearing the familiar tune. These are followed by a Teutonic burst of '*Hoch de Kaiser*', which is promptly answered by a fervent shout 'Curse the Kaiser.' Later a voice from the German trench calls out: 'When are you going back to Maryhill Barracks?' and a short exchange of badinage takes place, some Germans from Glasgow evidently having recognized our bonnets. Their merry making continues till the small hours of the morning, but C Company, physically cold and mentally dour, maintain a stiff reserve except when, as with the Imperial Toast, particularly irritating remarks are made by the Hun.[211]

Thus even in a single brigade, while some units were pleased to mingle with the enemy, others waited unmoved behind their defences. In some places, although not in 19th Brigade, the fighting actually continued. As Aidan had noted the RWF, like the 93rd, enjoyed more relaxed contact with the enemy, although they were careful to keep matters under tight control.

Our Pioneer sergeant 'Nobby' Hall, made a screen, and painted on it 'A Merry Christmas' which we hoisted on Christmas morning. No shots were fired. On the left we could see that our fellows were carrying the breakfast in the open and everything was quiet. Both sides got a bit venturous and looked over the top: then a German started to walk down the tow-path toward our lines and Ike Sawyer went to meet him. The German handed over a box of cigars. Later the Germans came boldly out of their trenches, but our men were forbidden to leave theirs, so they threw out tins of bully, and plum and apple jam etc, with plenty of sympathy in the shape of 'Here you are, you poor hungry bastards,' and other such like endearments. When Fritz rolled over two barrels of beer Captain Stockwell went out and spoke to two German officers: it was agreed to recall all men to the trenches and have no more fraternizing. But there was no more shooting, and the Germans were allowed to bury their dead.[212]

Aidan also found time to write home and reflected further on an extraordinary Christmas day.

Dear Mother,

Just a line to let you know I still flourish. It's freezing hard again now, started last night, which was gorgeous, beautiful moon and starlight. The Germans sang and played tunes. We encored them, and quite a conversation was held in one place between one of our men and a German who had lived in Glasgow. This afternoon the

Germans (who are a Saxon Regiment opposite here), started proceedings by rolling two barrels of beer into our trenches!! Most of our men and officers, including myself, went out and met them halfway, when we exchanged smokes, newspapers and various 'souvenirs' for over an hour. The whole time there was a continual boom a long way off on our left, where some battle was going on. On our right snipers were quite busy, but along our battalion and the next on our left, (i.e., as far as we could see), the whole place was crowded with groups of Germans, English, and Highlanders bucking away to each other. Quite a lot of them spoke English. I exchanged some tobacco with the gentleman from Glasgow, '*Soldat Enno Schneider*', for some quite good cigars.

They were awfully keen to get up a football match against us: whether it will come off or not I don't know. So in spite of the Kaiser, we had our Peace and Goodwill for the afternoon at any rate.

They were quite convinced that the Russians were absolutely beaten, and also the Serbians. Also that they would win, and the war would be over in 6 months at most. Their officers whistled them back after half an hour, and there was a lot of hand shaking and '*Auf Wiedersehen*'. Altogether a most astonishing show, they seemed quite peaceable. I asked one if he hated the English like the Prussians did. He denied the imputation most emphatically. They seemed very bored with the people on our left, who they thought fired too much during the day. All of which goes to show what a remarkable show this war is. One can hardly realize now, only an hour or so after that we are all on the lookout, waiting and wondering if they will attack, a thing headquarters rather expect them to do tonight for some reason or other.

There has been very little news out here lately, except for the snipers we are left pretty well alone.

Letters just going up, so goodbye,

Love to all from Aidan*

There is a great deal of speculation about whether a proper football match was ever held between the opposing armies on Christmas day, but it certainly seems likely that there were a number of 'kickabouts'. One such event was reported to have taken place by an Argyll sergeant from Longside in the *Glasgow News* of 2 January, but neither Aidan nor Hutchison made mention of it. Captain Jack though did hear word of these events, writing on 13 January:

There are extraordinary stories of unofficial Christmas truces with the enemy. It seems that on Christmas Day the 2/Argyll and Sutherland Highlanders (in trenches next to ours) actually arranged

---

* IWM JAL letter to EL dated 25 Dec 1914.

to play a football match versus the Saxons – whom we consider to be more humane than other Teutons – in No Man's Land that afternoon. Indeed, someone in my trench told me of the proposal at the time, but I scouted so wild an idea. In any case shelling prevented the fixture. . . There was no truce on the front of my battalion.[213]

On Boxing Day morning a few German shells were fired into the 93rd's positions, one going straight through a house to the rear that was used as an Orderly Room, but there were no casualties in either battalion or brigade. Brigadier-General Congreve's[*] 18th Infantry Brigade moved up to the lines in the afternoon, and the 93rd were relieved by the Sherwood Foresters. The Nottingham men started to come into the forward positions at about 5 pm, sending forward a platoon per company every quarter of an hour, so that the line was always fully manned. The relief was completed at 1930 and Aidan reported that the Foresters were 'were very bucked with our trenches after theirs within 25 yds of Germans'.[214]

It was then back to Armentières for the 93rd, although this time they were billeted around the Science College. Hutchison was billeted in an excellent house belonging to a *Monsieur* Johnson, and remarked upon the spacious rooms, tasteful decoration, comfortable beds and a piano! Aidan, who usually rejoiced in recording his own creature comforts, wrote nothing in his diary for three days. In the meantime the 93rd exercised, played soccer on the sodden ground, and took part in a long route march to Pont de Nieppe and Erquinghem. This left everyone very tired and very footsore, but the battalion marched again the following day. There was also the news from the Somerset Light Infantry that the body of Captain Henderson, killed in the light of the blazing farm at Ploegsteert, had been found and buried over the Christmas period. The burying of dead comrades was another small comfort to be derived from the unexpected truce.

On Tuesday 29 December the Highlanders marched again for the third successive day. However, Aidan made alternative arrangements, and accompanied by Anderson rode over to Steenwerck to see his friends in the Northumberland Hussars. As luck would have it, most of them were also on a route march, but there were a number of familiar and friendly faces. Aidan later explained to his father that these included 'Philip Smith, young Ridley, a Middleton and one or two others I know by name'. The Hussar Colonel, Peter Cookson, an old family friend, was delighted to welcome Aidan, and to catch up on news of the Liddell family, many of whom were still firmly rooted in the north-east. He

---

[*] Walter Congreve won a VC at Colenso in 1899 during the Boer War. His son Major Billy Congreve also won a VC in July 1916 at Longueves. Walter Congreve later lost his left hand in 1917, and was the only British Corps commander to be wounded. He finished his military career as a full General, The Congreves are one of only three father and son VCs.

generously offered the visitors lunch and afterwards they enjoyed a pleasant ride back to the 93rd. That evening Aidan wrote a lengthy and illuminating letter to an old Stonyhurst friend, in which he catalogued his war to date.

Dec 29th 1914

My dear old Flum,

I was so pleased to get your letter this afternoon. I've been out here since the end of August, when I brought the first draft from the 3rd Bn, under fire at La Ferté sous Jouarre on the Marne the day after I joined, but it was nothing very terrifying. We then pursued the Gs to the Aisne, where we squatted in reserve at a place called Bucy le Long, and later at Sept Monts just east of Soissons for a fortnight: our bivouac was shelled heavily incidentally. Next followed the journey by road and by rail to the north. We detrained finally at Blendecques near St Omer, which I suppose is the original Blandyke,* and took part in the attacks round Bailleul, mostly doing nothing except marching backwards and forwards. The first nasty show I encountered was on October 21st. We were suddenly dashed down from near Ypres to a village called Le Maisnil which had to be held. Unfortunately the middle of our line was held by 150 French cyclists, who decamped in the middle of the afternoon without anyone knowing. We had been unmercifully shelled from about 6 am until 4 pm when the Germans suddenly started firing from a farmhouse and wood about 50 yds from the edge of our line. I am machine gun officer, and moved my guns up within 100 yds of the edge of the wood. Two companies of ours were also brought up, and we held on until I actually had only three men left with the two guns and no ammunition. (The limber had been bolted about ½ a mile down the road by a shell.) The two companies lost 230 men and 5 officers, and a company of the Middlesex lost 100 men; all of this in the end of a small field not 100 yds broad. I was just behind and to the flank of all these poor devils, and it was a regular shambles.

There's no doubt we did a lot of harm, as I had both guns going hard for ½ an hour on the wood and house, and practically silenced the fire there.

However, the Germans got round on the other side of a road, and we had to retire.

After that I was detached with the MG section to help the Middlesex in the trenches. I was with them three weeks, and during the first fortnight we were shelled to blazes every day. Occasional night attacks. I had two gun emplacements absolutely blown to bits,

---

* Blandyke was the name for days out at Stonyhurst and was derived from the frequent outings to Blandecques when the school was at St Omer.

luckily no damage done to the guns or teams. During one of the night attacks I got a little bit of shell on the bridge of the nose. Bruised it and hurt like hell, but no damage done.   I joined the regiment again just to go straight into some other trenches, where I completed 43 days on end without a rest.   Pretty fed up by then! Another scratch, this time on the little finger, from a bit of shell in a night attack, and a bullet through both sides of my Glengarry without hitting my head, were the only incidents. A week's rest and more trenches, where we spent Xmas day. On that day everyone spontaneously left their trenches and had a meeting halfway between the trenches. Germans gave us cigars, and we gave them chocolates and tobacco. They seemed very pleased to see us! Some had lived in England for years, and were very bucked at airing their English again. We're out again for a week's rest again in a town which they shell pretty often. In fact they are doing so now, so the rest is more imagined than real. 24 days in and 8 out is what we are doing now.

You don't know how boring and nerve-racking this trench business is, and how long off the end of the war seems. It would appear that it has to go on until the Germans are quite exhausted, which might take a little time.

Bertie is with the 15th Hussars out here. He has been home on leave, but I haven't yet.

Lance is on the *Monarch*, 2nd Battle Squadron, and seems to be having a boring time doing nothing.

They are quite busy at Sherfield, where they have turned one wing of the house into a hospital, taking 25 wounded at a time. They've had about 60 of ours and 12 Belgians so far. Motor ambulance and everything complete.

Well Flum, this is a dreadful war, and now they have started using grenades and bombs with great frequency, it's a little worse than before. Some of the lines of trenches are only 25 yards apart, and all are full of water and mud. It's awfully cold and wet too, and I'm sure none of the 10,000,000 or so combatants would mind if peace was declared tomorrow. Do write again.

Yours ever,

Aidan L.[215]

The next morning some of the officers went off to Bac St Maur for a hunt, which met at 1400. Aidan was never particularly keen on riding or hunting, and stayed in the billets. Both Houplines and Armentières were shelled throughout the afternoon, with shrapnel bursting just behind his house, although it caused no damage. There was also a grenade throwing

54. *Company Bombers with Hale's Percussion Grenades. Photo Argyll and Sutherland Highlanders.*

course for some of the officers, and more route marching. Grenades or bombs, as they were usually described, were becoming an increasingly important weapon, and were well suited to trench fighting. Rifles and fixed bayonets were awkward to handle in confined spaces and could become clogged with mud and so all but useless. Bombs and weighted cudgels or knobkerries were often much more effective weapons in trench fighting, and the appointment of Brigade Bombing Officers and later Bombing Schools was evidence that these lessons were starting to be learned by the BEF.

The Germans had used bombs to good effect from October, but the British had not at first considered them an important adjunct to modern warfare and issued very few of their standard bomb, the Mark 1 Percussion Grenade, at the beginning of the war. Therefore, when the static trench war began the Tommies improvised, something that they were to become increasingly good at. The resulting jam-tin bomb was made literally from old junk, and was crude but effective. An old tin was filled with scraps of metal, and a detonator made of cordite or other explosive was placed down the middle. A hole was punched in the top to allow the addition of a fuse, and it was reckoned that every inch or so allowed a second's delay. The bombers lit them with a match or perhaps the glowing end of a Woodbine. But the lessons delivered in January 1915 were not about the jam tin, but concerned the official Mk 1 Percussion Grenade, or Hale's Percussion Stick as it was also known. It had an 18-inch cane handle and an explosive charge at the business end with a fragmentation jacket placed around it. On the top of the weapon was a detonator. Before being thrown a ribbon or tape some two feet long had to be attached to the stick, rather like the tail of a kite. The safety pin would then be removed to arm the weapon, which was then bowled over arm like a cricket ball to ensure that it landed nose-first to fire the detonator. It was a very cumbersome and unreliable weapon, and there were many instances of men getting tangled in the tail or bombs failing to clear friendly trenches and bouncing back with disastrous consequences. Presumably this was why in January 1915 the 19th Brigade staff were making a determined effort to properly train their battalions. Certainly, the 93rd bombers looked the part as a contemporary picture shows. In covered kilts, Glengarries and an assortment of other headgear and uniform, they look a wild crew, most clutching a long thin Hale's Percussion Stick. The much more handy jam tin bombs can be seen sitting in a recess in the trench wall above their heads.

Thursday was New Year's Eve, and in the tradition of the 93rd Athol Brose was brewed in the afternoon, and in the evening there was a concert for the men from 1730 until 2000. But the war was not so very far away, for there were also more classes in grenade throwing for the company bombers. Hogmanay in dirty billets in Armentières under the German guns was a far cry from Aidan's first New Year's Eve with the 93rd at Fort George in 1912, but as on that occasion the Athol Brose was downed with lip smacking relish and the Highlanders quaffed heartily on whatever else they could lay their hands on. The estaminets did particularly well that night for the 93rd were not only celebrating the New Year as only Scottish soldiers can, but they also knew that very soon they would be returning to the front. The next morning was a miserable wet day, with many sore heads and a particularly large attendance at the Orderly Room. New Year's greetings were exchanged by telegram with the other battalions of the Argyll and Sutherland Highlanders. There was also a special dinner for the men, accompanied by the distribution of more presents from friends of the battalion. Then at 1700 the anticipated warning order was received that the 93rd would relieve the King's Shropshire Light Infantry (SLI) at the front the following day.

They marched out of Armentières at 1900 on 2 January and for once it was a fine and very light night. The route took them about 4 km to Bois Grenier, from where the conditions began to deteriorate badly, and they soon found themselves wading through deep sticky mud to reach the trenches. They were taking over from the 16th Infantry Brigade and moved into a line of trenches running between Touquet and Rue du Bois, about three miles south of Armentières. The actual relief started at 2000. Everything was very wet, and the Highlanders experienced great difficulty in carrying their equipment to the trenches across over a mile of badly waterlogged ground. The machine-guns were a nightmare to manhandle forward and when Aidan eventually arrived in the trenches he found them to be no better and knee-deep in mud and water, even though in places they had been lined with bricks. He recorded 'One gun with C and one with D. Four men of latter coy lost their shoes on way in! Took six men to get one man out of mud between A and C'.[216]

But despite the awful conditions the Germans were active again and making their presence felt. One of the SLI machine-gunners was killed getting out of the trench and Captain Stirling of the Cameronians was also hit and killed during the relief. It was a grim, wet and dangerous night and at about midnight Aidan noted a heavy German bombardment on the right. The relief was not completed until 0030, and German snipers were active, firing at the stretcher bearers who were trying to bury the dead Light Infantry machine-gunner. They were cold, wet and hungry and the rations did not appear until 0300. It was not an auspicious start and Hutchison summed it up with a single line in his diary: 'Ghastly night and wicked trenches. The whole place a river.'[217] Unfortunately it was not going to get any easier.

Chapter Fifteen

Floods and Salmon Fishing

The problem for the 19th Brigade at the start of January was not so much German aggression as the unrelenting weather, which continued to worsen. It rained almost continually and the trenches that were shallow and close to the enemy were now utterly waterlogged. The 93rd occupied the forward positions with the Middlesex and the Cameronians, and the RWF and the Scottish Rifles were in reserve. The forward positions were under two feet of water in some places and there was also thick, sucking mud that made movement difficult, time-consuming and utterly exhausting. Throughout Sunday 3 January the Highlanders worked hard to make the trenches more habitable, but despite their best efforts the water levels continued to rise. Most communication trenches became impassable, which meant that the men repeatedly had to expose themselves to the enemy if the battalion was to function. Aidan noted that the snipers were very busy. Everywhere the rain fell, men baled and the water level rose to the extent that it became obvious that breastworks raised above ground level were the only practical method of protection. The brigade staff now set about securing engineering stores for this new task. That night hardly anyone slept.

Hutchison later recalled that first day in *Warrior*.

> Battalion Headquarters was connected with the line by a single alley-way, deep furrowed across the sodden fields. All attempts to keep this ditch free from water was soon abandoned, although every artifice of drainage, even the construction of weirs and sluices had been attempted by amateur engineers, with growing experience in such schemes. For most of its length this communication trench was waist-high with water. When summoned to Headquarters for what, as in Aldershot days, was still named a 'powwow', I took off my boots and hose, securing the former with their laces round my neck, then draped the kilt as a cloak over my shoulders: and holding my shirt high, I waded through thick slime, to hear the wisdom of those who presided over the destiny of the Battalion.[218]

The following day General Gordon made a tour of the forward positions and had his boots sucked off by the glue-like mud. Like Hutchison he finished his rounds wading barefoot through mud and water. Rather than risk losing their boots, many men took them off and carried them knotted round their necks by the laces. The worst trenches had to be abandoned to the rising water and Hutchison started to build a new defensive line with breastworks close to a building known as Culvert Farm. The only consolation was that the enemy were in a similar plight, and to discourage them further the British guns put a few shells into the German line opposite the 93rd during the morning. That night there was an alarm and Aidan fired flares with a Very pistol. 'Very good' he reported but presumably saw no suitable targets for he did not mention that his guns were in action. However, he did record some apparently excellent political news: 'Heard the Austrians had given in, and that Italy had declared war on Germany!'[219] News, good or bad, travelled fast in the front line, but both rumours were somewhat premature, the first by almost four years and the second by a mere four months! That night the Germans were sniping as well as baling and a man was wounded in the 93rd's headquarters support trench.

The next morning, Tuesday 5 January, Aidan noted that it 'Rained off and on most of the day'.[220] Water continued to rise in the British trenches, although there was some consolation to be derived from watching particularly accurate artillery fire bursting on the German front line at around 1100. At 1400 it was the Germans' turn to shell the 93rd, but despite hits on the parapets of the A Company forward trench and around the general area, there were no British casualties. In fact, the rain was causing greater damage than the German gunners, with dugouts collapsing and parapets sliding into the trenches right across the brigade frontage. The next day, the 93rd War Diary summed up the deteriorating situation:

Water still rising, having gained about a foot since the battalion came in on the 2nd. Most trenches only held by damming up communication trenches and baling. Headquarters trench about 1 foot in water except just near CO's and telephone shelters. Communication on raised planks. No communication with Coys except by telephone and by night across country.[221]

The weather was a little better during the day, but it poured again throughout the evening, making everyone extremely miserable. Hutchison, writing an omnibus entry in his diary spanning these few days, spoke for them all. 'Life in these days too hideous to write. Continuous rain and disappointment. Bitterly cold. Numerous casualties from shell and rifle fire. Many sick.'[222] It was very clear that illness was becoming an increasing problem.

Thursday 7 January was even worse, with no abatement to the rain, which poured down throughout the early hours after what had been a particularly dark and grim night. Aidan's part of the trench line was at least six inches deep in water, and as the water level rose parapets and traverses continued to slip and fall into the trenches. By midday it was waist-deep in places, and where there was less water there was thick sticky mud. A Company had to rescue a man who found himself up to his neck in mud and water, and there were only dugouts left for two men! Then the Officers' Mess fell in. The 93rd were like children on a beach, trying to hold back the tide with walls of sand. All their superhuman efforts to make the squalid trenches more habitable were simply being washed away as they looked on helplessly. At least Aidan's elusive but much anticipated leave appeared to be coming closer, and there was time to pen another rather damp letter home.

Jan 7th 1915

Dear Mother,

We have had a dreadfully tricky week in the trenches, and are in them for some time yet. It has rained incessantly and this brings great chunks off the side of the trench, which lies in the foot or so of water on the bottom, and soon gets churned up into a horrible slime. It is impossible to go along the trench without going over one's knees in several places. Of course one does what one can in the way of digging all this stuff out, but it gets so sticky that it won't leave the spade, which makes it very difficult. Added to which, all the ground behind is so poached up that it is awfully hard for rations or wood to be brought up.

I haven't had dry feet, or even boots without water slushing in them for a week, and our dugout leaks terribly, in spite of waterproof sheets hung on the ceiling, which have to be emptied every three hours or so.

So with wet straw to sleep on, and soaked blankets to cover one, and perpetual wet feet (our mess dugout is three inches deep in water), one would rather be elsewhere than soldiering. The only thing is that the Germans seem to have it a little worse than we do. They keep baling hard, but there are places their trench is so bad that if they want to get along, they have to go along the top behind their parapet, a game we manage to make very unpleasant for them. This morning they had a party bringing in planks, but we observed them and got the machine gun onto them, so there's been no more wood carrying since.

It's still raining hard, so heaven only knows what will happen. Very soon there will be very little trench left.

However, I believe my turn for leave ought to come soon, and if nothing unforeseen happens again, I ought to be home on 11th or 12th of this month. Perhaps I'll arrive before this letter, but I will be very glad of a rest, if only to get my feet warm again.

I had a letter from Cuthbert a couple of days ago, he seems to be enjoying himself pretty well now, having a good rest. Ypres must have been awful. We only just escaped being in trenches there, were within 4 miles of Ypres when we were hauled out of the frying pan into the fire at Le Maisnil.

Well, au revoir, on the 12th. Hope to goodness it comes off. Indigestion and rheumatics have become chronic now.

Love from

Aidan

By the afternoon it was quite clear that most of the 93rd's trenches were useless and untenable except in a few isolated patches. Major Kirk, still commanding though decidedly unwell, therefore decided that they would move out under cover of darkness and start work digging in immediately behind the existing line, making use of the back parapets which were flattened out to make a low bulletproof wall. Work began at about 1700 and a shallow trench was constructed. However, one of the major problems confronting the 93rd was a brook, a tributary of the River Lys, that flowed downhill through the German lines, crossed No Man's Land and then passed through their lines. When the front had been hastily established some eight weeks before, dry ditches and trickling stream beds had been quickly pressed into service as makeshift trenches, and where necessary dams and sluices had been fashioned by the amateur engineers to control the water flow. There was a great buttress that had been constructed at the point the brook crossed the line to protect Willow Trench. This was an old water course that now served as an accommodation and store area. It had bivvies and bays scraped out of the walls of the trench, where men could sleep and arms and ammunition were stored. This was clearly a vulnerable point in the line, but German attempts to shell the earthworks had been unsuccessful, and for a while the Willow Trench dam had worked well enough. However, with the Lys in spate and torrents of brown water rolling down the hill, the ingenuity of the British engineering was being tested to destruction.

At 1700 on 7 January the Willow Trench dam suddenly gave way without warning, releasing a wall of mud and water to flow down what was also the Headquarters support trench. At once the cry went up 'the dam's burst', and soldiers rushed to pull comrades out of collapsing bivvies and started to try to salvage rifles, ammunition and a machine-gun from the swirling water. Hutchison relates that three men died, trapped in a collapsed and waterlogged dugout before the heavy roof could be raised to free them. However, as neither Aidan nor the 93rd War Diary recorded casualties on this particular night, these deaths seem likely to have occurred at a different time. It was, none the less, a disastrous day for the 93rd and there was now very little shelter available for the men.

Miraculously, the CO's command post and the telephone shelter were still standing in Willow Trench. As the phone still worked, these continued to function for the time being, despite the freezing discomfort of the churning waters of Willow Trench. It was simply not practical to find an alternative location and relay the phone cables at that time, and the tenuous communication link had to be kept open.

After the excitement of the burst dam Aidan took command of a working party from 1200 to 0230, although before that he had briefly taken shelter at Grande Flamengrie Farm. In the relative dry and safety of the cellar he was able to eat a meal, and the next day the CO made the farm his new RHQ. Ten days later, after relief by the Cameronians, the cellar was a Company HQ. Captain Jack,* now recovered and back in service with his battalion, furnished a detailed description.

'C' Company's headquarters are in the vaulted cellar of this derelict farm, 250 yards from the front trench. . .The floor is awash with water which leaks in from the moat, and a hand pump works day and night. A small concrete platform in the corner, covered with damp straw, sacks and mackintosh coats, provides us with a dryish place on which to lie; a coke brazier maintains a moderate degree of warmth. The cellar roof is cracked and shaky from the concussion of shells, and we think that a direct hit from a howitzer gun would likely turn this sanctuary into our tomb. Although safe from bullets, we frequently hear them pinging through the empty doorways above or sputtering into the walls.[223]

Dawn on Friday 8 January was a truly desperate time as the 93rd attempted a 'stand to' and faced the enemy lines in the growing light. Some waited in the freezing water of the flooded trenches, and others tried to man the new line directly behind, which despite their frenzied nocturnal digging offered only three feet of muddy cover. The Highlanders, many soaked and with clothing and equipment lost in the flood, were heartened by the arrival of the Battalion Medical Officer who came up to the line, and did his rounds accompanied by a runner bearing a rum jar. Perhaps it was young Ditcham, but the records give no name. But the particular relief that freezing morning was the growing realisation, as dawn broke, that the Germans were in a very similar plight. Hutchison** explained:

The German trenches, too, were flooded. The cheerless, rain-swept morning found two companies of the 93rd seated upon a parapet, with such poor cover as may be provided by ammunition boxes, and sheets of corrugated iron, facing two companies of a Saxon regiment in a similar predicament. They waved feebly to us.[224]

---

* Captain Jack is included in Appendex Two, Notes on Persons Mentioned in the Text.
** Graham Hutchison is included in Appendex Two, Notes of Persons Mentioned in the Text

Throughout the day hostile activity from either side was minimal, as British and Germans were necessarily exposed, both to the continuous rain and to observation by their foes. On 8 January one man was killed and one wounded in the 93rd, and in the afternoon Royal Engineers arrived to provide professional assistance with the construction of the breastworks. These were now officially sanctioned by 19th Brigade, but although the theory might have been sound the practice was less so. As Aidan noted, 'Their stores however were bad at turning up, so very little was done' and like so many others he was also feeling 'very seedy'.[225] During the day Battalion HQ moved to Grande Flamengrie Farm, and Major Kirk, now too ill to continue, was evacuated to hospital. Captain Hyslop assumed command of the 93rd, and the one positive occurrence was the arrival of another draft of seventy men from the 4th Battalion.

It was about this time that Aidan packed up another little parcel of his souvenirs and sent them home to his mother. There was his Glengarry, which he modestly described as being 'not as tidy as it was', which was a reference both to its generally scruffy and lived-in appearance and to the bullet hole through the crown. There was also a clip of German bullets and a couple of irregular pieces of metal from a German shrapnel shell. These fitted neatly together in the shell case rather like a child's toy or a Christmas puzzle, but with the spaces in-between filled in with shrapnel bullets. Aidan explained how they worked to his mother.

> They have a layer of these iron pieces between each layer of bullets, so as to fill in the chinks. The regular shaped one is in the centre of the disc, then a circle of the irregular kind, and lastly a layer of triangular pieces. The bullets of course are in the depressions. These are from a 6 in. howitzer, which must contain an enormous number of bits. You can imagine these lumps make a horrible mess.[226]

Finally, he enclosed a shrapnel ball, and explained its provenance: 'The shrapnel bullet stuck in the ground about 6 inches from my elbow one day when I was having lunch, so I dug him out.'[227] One wonders what his mother must have thought of this grim little collection that so clearly illustrated both the dangers of the front and the luck that Aidan had so far enjoyed as a soldier. No doubt opened with some excitement, it would seem unlikely to have brought much joy and contentment to the Liddell breakfast table!

Saturday dawned and as usual it was still raining. A heavy bombardment of the German trenches was planned by 3rd Corps, but was then called off, although the gunners did drop a few registering shells around the enemy trenches to Aidan's front. The Germans then replied with half a dozen shells of their own in the 'tit for tat' of modern warfare. The Highlanders were still desperately trying to improve their defences, which meant having to move around in the open. Thankfully though, the Germans remained generally passive, although one man was killed. The particular task for the day was to complete 50 yards of raised breastwork with shelters for the men constructed behind. Sappers supervised the construction, and the Highlanders provided the labour, but it proved a hopeless task. Eventually, these breastwork structures would be six feet high and up to eight feet thick and be almost as effective as trenches, but that was still far off in the future.

For the present, the problems of constructing adequate defences seemed insurmountable. Aidan explained the difficulties 'Everything swamped, men incapable of throwing a shovel full of earth.'[228] The other problem was that the stores carried forward were woefully inadequate, and this was in part owing to the poor road and flooded fields and ditches that the carrying parties had to cross to reach the line. There were timber frames for the parapets, large brushwood hurdles to provide a framework for sandbags and earth, and sheets of corrugated iron; but there was never enough of any of it. After immense effort only 20 yards of parapet was put up and that was not finished. That night the Germans used one of their big searchlights to illuminate their own line and Aidan saw them digging hard. The men of the 93rd were physically and mentally exhausted and seven of Aidan's Machine-Gun Section were now sick.

The next night they tried again to complete the 50 yards of breastwork, but during the intervening day the men had to sit very still in their positions, making the best use of whatever limited cover was available. Movement was severely limited because of the lack of protection and soldiers were constantly exposed to the elements, becoming increasingly cold, wet and miserable, and then eventually ill. There followed another wet, miserable night with the prospect of backbreaking and frustrating work as the War Diary recorded. 'RE material commenced arriving at 9 pm but was not all up till 2 am. What did arrive was totally inadequate and various essential parts were omitted. One of the shelters put up the night before fell in, damaging four men, fortunately not severely.' [229]

For Aidan though that Sunday was altogether different, for at long last his much anticipated leave came through. He was woken late, and while his comrades huddled in their wet open trenches, his instructions were to make his way back down the line and get to Bois Grenier during daylight. From there he rode into Armentières, where he had a bath and put on clean clothes. Life was getting progressively more comfortable as he moved further away from the line. Looking and feeling much more like his old cheerful self, he met up with Bucknall, an officer he knew from the Middlesex, and together they drove to Merville and dinner. The following day there would be a train, a troopship and England.

There is no clear record of how Aidan spent those few days of home leave that he had so long looked forward to. There was certainly no serious sweetheart awaiting the return of her soldier boy and demanding his attention, for Aidan like many young men of his wealth and background did not rush to romance, and late marriages were commonplace among his peers. Clean clothes, roaring fires and hot baths must have been a very high priority, and the unaccustomed luxury of clean sheets on a warm, dry and comfortable bed.

First he doubtless returned to Sherfield Manor and his family and friends. There was the hospital to see, and much to tell and be told of the last five months. His car and motorbike awaited and London, with clubs, shows, favourite restaurants and more friends was only a short train journey or drive away. There was also the opportunity to shop, to visit the military tailor, the hatter and boot-maker and acquire the very latest in front-line fashion and gadgets. Aidan probably did all of these things, but the one fact that is known with certainty is that he travelled north to Cumberland to stay at Warwick Hall, and partake of the fishing on the River Eden. This was the home of his uncle, Charles Liddell, one of his father's brothers, and of his aunt Madeleine.

Charles was a particularly keen fisherman, and the estate included three miles of excellent salmon fishing. The River Eden flowed into the Solway Firth, and fed by Pennine and Lakeland streams, offered great sport for salmon. It also fished particularly well for sea and brown trout and grayling. It was a favourite place for Aidan and salmon aside, he was also very fond of his young cousin Ailleen, and would certainly have enjoyed her company if she had been there. However, as she trained and served as a nurse on the home front, her presence was by no means certain and is not recorded. Good fishing, however, was almost guaranteed at Warwick Hall and Aidan killed six salmon in a fine three days of sport.

Aidan had only a single week of leave, from Monday 11 January until Monday 18 January, and it is interesting that he spent three of those precious seven days on a river bank by the swollen Eden in windswept and wintry Cumberland. It might seem extraordinary that after the cold and discomfort of the last few months, he should elect to do something that at first sight might appear to offer more of the same. But he had had much time to dwell on his leave and opportunities that it might present. Indeed, judging by his letters home it was becoming close to an obsession. Soldiers home from the war make carefully considered choices and Aidan set great store by his fishing, which was clearly very important to him. Inevitably, there must have been the consideration that this could be his last opportunity to fish the Eden. So Aidan indulged himself and did what he really wanted to do, despite the cold and the wet and the rain!

While in the trenches Aidan had dreaded the thought of returning to France after leave, likening it to going back to boarding school after the holidays. Well soon 'the holidays' were over and on Monday 18 January he arrived at Victoria station bright and early to catch the 0815 train to the coast. Troop movements to France were now well practised, swift and efficient. He travelled first by troopship to Boulogne, then by another train to Hazebrouck, and finally by bus to the 19th Brigade area at Nieppe. Here, he was lucky enough to be able to get a lift to the front in the Middlesex mess cart, and arrived at the 93rd's second echelon at about 2300. He was back with the battalion and on active service only fifteen or so hours after leaving smoky London, but this time he was a veteran and knew exactly what to expect.

Little had changed in his absence and the particular challenge was still to construct adequate raised breastworks. The trenches remained waterlogged and were still virtually uninhabitable. The engineers had been trialling various models of defensive structure, most of which were judged useless by the infantry. The Sappers though had devised 'hencoops', a sort of wooden shelter rather like a packing case, which could be dug into trench or breastwork to provide a rudimentary shelter. That helped a bit, for it was fearfully cold and some cases of frostbite were being reported. Fortunately, the Germans were still in a similar predicament and what amounted to an unofficial truce had developed. Both sides allowed each other to work in the open unchallenged, although most of the serious construction work still had to be done at night. When eventually after many weeks of work the defensive lines of both sides were completed to their satisfaction, both sides tested the strength of the others' fortifications constructed under such trying conditions. The British works appeared massively made and looked much more substantial than the flimsier German constructions. But a one-hour bombardment blew several holes in the 93rd's line, and when the British replied in kind it was discovered that the Germans had riveted their defences with concrete, which made them an altogether tougher proposition. But that was in the future and for now the siting of the new raised defensive line was being hampered by the legacy of the autumn fighting. Excavating an old company latrine was unpleasant and unhealthy, and both the RWF and the 93rd also encountered bodies buried during the earlier fighting. The 'most gruesome stories' about dugout walls collapsing to reveal corpses that Aidan had dismissed in December were sadly not as 'tall' as he had at first imagined.

He found that the 93rd had been relieved by the Cameronians in the middle of the previous week, and that there was now a new CO, Lieutenant-Colonel Gore. When Aidan returned they had just moved out of billets and had taken over a new set of trenches from the Middlesex. There was also now a new regime whereby battalions did five days in the line followed by five in reserve, so that the brigade operated with two and a half battalions forward and the balance in reserve in billets. The Middlesex and the 93rd worked the left side of the frontage and the RWF and the Cameronians the right. In the centre were the Scottish Rifles who maintained an alternating two-company frontage. This was perhaps not purely coincidence for it was observed by the RWF that 'The Scottish Battalions of the Brigade did not work well together'.[230] Whatever the reasons for these present arrangements, which meant that the 93rd rotated with their old friends the Middlesex, they proved generally satisfactory.

Aidan slept that night at the 2nd echelon farm, and had breakfast there before making his way forward to report to RHQ, arriving after lunch. At dusk he went forward to the trenches and inspected his guns which were deployed with D Company. The 93rd were not impressed by what they had inherited from the Middlesex, as the War Diary explained. 'Trenches taken over were in a bad state, fire-trenches impassable and only tenable in places. Very little work had been done with breastworks. Our left (D Coy) was opposite Saxons who never fired, so work proceeded by day.'[231] Aidan's diary note read simply 'Lots of mud. Things very quiet'.[232]

The next day he paid a call on the neighbouring battalion, and was able to see for himself just how relaxed both sides had become in some places. He also noted the increasing amount of sickness amongst the officers:

> Walked up to Headquarters for a court martial, which was postponed until tomorrow. Went to call on the Leicesters who are on our left, and are within 40 yds of the Germans. Both sides hard at work building breastworks. German officer sitting in chair directing operations. In front of D coy similar quiet, only 200 yards apart. Opposite C coy. however are Prussians who snipe continuously. Jim Younger arrived in evening, Nichol a few days ago. Kirk and Moorhouse home sick. Anderson, Stewart more recently. Slight alarm 9 pm.[233]

It continued to be very wet and cold on the Thursday and through the early part of Friday, although later the sun came out, and Aidan watched a number of aeroplanes flying overhead. He was starting to feel unwell, but endured another freezing day in the line. When the 93rd were relieved by the Middlesex on Saturday 23 January, he immediately lay down on arrival at the billets, although he found time to record 'Felt pretty seedy'. He was no better on the Sunday, noting 'Remained lying down'.[234]

It was now clear that this was no passing chill, but a serious medical problem that warranted proper treatment beyond the rudimentary care available within the battalion. On the Monday morning, seeing no signs of recovery, the Medical Officer arranged for him to be taken by wagon to the Field Ambulance at Erquinghem. Once admitted he stayed on a mattress on the floor. The 93rd briefly recorded the day's events and noted Aidan's departure: 'Route marching by companies. Lieut Liddell sent away sick. 5 pm. Draft of 95 men under 2nd Lieut IM Miller arrived.'[235] For the Adjutant scribing the War Diary it was another uneventful day in billets, with the endless grind of military training, the departure of a sick officer and the arrival of a fresh one to replace him. He probably thought it very convenient. But for Aidan it marked the end of an extraordinarily eventful chapter in his life. Although he did not know it then, he would not return to the 93rd.

Chapter Sixteen

England Again

On Tuesday 26 January Aidan's terse diary entry described the next stage of his rather slow progress to the rear. 'Motor ambulance left at 10 am for Clearing Station (No. 2) I think, at Bailleul, reached about 12, bed at once.'[236] Meanwhile, the 93rd were route marching by companies, and the forward battalions of the 19th Brigade were watching the fall of shot as the supporting batteries tested their concentration of fire against the German wire and breastworks. The following day, 27 January, was the Kaiser's birthday, and there were concerns about enemy troop concentrations around Lille and the strong expectation of a powerful attack to mark the day. General Gordon intended to be ready and exercised his supporting batteries accordingly. In the event, however, there was no great assault, although the 93rd were stood to arms in anticipation of one. The only remarkable thing about Kaiser Wilhelm's birthday was that it stopped raining. For Aidan, it was just as well that there was no attack and resultant streams of British casualties, for it meant that his measured progress to the rear could proceed unimpeded. He was taken by stretcher to an ambulance train, which left at about 1030 and arrived in Boulogne station at 1600 from where, like Captain Jack before him, he was transferred to No. 7 Stationary Hospital. He continued to feel feverish, weak and unwell, but still found the strength to record the day's events briefly in his diary, and then pen a short note home.

> Wednesday Jan. 27th
> No. 7 Stationary Hospital
> Boulogne
> Dear Mother,
>
> Here I am with flu, or at least that's what I imagine most of it is. Went sick on Saturday, and have had a weird journey here in ambulances of all kinds, horse, motor, trams, and am now at the above No 7, feeling very washed out. I was pretty run down before I went on leave, but thought that would put me right. However the germs have got the better of me now. Will write again shortly.
>
> Love from
> Aidan[237]

The stay in Boulogne was very brief, and the following morning Aidan was taken aboard the Hospital Ship *St Edward*, which sailed for Dover at about 1300 and arrived in England two hours later. Following disembarkation he was conveyed by Hospital Train to Woolwich, where he was admitted into the Herbert Hospital and was examined by Dr CH Robson, a lieutenant in the RAMC who made the following record of the admission on Army Form I 1237 or the Medical Case Sheet:

Pt went out with Expeditionary Force on Aug 30 1914. In action nearly all time until he had leave from 11–18 Jan. He was feeling seedy when he got back. He went sick on 23rd. He had a sore throat, pains in back and legs and head. He was invalided home and arriving at Herbert on 28 inc. Whilst in France pt says he suffered from headaches indigestion etc.[238]

Dr Robson's assessment of Aidan's present condition was that 'Pt seems to be recovering from an attack of influenza and still seems weak', which was pretty much what Aidan had told him. Indeed, even the word 'seedy' seems to have been plucked directly from his patient's lips. The remedy was easily administered, and with good food, a warm bed, clean sheets, and proper medical attention Aidan's condition improved rapidly. His recovery was assisted by the care of attentive nurses, and the opportunity to sleep soundly and enjoy the peace and rest. Two days later on 30 January, he appeared before a medical board, which solemnly declared that 'He is now recovering from an attack of influenza'.[239] He was judged unfit for General Service, or indeed for Home Service, and was discharged from hospital and awarded three weeks' leave.

Aidan returned at once to Sherfield Manor to continue his convalescence. There, a week later, came the splendid news that Cuthbert had been Mentioned in Despatches for his service with the 15th Hussars.* The award was gazetted on 7 February, and the news greatly cheered the Liddell household. A little over a week later there was cause for another round of celebrations, for Aidan heard that he too had been Mentioned in Despatches. That news had also reached the 93rd and on 19 February the War Diary recorded that 'The following names appeared in the Gazette dated 17/2/15 as Mentioned in Despatches. Major Kirk , Major Hyslop, Capt Thorpe, Lieut Clark, Lieut Liddell, Sgt Major Kerr, Pt J Campbell, Pt J Hadrion'. Two days later there was a second entry: 'The following honours have been posted in the *London Gazette* of 18th February. Major Kirk to be Brevet Lt Col, Major Hyslop DSO, Capt Thorpe DSO, Lieuts Clarke, Liddell (3Bn) and Sgt Major Kerr Military Cross.'[240]

The Military Cross (MC) was a new decoration, and although no citation survives, friends in the 93rd had no doubt that Aidan's cross was awarded for the action at Le Maisnil, given in recognition of the crucial

* Bertie would receive a second Mention in Despatches on 22 June 1915.

role he played by advancing his machine-guns and holding back the main German assault at the critical point in the battle. The Military Cross had been approved by the King on 14 October 1914, just a week before the action at Le Maisnil, in order to provide a gallantry award for the Army that matched the Distinguished Service Cross (DSC) which was a Royal Naval decoration only. Making the DSC available to the Army but with a different coloured ribbon was considered, as was a Conspicuous Service Cross, but finally the designation Military Cross was suggested. Approval having been given, the fine detail had to be agreed and this proved a slightly more complicated process. FEG Ponsonby, an official of the Privy Purse Office at Buckingham Palace, wrote to Lord Kitchener on 10 December with some possible ideas.

> With regard to the ribbon it has occurred to me that orange has never yet been used with British Decorations or Medals. The plain orange ribbon would be quite distinctive and would never be confused with another medal. If however you think it necessary to have more than one colour, either red or blue borders could be added. The red white and blue ribbon that was suggested seems more appropriate to a War Medal than for a Cross. It is also rather too French, which is hardly advisable in view of the fact that at some future time we may be at war with France.[241]

Ponsonby's reflection on the French is interesting, but in the event it was the King that chose the colour, aided by Lord Kitchener. They met on 21 December and together viewed the book of medal ribbons that had not been previously chosen, in much the same way that one might select a design from a pattern book for curtains. Fortunately, His Majesty did not share Ponsonby's predilection for orange. Even so, the choice was not an easy one, although he had already issued instructions regarding the Cross itself. Ponsonby had written on 19 December:

> The King has approved of the enclosed design for the new Military Cross. His Majesty is however very much opposed to iron of any description, or black metal resembling iron being used. He does not wish there to be any suspicion of our copying the Germans.[242]

There had also been suggestions of a silver and bronze cross, but these would be expensive to produce, so finally Ponsonby concluded 'His Majesty also thinks it would be best to have the whole Cross made of silver'.[243] The finished item was thus a silver cross with the imperial crown at the end of each arm with the Royal Cipher in the centre. It was attached on a plain suspender from a white ribbon with a central deep purple stripe, and it must be said looked very handsome indeed. It was anticipated that some 5000 might be needed during the course of the campaign, but in fact over 38,000 were awarded during the Great War. The Royal Warrant instituting the new Decoration was signed at His

Majesty's Command by Lord Kitchener on 28 December 1914, and the first ninety-nine recipients were gazetted on 1 January 1915.

Aidan's award in February was thus among the first MCs to be gazetted, but there were some among the 93rd who believed that he had deserved the DSO for Le Maisnil. The alternatives to the MC at that time were the superior DSO or the much less significant 'Mention in Despatches', and interestingly at the time of the action the MC had not yet been instituted. However, there is no evidence to suppose that Aidan felt hard done by, despite others' protestations on his behalf. He never actually referred to the MC in letters or his diary but this is easily explained by his sick leave, which precluded both the need for family letters and extensive diary entries.

However, the new MC and a 'Mention in Despatches' must have been a splendid tonic for a convalescing soldier, and Aidan was not the sort of man to feel slighted. As a new decoration, the minting of the medal and

the production and issue of the ribbon would have taken some time. Sadly there are, therefore, no photographs of him wearing either the cross or the ribbon. His studio portrait taken in June 1915, the last of him taken displaying his tunic front before his departure to France, shows him still unadorned, without the purple and white MC ribbon.

The three weeks of sick leave soon passed, but although he was feeling rather better, he was still not judged to be entirely well. On 24 February he returned to Tidworth for a second medical board. The assessment was that 'He has recovered from influenza but has developed rheumatism in the right shoulder from standing in a wet trench'. He was judged unfit for General Service or even light duties at home, and was awarded a further three weeks' sick leave. The wet and damp had probably left its mark on a man who had for years suffered from physical weakness at Stonyhurst College and Oxford, or perhaps it was simply an understanding MO who was

55. Portrait, June 1915, Dover Street Studios Mayfair. Photo Mark Liddell.

56. *Portrait, June 1915, Dover Street Studios Mayfair. Photo Mark Liddell.*

prepared to stretch a point for an officer now decorated with the new MC.

Three weeks later he returned again to Tidworth and this time he was found to have completely recovered from illness, and pronounced fully fit for General Service. He returned to duty with the 3rd Battalion at Woolwich, where he met up with a number of old chums, including James Cunningham, who had by now recovered from being shot through the mouth at Ploegsteert Wood the previous November. There was also Philip Anderson and 'Nut' Calquhoun, and the four of them whiled away their off duty time in the bright lights of the West End. A particular favourite was the Cavendish Hotel off Jermyn Street, where Mrs Rosa Lewis, dubbed the Duchess of Duke Street, welcomed young officers who had returned from France and showed them kindness and considerable hospitality.

Mrs Lewis had made her reputation cooking for royalty and the nobility and Edward VII was said to have particularly relished her quail pudding. She was probably the first celebrity chef, and made her money catering on a lavish scale for the rich and famous, and was a hostess of some renown. Indeed, such was her fame and celebrity that she inspired Evelyn Waugh's character Lottie Crump, the proprietor of Shepheard's Hotel, in *Vile Bodies*. During the Great War Rosa Lewis kept an open house at the Cavendish Hotel for young officers and said that it was her war effort. The champagne flowed and the music played and Rosa helped the young men to forget their troubles. When Cunningham and Anderson were returning to France they found two hampers packed with food and other luxuries awaiting them in Southampton. There was no charge; they were simply another gift from the Duchess of Duke Street. Thirty years later, in another German war, she was still showing this exceptional kindness. Soldiers raised their glasses to her as the Cavendish jazz band played and the notes of her favourite 'Tipperary' once again echoed along Jermyn Street.

London could be fun, and soldiers destined to return to the war deserved the opportunity to relax and enjoy themselves. Aidan made the most of it, but he also took the time to do some very serious thinking about his future. He had clearly demonstrated his value as a courageous and highly competent infantry officer, and had become a popular figure in a battalion that, when he joined it, was still dominated by the peacetime regulars. For a Special Reservist that was no mean feat. But Aidan was also a trained and qualified pilot, and as he had witnessed from the ground and noted in his diaries, aircraft were increasingly seen over the battlefield and had a vital role to play in modern warfare. It is, therefore, hardly a shock that in the spring of 1915 he decided to apply for a transfer to the RFC. Indeed, perhaps the most surprising thing was that it took him so long to do it.

In the summer of 1914 the RFC had been in every sense a fledgling service, with few machines and equally limited numbers of pilots and mechanics. The sole operating base was at Farnborough and when on mobilisation the RFC was required to prepare all available air assets for despatch to France, they did just that. The four squadrons that deployed took with them almost all the effective pilots and most of the serviceable aeroplanes. Sixty-three machines were sent to France, but although a further 116 remained at home, the figures were somewhat misleading, as the Official History explained: 'About 20 of them, more or less old fashioned, were used at the Central Flying School for the purposes of training; the rest were worn out or broken, and were fit only for the scrap heap.'[244]   But the four squadrons that went to France had rapidly established their credentials as the eyes of the Army, and performed invaluable work during the early battles of manoeuvre, when the Germans had come so close to encircling the Allied armies and taking Paris. Aerial reconnaissance was a vital form of intelligence and helped to guide the redeployment of the reorganised French armies, enabling them to thwart the planned German envelopment. The four squadrons of British aircraft contributed significantly to that achievement.

After those early battles Sir David Henderson, commanding the RFC, provided a prophetic vision of the future: 'This is the beginning of a fight that will ultimately end in great battles in the air, in which hundreds, and possibly thousands, of men may be engaged at heights varying from 10,000 to 20,000 feet.'[245] Men and equipment were now required to meet that challenge, and in the same way that Lord Kitchener engineered the expansion of the regular army by the creation of the New Army, so the RFC conducted its own parallel exercise. The requirement was for new aircraft, the mechanics to service them, and above all for pilots to fly them. In the spring of 1915 Colonel Sefton Brancker, the Deputy Director of Aeronautics, produced a plan that called for fifty squadrons. When it reached Lord Kitchener, the Secretary of State for War, he returned it almost at once with the simple notation 'Double this. K'.[246] So the resolve was there at the very highest level to finance and build a powerful air force to complement the New Army that would be needed to win the war, and the call went out for volunteers to fight not just on land but in the air.

Aidan never explained his reasons for transferring to the RFC, or if he did they no longer survive, but they were probably not difficult to understand. In 1914 Aidan went to war with people that he knew, and as a Special Reserve officer doubtless felt that there was something to be proved, both to himself and to his comrades. To have transferred back from the deprivation and danger of the trenches during the autumn fighting of 1914 would have felt like the soft option and as if he was walking out on his friends. Now, however, there had been a clean break of several months at home, and very few of the old 93rd remained. What is more, the RFC was expanding rapidly, and pressing hard for volunteers. The biggest catch of all was a trained pilot, and Aidan, as a patriotic Englishman, must have realised that he was of much greater value to his country in a cockpit than in a muddy ditch with the 93rd. Military aviation seemed to offer the ultimate challenge, and with it came the tantalising prospect of flying some of the most modern machines then available. It would he knew be very different from his Brooklands days and the good old Vickers Boxkite.

By the time Aidan transferred to the RFC, the planned expansion was already well under way and the single airfield at Farnborough had been supplemented by the takeover of the civilian facilities at Hounslow, Shoreham, Joyce Green and Brooklands. The aerodromes at Gosport, Dover, and Netheravon were also requisitioned by the RFC as training stations, and new airfields were established at Northolt, Norwich, Catterick, Castle Bromwich, and Beaulieu. At the operational level, command and control was to a degree decentralised by the grouping of squadrons into wings. Aircraft supply had also been stepped up, and new types ordered before the advent of war were now appearing in the front line, supplemented by French machines and engines. Aeroplanes were faster, flew higher, and carried more weapons than ever before, and the flying services were catching the eye and firing the public imagination. This process was accelerated by the gallant and much publicised actions of 2nd Lieutenant Rhodes-Moorhouse on 26 April.

Willy Rhodes-Moorhouse was a wealthy young man, educated at Harrow and Trinity College Cambridge, and like Aidan enjoyed speed and modern technology. He raced cars at Brooklands and gained his pilot's ticket at Portholme Meadow, Huntingdon, in 1911, after which he became a celebrated pioneer airman, and inevitably joined the RFC. On 26 April he piloted a BE2b of No. 2 Sqn against enemy rail communications, in an effort to prevent German troop reinforcements arriving in the Ypres salient. He flew without an observer to compensate for the single 100-lb bomb that the aeroplane carried, and had been ordered to attack the railway lines adjacent to Courtrai station. Similar attacks, each by a single No. 2 Sqn machine, were to be made against other nearby locations.

Before he left he handed his Flight Commander a farewell letter to be sent to his wife in the event of his death. It finished 'I am off on a trip from which I don't expect to return but which I hope will shorten the War a bit. I shall probably be blown up by my own bomb or if not, killed by rifle fire.'[247] Willy was an experienced pilot and navigator and found the station with no difficulty. He made his attack at low level, coming down to 300 feet on his bombing run. He dropped his load accurately on the railway line to the west of the station but during the approach he was subjected to heavy rifle and machine-gun fire from troops on the ground. He was also fired on by a machine-gun mounted in the bell tower of Courtrai church, which was particularly effective as it was able to track the aircraft as it flew past and fire into it from a similar level. The bomb detonated on target, and the aircraft was so low that it was peppered with shrapnel from the blast. Immediately afterwards the pilot received a bullet wound to the abdomen, and was wounded twice more to the hand and thigh as he struggled to take the damaged aircraft home. Rhodes-Moorhouse was mortally wounded and very weak from loss of blood, but he brought the badly damaged BE2c back and landed safely at Merville. There, instead of being taken to hospital, he insisted on being carried from the bloody cockpit to a nearby office to report on his mission. This he did in the presence of his Wing Commander, the newly promoted Lieutenant-Colonel Hugh Trenchard. Mechanics counted ninety-five bullet and shrapnel holes in the aircraft. Willy Rhodes-Moorhouse died the next day in hospital and Trenchard's recommendation of a posthumous Victoria Cross (VC) was upheld, and gazetted on 22 May. There is no doubt that it was an exciting time for an infantry officer to be joining the RFC.

Aidan's first posting in the RFC was to Shoreham on 4 May. This was the home of No. 3 Reserve Aeroplane Squadron, but he was not to stay there long. In under two weeks he was transferred to No. 15 Sqn, at Dover. He is listed on an intake that arrived there on 26 May, although his diary records that he did not actually reach Dover until the first week in June. Perhaps he remained longer at Shoreham or managed to take some additional leave, for he was photographed by Sligger at Balliol in May. However, in early June he was on the strength of No. 15 Sqn at Dover and living comfortably at Burlingham. There would have been lectures on engines and aeroplanes, on meteorology and wireless

57. Aidan at Balliol College
Oxford May 1915.
Photo Mark Liddell.

telegraphy, and on rudimentary tactics. However, the real emphasis was on the practical, and the principal aim of the instructors was to turn out safe pilots in the minimum number of hours. Learning to fight and stunt was not at this stage of the war part of the curriculum, and had to be learned, or not, on a squadron in France. Even this modest training was to prove hazardous, and at Central Flying School (CFS) they called the students 'Huns', because of the numbers of instructors they killed. Indeed, flying had now become a dangerous business, even without the enemy. Of the more than 14,000 British pilots who died during the war, over 8000 were killed during training in Britain.

The talk in the RFC messes at Shoreham and Dover must have been of Rhodes-Moorhouse and the first RFC VC, but very soon there was to be another flying hero. On 7 June Flight Sub-Lieutenant Rex Warneford of the Royal Naval Air Service (RNAS) destroyed a Zeppelin, the first to be downed by an Allied aircraft. Warneford was serving with No. 1 Sqn RNAS at Dunkirk and one of the squadron's roles was to intercept Zeppelins that attempted to cross the channel to England or to catch them on their return. On 17 May he had already encountered the enemy while on an anti-Zeppelin patrol, and although he had closed in and opened fire the airship had jettisoned ballast and climbed quickly out of harm's way. On 7 June he had a second chance when he took off with another aircraft, to try to intercept three Zeppelins that were known to be returning under cover of darkness from a bombing sortie over England. The RNAS pair was flying Morane Type 'L's and each carried six 20-lb bombs, but no guns. Soon after starting out from Dunkirk, Warneford noticed the unmistakeable pencil silhouette of a Zeppelin on the far horizon, and climbed in pursuit. The other aircraft was quickly forced to break off when its instrument lights failed, and Warneford was left to carry out the long nocturnal chase alone. He gradually overhauled the enemy, which was watching his approach, and after about three quarters of an hour he came under enemy machine-gun fire from the gondolas.

The airship was aggressively handled and nearing home. Warneford knew that if he pressed the attack too vigorously, it would probably shed ballast and climb away as had happened on 17 May. This time he pretended to be driven off by the machine-guns and was able to climb to 11,000 feet, and attack the enemy from above. Cutting his engine he dived down and glided along the whole length of the airship, releasing his bombs as he passed about 150 feet above the huge envelope. At first nothing seemed to happen, but then suddenly there was a massive explosion that tore the airship apart, tossing the little Morane high into the air and flipping it onto its back.

While Warneford struggled to control his damaged aircraft, blazing pieces of the Zeppelin fell to the ground at Ghent. Twenty-seven of the twenty-eight men on board the Zeppelin were killed. The sole survivor was the coxswain, who had a miraculous escape when he fell through the roof of a nunnery and landed on a feather bed. Meanwhile Warneford, found that his engine had stopped, and had to make an emergency landing behind enemy lines. At first he considered destroying the aircraft, but then quickly identified the problem as a damaged fuel line. After about thirty-five minutes on the ground, in the true tradition of the pioneer aviator, he managed to improvise and made a repair with his cigarette holder. As he readied himself for take-off, German troops emerged from a nearby wood and started firing at him with carbines. However, he was able to get airborne and had sufficient fuel to cross the lines where a hero's welcome awaited.

On 8 June he received a telegram from the King conferring on him the Victoria Cross, and suddenly he was a national hero. Sadly he did not have long to rejoice in his celebrity. On 17 June, after a trip to Paris in which he received the Legion of Honour, Rex Warneford was fatally injured in a flying accident when the Henri Farman that he was piloting broke up in mid-air. An American passenger also died in the incident. It was another tragic reminder of the fragility of contemporary aircraft and the ever present dangers to the men that flew them.

Aidan remained with No. 15 Sqn, effectively a flying training unit, until 20 July, and having been awarded his RFC wings was gazetted as an RFC officer in the rank of captain and ordered to report to RFC HQ at St Omer. His induction into the RFC and reacquaintance with flying had been accomplished in two and a half months. He was ordered to proceed to Farnborough from where it was intended that he would fly to France in a replacement aircraft.

Now on active service once more, Aidan returned to his practice of writing a daily diary, recording his first entry for several months: 'Wed 21 July. Sent to Farnborough with instructions to be ready to proceed to France at short notice. Told would fly over a BE2c, but none ready. Rained in torrents so went home.'[248] He was fortunate that Sherfield Manor was conveniently located only sixteen miles away.

*58. 23 July 1915. Aidan prepares to
leave Farnborough for France.
Photo Mark Liddell.*

The following day the weather was no better, and Aidan remained at Sherfield, returning to Farnborough on the Friday morning. However, when he got there he discovered that there was not to be a cross channel flight to France after all. Instead, an RFC tender was made available to convey him to London. There he caught the 1340 train from Victoria to Folkstone, and then boarded a troopship to Boulogne. There was time for one last photograph at Farnborough, and this shows him in the now familiar Glengarry, standing alongside the large RFC staff car, with his newly won RFC wings concealed beneath a capacious mackintosh. Walter Raleigh wrote in *The War In The Air*, 'The air service has its own advantages, its own trials, and its own marks of distinction. Life in the air service was lived at high pressure, and was commonly short'.[249] After almost six months at home, Aidan was returning to France and to a very different sort of war.

Chapter Seventeen

Per Ardua Ad Astra[*]

Aidan arrived at St Omer at 0330 on Saturday 24 July. He reported to RFC HQ, which was located in a small red and white painted stucco château that stood on a hill between the town and the aerodrome. There he was given his orders to join No. 7 Sqn, which was the only RFC squadron operating from the adjacent airfield at that time, the rest being deployed closer to the front. The four RFC squadrons that had flown to France in August 1914 had by now expanded to eleven, and each comprised about a dozen machines, and with luck enough pilots and observers to fly them at the required rate. Despite the already dramatic expansion, the RFC was still a small and intimate force in which the pre-war personalities dominated – a very far cry from November 1918, when the RAF had ninety-nine squadrons in the field in France, and boasted 22,000 aircraft.[250]

Clearly Aidan was keen to meet his twenty or so new flying comrades, to find out all he could about the routine and to get to grips with the front-line fighting machines. But in his diary he was somewhat dismissive of the aircraft that he found at St Omer noting, perhaps with a little disappointment, 'Voisins and a few REs only'.[251] He was probably hoping for something faster and more modern. No. 7 Sqn had deployed from Netheravon on 8 April 1915 and was by now well established at St Omer. Initally it had operated a mixed fleet of aircraft, with two flights of RE5s (the designation was for Reconnaissance Experimental) and a flight of four Vickers FB5[**] 'Gunbusses'. However, the FB5s were quickly detached to protect Boulogne, and were subsequently transferred to No. 5 Sqn at Abeele. To replace them C Flight was resupplied with French-built two-seater Voisins. There was also a sole single-seater Bristol Scout that Aidan might have found more to his taste, although in the event he was not to have the opportunity of flying it.

Most of the squadron was thus made up of the large RE5 two-seater, twenty-four of which had been ordered from the Royal Aircraft Factory at Farnborough in late 1913. This aeroplane had a wingspan of over 45 feet, some variants were even wider, and a triangular seven-foot tail fin supported a substantial rudder and ailerons. The two-or four-bladed propeller was driven by a 120 hp Austro-Daimler engine, which delivered

[*] Per Ardua Ad Astra, 'Through Struggle to the Stars', was first the motto of the Royal Flying Corps and then inherited by the Royal Air Force.
[**] The FB designation was for Fighting Biplane.

236

a maximum speed of 78 mph. One of No. 7 Sqn's Flight Commanders, Captain Norman Spratt, had established what was then an altitude record when he took an RE5 up to 18,900 feet in May 1914. The front of the machine was covered by an aluminium cowling that surrounded the engine area, and steel tubing was used extensively in the construction of the fuselage, which was fabric-covered, apart from plywood sections adjacent to the cockpit areas. It has been suggested that the dope on some examples was coloured to give a disruptive camouflage effect. This certainly looks to have been the case and can clearly be seen in some contemporary photographs. The pilot and observer were accommodated in two large cockpits, with the pilot sitting in the rear seat. However, although close together the only means of communication in the air was by hand signals or a slate board and chalk. The RE5 had been the first aircraft to be produced in quantity at the Royal Aircraft Factory, and although it was by now being phased out of front-line service, it was still an effective reconnaissance machine and light bomber. No. 7 Sqn was the only RFC unit to operate the RE5 in numbers.

St Omer had been an active airfield even before the war, and had been the point of arrival in France for the deploying RFC in August 1914. However, even in July 1915 it was still very much a canvas camp, with various light, portable field service hangars erected for housing aircraft and workshops and a large number of bell tents to accommodate the men. The RFC knew how to live well; the officers had comfortable billets with plentiful hot water, and could look forward to leisurely breakfasts and the opportunity to read a newspaper, still less than twenty-four hours old. The Officers' Mess was set up in an estaminet at Drogtlands, run by a cheerful French family, comprising Madame, three attractive younger women, presumably daughters, and their small children. The men were not represented in contemporary photographs and were doubtless under

59. No 7 Sqn Lines, the airfield, St Omer, July 1915. Photo Mark Liddell.

60. *French family at the estaminet which was the mess. Photo Mike Pearce/Sir Piers Benegough.*

arms for France. This comfortable life was all a far cry from the cold and discomfort of soldiering with the 93rd, and that summer the squadron officers relaxed and enjoyed tennis and a glass of 'fizz' with the locals. One commented somewhat ungallantly on the appearance of the girls, writing 'None very striking, but some could play tennis rather well'.[252]

For the present, however, Aidan's concern was to fly rather than swing a tennis racket, and that would have been the first priority of his CO too. New pilots arrived from training with the bare minimum of flying hours, and although Aidan had obtained his 'ticket' at Brooklands the previous year, he was still very much the novice and needed all the experience that he could get. Having settled in and recovered from his journey, on Sunday 25 July he was allocated one of the new BE2cs that had only just arrived with the squadron, but his anticipation and excitement were short-lived. The machine had a bad engine that could not be fixed, and so his first flight with No. 7 Sqn had to be abandoned for the day. It was of course a disappointment, but as a new pilot there was still much to be learned and understood.

No. 7 Sqn had just been transferred to the direct control of RFC HQ, and its major role was strategic reconnaissance, in which aircraft penetrated deep into German territory to observe the enemy lines of communication and watch for significant troop movements. It was an increasingly hazardous task, as ground forces were becoming more efficient with their anti-aircraft measures. Aerial combats were starting to occur, although aircraft were still unable to fire forward through the propeller. Reconnaissance was the first priority for military aviators, but both sides now looked to deny such intelligence to their enemies by aggressive patrolling. However, at this early stage of the air war scout or fighter aircraft almost always hunted alone. No. 7 Sqn's record book clearly indicates how the a situation was changing in the early summer of 1915.

Although the squadron had arrived on 8 April, their first combat casualties had not come until 23 May, some six weeks later. An RE5 was hit by anti-aircraft fire near Vieux Berquin and broke up at about 300 feet, with the loss of both crew. June proved to be another casualty-free period, but on 3 July a second RE5 was lost, having been damaged by enemy fire near Ghent. When the engine failed the pilot, Lieutenant Adams, put his machine into a shallow glide and flew over the border into neutral Holland where he managed to land safely. The crew then set fire to their aircraft. It was Adams who had written of the pleasant life at St Omer and of the joys of mixed doubles and champagne. For this particular pilot and his observer, life would not be so comfortable again for quite some time, as shortly afterwards they were arrested by the Dutch and interned for the duration of the war.

Three days later another No. 7 Sqn aeroplane, this time a Voisin, was shot up by an enemy aircraft while on a dawn reconnaissance in the vicinity of Armentières. The combat lasted for twenty minutes and both the British airmen were wounded by exploding cartridges, before the Voisin was able to break away from the engagement. The observer was an experienced officer named Roland Peck, who had served with No. 7 Sqn since February. Fortunately neither man was seriously hurt, and the aircraft was able to recover safely to St Omer without further incident. Two weeks later, another RE5 was lost when the engine stopped after an encounter with an enemy machine and the crew landed safely in Holland. Again they destroyed their machine, before being interned by the Dutch authorities.

The pace of the air war was quickening, as equipment and weapons improved and the airmen on both sides became bolder and more aggressive. Indeed, that very day, as the frustrated Aidan talked to his new comrades about the war that they had experienced in the air, Captain Lanoe Hawker of No. 6 Sqn was busy demonstrating that the Germans were not necessarily having things all their own way. In the most successful British air combat of the war to date, Hawker, piloting a Bristol 'C' Scout on an evening offensive patrol, accounted for three enemy aircraft. For his courage and skill he was recommended for and was shortly to receive the Victoria Cross. This was to be the third air VC, and although that news would not be known until the middle of August, his success against three opponents on 25 July reverberated around the messes and crew rooms of the RFC in France.*

The next day Aidan tried out the RE5, although he did not record his first impressions. Little commentary on the type survives, but a brief pamphlet entitled *Notes on Flying Various Aeroplanes* does include three short but illuminating paragraphs:

The RE5 practically flies itself; a beginner may find her apt to drop on her turns, and should be careful not to let his engine race.

* Lanoe Hawker VC was killed in aerial combat with Manfred von Richthofen, the Red Baron, on 23 November 1916.

The machine can be left to take herself off the ground; her tail should not be helped up with the elevator as there is a danger of the skids touching the ground if her tail is at all high.

In landing the machine there is a tendency amongst beginners to flatten out too late. It is far better to 'pancake' a few feet than land fast. The undercarriage will not stand fast bumpy landings, but almost any liberty can be taken if the machine is landed slow with no drift.[253]

Later that day Aidan was allowed to give joyrides to passengers in the BE2c, but as a reminder that the war was not far away, a Voisin crew returned safely with tales of how they had successfully driven off a German attacker. He would have discussed their experiences in detail with them, not just from personal interest, but because the Squadron Commander, Major Hoare, had appointed him Squadron Intelligence Officer, and it was one of his tasks to debrief returning crews. The next day there was another opportunity to fly the RE5, and it may have been one of the long-wing variants, at least one of which is believed to have been operated by No. 7 Sqn.* In the evening he was warned of a long reconnaissance the following morning. Modern airmen may find it extraordinary, but after a brief period of flying training and only two days of local flying, Aidan was poised to undertake a long-range mission of four hours that would take him deep into enemy territory.

That night he slept in the C Flight office as he was expecting to fly at

61. RE5 with extended wings at St Omer. Photo Mark Liddell.

*The photograph of the long winged RE5 appeared in the Liddell family album with the legend 'The aeroplane in which Aidan did his last flight and gained his VC'. This was not the case but he may, however, have flown it prior to the last mission.

dawn, but it proved to be a particularly windy morning. The prevailing wind was westerly, and this assisted the RFC to cross the German lines on the outward leg of a mission, but meant they had to battle back against the wind on the return journey. With the low airspeeds of aircraft in 1915 the weather was an absolutely critical factor, and the mission was aborted before it had even begun, although it did not deter German aircraft from launching a night bombing raid on St Omer at midnight. They also dropped a somewhat chilling message that they would bomb St Omer daily for a week until it was destroyed. It was not a convincing threat as the damage done was slight, affecting only a bread shop and a single home.

The next day, Thursday 29 July, the wind had dropped and Aidan prepared to take off at around dawn on another long reconnaissance mission, on which he was to be accompanied by 2nd Lieutenant H H Watkins, a brand-new observer, who had also joined No. 7 Sqn on 24 July. The first war sortie is a daunting prospect and neither of them can have much enjoyed their early breakfast. It must have been a tense walk to the flight line for the rookie crew, as they focused their minds and carried their haversacks and other equipment to the waiting aeroplane. Muffled against the elements by their long leather coats and sheepskin flying boots, there would have been the opportunity for a final word, a last look together at the flight plan. Aidan would then have inspected the exterior of the machine, before the two of them clambered into their large cockpits to check the equipment and prepare for take-off. Strapped in, helmets on, a last polish of the goggles, and then the mechanic was priming the engine. With the yell of 'contact' Aidan would have fired the magneto and heard and felt the 120 hp Austro-Daimler roar into life. While the engine warmed up for several minutes, it was the pilot's job to check his instruments and to test the controls and throttle. Then suddenly, tighten straps, thumbs up, 'chocks away' and the RE5 taxied out for the take-off into wind.

The flight was a success, although not without incident, as Aidan later described in his diary:

> Got going about 3.45 am via Dunkerque, Ostend, Bruges, Ghent. At Ostend a Hun arrived and opened fire with MG. Paused at Bruges while we were Archied.* Then tried to hustle, no cast.** Managed to get to West, and MG jammed at Ghent. Kept on with rifle and pistol, and Hun sheered off at Heerstert. Watkins scratched on finger. About 11 holes in planes. Bracing wire broken and a flying wire hit. Altogether 3 hours 50 minutes in air. Archies were rather close.[254]

It had been an excellent first effort from a novice crew, and both men

---

* The larger anti-aircraft shells earned the nickname 'Archie' after a popular music hall song that ended in the resounding chorus 'Archibald, certainly not!' 'Archie' not only harassed aircraft, but also signalled their presence to attacking aircraft.
** The meaning is not clear from the transcripts. It might have actually read no(rth) east.

had acquitted themselves well in a prolonged battle with a persistent foe. The RE5 carried a Lewis gun in the front cockpit, which was mounted facing backwards. Forward fire was clearly impossible without damaging the propeller, and firing to the rear was restricted by both the pilot and the fuselage and tail assembly. The gun was heavy and awkward to handle, even though the cooling fins had been discarded to shed weight, and because in theory they were unnecessary as the weapon would be cooled by the slipstream. Unfortunately, the slipstream also caused the lubricating oil to freeze, and as they found out that day, stoppages were a constant danger. All in all it was hardly an ideal arrangement, which was why additional weapons in the form of rifles, carbines and pistols were often carried. Aidan, who was always keen to have the very best equipment, had acquired a German Mauser automatic, which was something of a favourite among RFC officers. It cannot have been a very effective weapon, but Aidan used it when the Lewis gun jammed and Watkins was trying to engage the Hun with a rifle. It seems unlikely that either of them would have done the enemy much harm, but they probably felt much better for their efforts.

Early next morning, the Germans returned as promised to St Omer with an attack at 5.45 am, dropping three bombs on the town. Maurice Baring, Major General Henderson's ADC at RFC HQ was awakened by the thud, but Aidan made no note of it. Major Hoare routinely drew up the operational tasking for the squadron in the late afternoon so that everyone knew what the morrow would hold for them. Aidan was warned to be ready to fly again on 31 July on another long-range sortie. This time he must have been reassured to hear that he was to be accompanied by the experienced observer 2nd Lieutenant Roland Peck, who only a few days before had been involved in fierce aerial combat.

Although of course they were unaware of it Saturday 31 July was to prove a particularly eventful day for No. 7 Sqn crews. Lieutenant Broder and 2nd Lieutenant MacPherson suffered engine failure in their RE5 and made a forced landing behind enemy lines, so ending their war in captivity. One of the Voisins was also in action, and twice tried to engage enemy machines, although each time the Hun dived away and evaded. It is a clear indication of the courage and tenacity of the British crews that even in a lumbering Voisin they were prepared to look for combat and take on not one but two of the enemy. But the most remarkable action of the day was that performed by Aidan Liddell and Roland Peck.

Their mission was the standard Long Reconnaissance, designated 1(a) in the Squadron order book, and similar to that which Aidan and Watkins had previously carried out. It involved crossing the front line in the north and then circling round Ostend on the coast and proceeding in an arc to Bruges and Ghent. Once again it was to be a morning flight, although this time with the more civilised planned start time of 0800, although take-off was delayed and they did not get airborne until 0915. Even then though, things were not entirely straightforward. Work had been carried out on RE5 2457 after its previous sortie, and seven fabric patches had been applied, five to the top plane and one each to the bottom and tail plane and a compensating wire had also been renewed. As the RE5 was to undertake a four-hour mission, most of it behind enemy lines, an air test was deemed appropriate before the sortie. Aidan and Roland Peck flew around St Omer for thirty-five minutes to test the machine before returning briefly to the airfield, where they indicated that all was well. They took off again almost immediately at 0950 and commenced the Long Reconnaissance. The distinguished airman Cecil Lewis described flying out of St Omer in a BE2c in 1916, and paints a vivid picture of the local area and challenge of air navigation.

At five thousand over the aerodrome I turned north. The flat country stretched to the four horizons. To say it looked like a map was a cliché. There was a resemblance of course, as between sitter and portrait; but the real thing had a bewildering amount of extra detail, a wealth of soft colour, of light and shade, that made it, at first, difficult to reconcile with its printed counterpart. Main roads, so importantly marked in red turned out to be grey, unobtrusive, and hard to distinguish from other roads. Railways were not clear black lines, but winding threads, even less well defined than the roads. Woods were not patches of green, except in high summer: they were dark browns and blacks, merging, sometimes imperceptibly, into the ploughed fields which surrounded them. Then there were cloud shadows, darkening patches of landscape and throwing others into high relief; ground mist, blurring the horizon and sometimes closing in around you to a few miles, or even a few hundred yards, an implacable wall of vapour, mysteriously receding as you advanced. It was not always easy to find your way, or read your map.[255]

Aidan first flew the machine towards Furnes, and passed safely over the Belgian-held front line, flying at around 5000 feet. At this point the crew spotted a German aircraft some miles away and to the south-east. It was several thousand feet higher than them and was clearly a threat, so they watched it carefully but eventually lost sight of it. After passing over Ostend the RE5 swung inland and set a course for Bruges. Both men were now constantly scanning the sky for hostile aircraft, as well as noting carefully the strategic points they passed for tell-tale signs of significant enemy activity. The work rate in the aircraft was high, and Peck had unstrapped himself so that he could move around in the cockpit to increase his all-round observation and properly use his field glasses. He was also better able to handle his weapons, the Lewis machine-gun and the lighter more manoeuvrable rifle that he was also carrying on board.

They were approaching Bruges when suddenly the aircraft came under heavy machine-gun fire from above, although they did not see the enemy or precisely where the fire was coming from. Then suddenly Peck saw it, an enemy two-seater aggressively handled, and was able to fire off a full drum of ammunition at it. He immediately reloaded the weapon and prepared to continue the fight. In his combat report he described the enemy as a 'Tractor biplane, covered in fuselage, similar to a Bristol Scout but at least twice as large, crosses on both lower planes. Armed with a machine gun. Speed about 90 mph'.[256]

Then disaster struck, as the German machine made another unobserved pass and raked the RE5 with machine-gun fire. Peck recalled, 'I had just reloaded when our machine nosedived and then turned completely over, and all the remaining ammunition fell out'.[257] The attack had badly damaged the RE5, cutting the throttle cable, smashing the control wheel in the pilot's hands, and damaging much of the left-hand side of the aircraft. Aidan was badly wounded in his right leg and thigh. One bullet smashed into the Mauser automatic pistol by his side, and another grazed the twelve-round magazine. His leg was broken and he instantly lost consciousness as the RE5 dived out of control and flipped over onto its back. It looked a certain kill, and the German pilot was so sure of this that he did not bother to follow the RE5 down. Peck, who was still unstrapped, was in grave danger of falling from the inverted aircraft, but somehow he managed to cling on, although the rifle, spare ammunition and other items of equipment fell out and tumbled to the ground below. Then suddenly, Aidan regained consciousness and as his head cleared he instinctively appreciated the nature of the emergency. He focused his strength and skill to recover the machine as he explained in a typically self-effacing letter home:

It was a weird sensation falling like that. I thought at first a shell had hit us and knocked the tail off, a piece getting me in the process. I was waiting for the bump, when suddenly I thought it might be a good thing to straighten her out and try to recover flying position. Just as well I had that brainwave, what?[258]

Despite his grievous wounds he managed to control the badly damaged aeroplane, which had plunged 3000 feet before he was able to get it flying straight and level. His first thoughts were for his observer and he later remarked:

Poor old Peck must have had a terrible shock, not knowing whether I was dead or not, or whether he was going to hit the ground with the machine, or going to fall out, as he had undone his straps so that he could use the machine gun: glad I wasn't him really.[259]

244

A few more moments of unconsciousness and all would have been lost. But for the moment, despite the shock and Aidan's pain and disorientation, the priority of the crew was to plan what to do next. Cecil Lewis knew how easy it was to get disorientated and make mistakes.

You could get lost in the air as easily as in a forest, and you were just as likely to fly in circles as walk in them on the ground. True, you had a compass to give you general sense of direction; but compasses in those days, owing to the vibration of the machine, had a maddening habit of spinning like tops. Once lost there was a tendency to panic.[260]

But Aidan kept his head. He realised that he was badly wounded and that he would get weaker. The obvious option was to crash-land behind enemy lines, or even head for Holland, which was much closer than friendly territory. However, by experimenting he found that despite his wounds and the severe damage to the RE5, he could still manage to fly the machine. The throttle cable had been severed so he had no control over the engine, and the rudder was also damaged. However, he was able to make the rudder control work with one hand by pulling the cable, and with the other he nursed the shattered control wheel. The aircraft was now low, probably only around 2000 feet, and it was difficult to control and manoeuvre. It was obviously very vulnerable to ground fire or to another attack from the air, and although Aidan may not have realised it, Peck had lost his spare ammunition and now had only the single magazine that was loaded onto the Lewis gun. He had lost his rifle too, and Aidan's Mauser was smashed and useless, even if he had been able to find a free hand to fire it!

Their position was critical but Aidan decided to take the aircraft home, as he later explained to his mother. 'I must say I was only too glad when I found I could fly the machine, and would have willingly gone on for another two hours rather than land in the German lines, or even in Holland, which was much closer.' He added with customary modesty 'Nothing except the instinct of self preservation and the desire to get near a decent hospital urged me on'.[261] Aidan then gently raised the RE5's nose and, battling against the prevailing wind, did his best to make the damaged machine gain height for the hazardous transit over the lines. They crossed at 2800 feet, which was still dangerously low, and the RE5 was heavily fired upon by 'Archie', although it escaped further damage.

Communication in the air was difficult, particularly when trying to address a complex mid-air emergency, but Aidan wrote an abbreviated message on the blackboard and passed it forward to Peck. He indicated that his leg was broken and that he intended to land on the open sands west of Nieuport, because he felt unable to steer sufficiently accurately to find a field and make a forced landing in the enclosed Belgian countryside. But Peck realised that the friendly airfield of La Panne near Furnes was closer and more suitable and also offered the prospect of rescuers and medical attention. He somehow managed to convey this to Aidan, who signalled his agreement and turned the machine onto a heading to approach La Panne. The RE5 was never an easy machine to land, and with half the controls shot away and no way of adjusting the throttle, Aidan had only one chance to get it right. He drove the machine down with the power on, steering with the damaged rudder cable, and at the appropriate moment killed the engine and executed a perfect landing. Little more than half an hour had passed since the successful German attack.

It had been a truly extraordinary effort by the badly wounded Aidan Liddell. He had displayed great courage and airmanship of the highest order. It must be remembered that he was a brand-new operational pilot and had been flying the RE5 for less than a week. The easy option would have been to land in occupied territory or Holland, but he had brought his aircraft and observer to safety behind Allied lines. Roland Peck had also done very well, and although the two men had never flown together before, the sortie was a model of crew cooperation. On landing, Peck jumped from the aeroplane and was quick to summon assistance from the Belgians who were soon surrounding the damaged RE5. Aidan's immediate reaction was to chastise the first Belgian officer to appear because of the inadequate directional arrow markings on the airfield.

Among the crowd that clustered around the damaged aircraft was a photographer, who took a series of high quality photographs that graphically caught the action as events unfolded over the next three quarters of an hour. Aidan realised that his leg was very badly smashed, and that he had already lost a great deal of blood. He needed help, but was very concerned that unskilled rescuers hauling him from the cockpit would be likely to make the situation worse. He therefore told Peck, who stood guard beside the fuselage, that he would not allow himself to be moved until a doctor arrived to supervise. In the meantime he fashioned a splint for his leg, and then applied a tourniquet to check the bleeding. Photographs show Peck handing him a drink of water with rescuers sitting astride the fuselage. After about half an hour the medical team arrived, and he was gently lifted from the cockpit by a score of willing hands and lowered carefully to a stretcher on the ground.

It was said of Aidan that 'he was always so bright'.[262] His friend Major Maxwell Rouse wrote: 'In snow, in muddy trench, or ante-room he kept us laughing and his influence will last'.[263] Now, lying on a blood-stained stretcher, with a smashed leg from which it was said four inches of the bone had been shot away, he smiled for the camera, smoked the inevitable cigarette, and gave a cheery wave as the camera caught the

62. *(Top) After the descent to La Panne. The Belgian crowd. Photo Mark Liddell.*

63. *(Left) Aidan's Observer Lt Peck offers a glass of water to his wounded pilot. Photo Mark Liddell.*

64. *(Right) First aid in the cockpit. Photo Mark Liddell.*

65. *(Top) Lifting out of the aircraft.*
Photo Mark Liddell.

moment for posterity. Aidan was then borne away to the nearby Red Cross Hospital at La Panne and to specialist surgical attention. Meanwhile, the news of his actions began to travel around the RFC.

Having seen Aidan into safe hands, Roland Peck returned at once to St Omer to make his combat report. Having read the account, the Squadron Commander, Major Hoare, at once added his own unequivocal and detailed endorsement, stating that 'in my opinion, it was a remarkably good piece of work by both pilot and observer in bringing their machine safely back'.[264] The next day the Commandant at La Panne wrote to Hoare to give the

66. *First aid on the ground.*
Photo Mark Liddell.

67. *A remarkably cheerful Aidan responds to the crowd with a smile and a wave. Photo Mark Liddell.*

68. *RE5 2457, the aircraft in which Aidan won the VC. Photo Mike Pearce/Sir Piers Benegough.*

From:-
     O.C. Number 7 Squadron,

To:-
     G.S.O. 1,
       R.F.C., H.Q.

1. In forwarding the attached report by 2/Lt. Peck on an encounter
with a hostile aeroplane, I should like to call attention to the
following points, as, in my opinion, it was a remarkably good
piece of work by both pilot and observer in bringing their
machine safely back.

2. Capt. Liddell is a comparatively young pilot and was on only
his second reconnaissance.
He has had 1 weeks experience of flying R.E.5 machines,which
undoubtedly require more judgement than most to land.

3. In spite of his leg being broken very badly, with apparently
4 inches of bone shot away, he flew his machine back over the
line at a height of 2,800'.

4. An experienced pilot would have difficulty in flying and
landing the machine under the circumstances in which he was
placed; with one hand he worked the wheelcontrol , which was
broken in half by bullets, and with the other he worked the
rudder.
His throttle control was shot away but he rightly drove the
machine down with his engine on in order to make sure of
hitting the aerodrome, and then switched off.

5. Whilst over the lines he was heavily fired on, and was flying
for over half an hour from the time he was wounded until he
landed.

6. The observer, 2/Lieut. Peck, who has had several encounters in
the air previously, kept his head, and was evidently of considerable assistance to the pilot.
He was not strapped in, but though everything loose fell out
of the machine, he managed to retain his gun whilst holding
himself in.

7. I should add that after making a perfect landing, Capt. Liddell
sat for half an hour in his machine to await the arrival of a
doctor, as he considered his leg would be still further damaged
if inexperienced hands lifted him out of the machine.
He then put a splint on his leg and himself applied a tourniquet,
to stop the bleeding.

                                        Major,
                 Commanding Number 7 Squadron,   R.F.C.

In the Field,
  31-7-15.

69. *Major Hoare's Report, sent to Mrs Liddell by Lt L de Burlet, 1st Belgian
Lancers, Military Aviator, 3rd Escadrille, Furnes. Photo Peter Daybell.*

July 31st. 1915.

Squadron   7.

Type R.E. 5   2457.

Armament.   Lewis Gun and Rifle.

Pilot.   Capt. J.A. Liddell.

Observer.   2/Lieut. R.H. Peck.

Locality.   Ostend - Bruges.

Height.   5,000'

Duty.   Reconnaissance.

Remarks on Hostile Machine.

Tractor biplane, covered in fuselage, similar to a Bristol Scout but
at least twice as large, crosses on both lower planes.
Armed with a machine gun.
Speed about 90 m.p.h.

Narrative.

Whilst on the reconnaissance Ostend-Bruges-Ghent this morning, shortly
after leaving Ostend we were attacked by a hostile machine.
We first saw the machine when crossing the lines, some miles away to
the S.E.
We were flying at about 5,000' and the German machine was several
thousand feet higher. We continued with the reconnaissance and I
finally lost sight of the machine.
When near Bruges we were heavily fired on from above but were unable
to see the enemy. We then got a brief glimpse of him and I was able
to fire one pan of ammunition at him which caused him to withdraw.
I had just reloaded when our machine nose dived and then turned completely over and all, the remaining ammunition fell out. The pilot
had apparently momentarily lost consciousness, but regained control of
the machine after dropping 3,000'. Capt. Liddell then handed me a
message stating that his leg was broken and that he proposed landing
on the sands, xx West of Nieuport, as he could not steer sufficiently
to land in enclosed country.
I then pointed out the aerodrome near Furnes and Capt. Liddell working
the rudder control with his hand by holding the cable was able to land.
He was unable to throttle the engine down owing to the throttle control
being shot away, but switched off shortly before reaching the ground.

R.H.Peck

                                                   2/Lieut.
                 Dorsetshire Regt, Attached R.F.C.

70.   Lt Peck's Report, sent to Mrs Liddell by Lt L de Burlet, 1st Belgian Lancers,
      Military Aviator, 3rd Escadrille, Furnes. Photo Peter Daybell.

Belgian view of the incident.

> To Major Hoare
>
> La Panne
>
> 1 August 1915
>
> I, the undersigned, Dhanis, of the 1st Regiment of the Guides, Flight Lieut and Commandant of the 3rd Escadrille of the Belgian Flying Corps, consider it my duty to bring to your notice the magnificent conduct of Capt Liddell and of Lieut Peck, both of them aviators under your command.
>
> These officers, who were flying in a Beardmore aeroplane, Type RE 5, 120 hp, were compelled to land on our aviation ground on July 31st, the pilot having been severely wounded. His right thigh was broken by bullets in an engagement with a German aeroplane. Thanks to his coolness and conspicuous energy he has saved his aeroplane, his companion and himself from the hands of the enemy, having had the incredible strength of will necessary to make a faultless landing on our camp. He has thus given us all a magnificent example of endurance, and one which deserves to be both mentioned and rewarded.
>
> W. DHANIS[265]

It was a ringing endorsement and made plain the growing feeling that the events of 31 July had been truly exceptional. Dhanis probably also spoke to Major Hoare when the latter visited La Penne on 1 August with a fitting team dispatched from St Omer to assess the aircraft and, if possible, recover it. Major Hoare must have also hoped to visit Aidan, but that was not yet allowed. The fitters and riggers found the battle damage to RE5 2457 was extensive, as the Engineering Log Book recorded:

> Rudder, left hand top aileron, rear inside left hand wing inside strut, left hand front undercarriage strut, left hand undercarriage wheel, left hand front centre bracing wire, shot through. Numerous shots in fabric in planes and fuselage. Bracing wire and rib of lh top plane shot through. Rib in left hand bottom plane broken near nacelle. Form section in fuselage shot through.[266]

Running repairs were carried out by the recovery party to make the machine airworthy and safe to fly, and then Major Hoare and Lieutenant Birch flew it carefully back to St Omer, where over the next three days extensive repairs were carried out. It must have been a sobering experience for the CO to examine the blood-stained and battle damaged machine and then gingerly nurse the RE5 home. Roland Peck must have had even stranger feelings when he flew in 2457* on another operational sortie on 14 August. To his relief that mission turned out to be uneventful.

The next morning, Major Hoare wrote Aidan a personal letter, which greatly cheered him when he read it. The GOC Major-General Henderson had summoned the Major to RFC HQ and congratulated the squadron on the great achievement, explaining that he would be personally reporting the circumstances to the Commander-in-Chief, Sir John French. Stiff and formal in its traditional salutation, it was written airman to airman and carried with it the warmest congratulations and admiration of No. 7 Sqn.

> 2 August 1915
>
> Dear Liddell,
>
> In case I can't come over to see you before this arrives, just a line to say how damned sorry I am that you've been so badly winged. I'm afraid you will have a bad time, but you will have this much to buck you up, that you have done one of the finest feats that has been done in the Corps since the beginning of the war. How you managed to get back God only knows, but it was a magnificent effort and the General is giving a detailed report on it today to French. I cannot express to you the admiration we all have for what you did. You have set a standard of pluck and determination which may be equalled, but certainly will not be surpassed during this war. Everyone's best wishes for a speedy recovery, we shall miss our 'intelligence officer' sadly.
>
> Yours
>
> C Hoare[267]

On 3 August Aidan was well enough to pen his own long and detailed letter home. Written in a strong firm hand, and well-constructed and absolutely clear, it is quite apparent that the patient was doing very well. In fact, he said as much himself:

> Still very flourishing, on full diet, temperature all the time round about normal, smoking like a chimney, and sleeping between whiles. Indifferent night last night, only because the muscles of the small of my back were resenting their enforced inactivity by cramping; however, I did without morphia, and got in a quite long sleep later. My leg doesn't hurt at all, except of course the dressings are painful – irrigation with peroxide, washed all around the edges with ether, and the packing. They are getting much less tiresome each time, and they are awfully quick and gentle with it.[268]

---

* See Appendix Two for further details of RE5 2457.

He described in some length the incident itself, as quoted earlier in the chapter, and went on to cheerfully explain the advantages of this 'little inconvenience' and the advantages it bestowed:

However, the result of the whole thing is that I met with an accident which has caused me just a little inconvenience, and apparently gained me quite a reputation. Generals, English and Belgium, keep on coming to see me – Poincaré yesterday! Altogether, considering it will also mean several months holiday when finished, I think it rather a blessing in disguise. Reconnaissance over the German lines for three hours at a time at least once every two days, sometimes every day, promised to be a little too exciting for my nerves.[269]

It must have been a very heartening letter for John and Emily Liddell, who had only received the shocking casualty telegram on the day this lengthy note was drafted. He was already being fêted as hero, and the visit by *Monsieur* Poincaré, the President of the French Republic, was clear evidence of his growing celebrity. He was now well enough to begin the inevitable list of requests, and his mind was clearly still on the task in hand for he asked for the current editions of the aviation magazines F*light* and *Aeronautics*, as well as for books to read. One imagines English novels were in short supply in a Belgian military hospital. Aidan's parents would have also been greatly reassured by Major Hoare's generous decision to send Roland Peck back to England to personally offer them an account of the action. It had been a tough experience for Peck too, and he had kept his head and been of tremendous support to Aidan. He must also have welcomed a few days of home leave, and the opportunity to visit his invalid father in Bournemouth.

The Liddell family of course knew all about nursing wounded soldiers from their experiences at Sherfield Manor Hospital, and in a cheeky postscript to his first letter home Aidan remarked 'The Toad ought to come and nurse the braves Belges here. I am afraid there are no vacancies though.' There was a second afterthought, and a typical dash of humour: 'PS Don't go advertising me to all the old dowagers of your acquaintance for the Lord's sake.' The news was therefore good and everyone's spirits were high.

Soon, one or two newspapers were carrying the story of an unnamed aviation hero, and his remarkable airborne feats. Before long the story was repeated in papers right across Great Britain. Then when Aidan's name was released, the story was run again, and this time photographs were available so that an amazed and fascinated public could not just read about it but actually see what had happened. The culmination was the picture spread on the front page of *The Daily Mirror* of 14 August, complete with four of the Belgian photographer's remarkable photographs and the eye-catching, although somewhat ponderous

headline 'BRITISH AIRMAN WITH FIFTY WOUNDS IN HIS LEG:
UNCONSCIOUS WHEN HIS MACHINE TURNED TURTLE'.
    Aidan was already a national hero, but he was also a hero to a young

*71. The Front Page of the Daily Mirror, Saturday 14 August 1915. 'British Airman
with fifty wounds in his leg: unconscious when his machine turns turtle.'*

Belgian pilot at La Panne who had been involved in the arrangements for his medical care. This officer had in his official capacity requested copies of the British reports of the incident from Major Hoare. It was obviously thought appropriate that the Belgian authorities should be formally informed as to the circumstances, but Lieutenant Burlett saw it very differently once he had the documents in his possession. Immensely moved by what he had seen and read, he took it upon himself to divert the official papers to the Liddell family in England. He accompanied them with a touching and heartfelt note, written carefully in his best and somewhat ponderous English.

Friday August 13 1915

Mrs Liddell,

Having had the luck to be on the flying field when the Captain Liddell landed, wounded, I cared specially for him and had him brought to a good hospital, and also in the hands of the best doctor. You can be absolutely in rest about him and the cases which are given to him. I don't really think he could be better (cared for). I see him every day and he is doing well – I cannot enough say to you how much his splendid performance and courage filled us with admiration, and myself I was sad and cried to see such a splendid boy as yours suffer – now as I say he is quite well.

I had asked for myself of the Major Hoare the official report on his performance, but I don't hesitate one moment to deprive myself of it for you, his mother, for whom it is a precious testify of your dear son.

I dare say I love and care for the Captain Liddell as if he was my own brother. Please accept these two official reports Mrs Liddell, but have the kindness not to show them to the military authorities because they were sent to me alone – and I want you to keep them rather than me, because if I had done such a thing, I think my mother would be proud to have such an official report of her son. I think well doing in saying to you Mrs Liddell to be entirely in rest about your dear son – he is awfully well cared for and happy, and as soon as well enough shall be brought safely to you.

I am most respectfully your devoted

Lieutenant L de Burlett
of the 1st Belgian Lancers

Military Aviator

3rd Escadrille

Furnes

NB I am so happy to do something for the good people you are all of you British - Excuse my writing, I am only a Belgian.[270]

Then, on 17 August another telegram was received at Sherfield Manor. This time it was from Aidan. It simply read 'Have been given Victoria Cross. Will be in Gazette Saturday'.[271] It would be the fourth VC for the Air Services and the second of the three crosses won by Stonyhurst men in the Great War.*

72. *Aidan's telegram home announcing the VC. Photo Peter Daybell.*

*The third was won by Gabriel Coury on the Somme. See Appendix Two for details.

Chapter Eighteen

The Journey Home

Celebrations were short lived, for despite the excitement of the award, it had become clear that Aidan's condition was deteriorating. On the day after he had received the momentous news of the VC, the doctors reluctantly agreed that he must lose his leg and decided to operate at once. A British surgeon had been sent across from GHQ to confirm the opinion of the need for amputation as Major Hoare dutifully explained in a letter to the family:

> I cannot tell you how sorry I am to have to tell you that your son will lose his leg. Everything possible has been done. Wallace from General Hdqrs was sent over for a consultation and was of the same opinion. I went over yesterday to see him, he had a lot of fever, and I felt myself it was better he should lose his leg than risk his life.[272]

The operation was carried out on the morning of 18 August by a Belgian surgeon that everyone agreed was a first class man, and it was hoped that an improvement would quickly follow. However, on Saturday 21 August, the day that Aidan's VC and that of Lanoe Hawker were gazetted, his condition was found to have deteriorated to the extent that it was felt necessary to inform the family. General Bridges from the British Mission at La Panne wired Sherfield Manor with the terse message 'Your son's condition not so satisfactory suggest your coming to see him. Will have car for you at Boulogne if you wire time of arrival there'.[273]

Emily Liddell left at once, with no time to pack properly or organise the house. Indeed, in her first letter from La Panne she asked for parcels of dresses and under linen to be made up and sent, and included detailed instructions to the staff for the running of the Manor. When she arrived in Belgium she found that the news of Aidan on Monday 23 August was perhaps better than might have been expected, for he had enjoyed a fair night and was interested in all the newspapers in the morning. This was probably the day that the citation from *The London Gazette* would have reached him, and he must have been very bucked by what it said. It read:

> For most conspicuous bravery and devotion to duty on July 31st, 1915. When on a flying reconnaissance over Ostend-Bruges Ghent he was severely wounded (his right thigh being broken), which caused him momentary unconsciousness, but by a great effort he

recovered partial control after his machine had dropped nearly 3000 feet, and notwithstanding his collapsed state, succeeded, although continually fired at, in completing his course, and brought the aeroplane into our lines – half an hour after he had been wounded.

The difficulties experienced by this officer in saving his machine, and the life of his observer, cannot be readily expressed, but as the control wheel and throttle control were smashed, and also one of the undercarriage struts, it would seem incredible that he could have accomplished his task.[274]

Later that day Aidan suffered a shivering fit and his temperature became very high. 'His leg is going on wonderfully, it is the blood poisoning one fears'[275] his mother reported. She added the reassurance in her letter home that he was taking nourishment.

The next bulletin to Sherfield Manor was on Thursday 26 August when Emily wrote:

Aidan is pretty much the same this morning. Yesterday they made two slight incisions one in each arm which were very swollen and inflamed and got a lot of matter away. His temp went down then to normal and he was quite chirpy. This morning his temp is up again, but his mind is quite clear and he is much interested in his mail. On Monday he was delirious nearly all day, and didn't seem able to get away from his flying machine and everything connected with it.[276]

It must have been enormously difficult for Emily Liddell, who wanted to keep the family informed of progress, but was clearly trying to be positive and strong as well. She concluded 'I am going to buy some grapes for the boy now, he likes them so much'.[277] What was to be the final report, written on 28 August, was even more positive and still presaged hope for the future:

Aidan is I am glad to say a little better this morning. His temperature is better, he doesn't seem so desperately weak. The wound is most healthy. I haven't seen it as he is taken at his own wish down to the theatre each day to have it dressed. They amputate here like 'Macs' leg was done...all on account of gas gangrene which seem to be the trouble in these parts. Today he is to have some fluid drawn off his lungs, his chest is tight, and I hope then he will show even more improvement. He can move his arms a little better, when I came he couldn't move his arms at all. He has soluble gold injections... And his appetite is good. Yesterday he had 4 eggs. . .[278]

It was clear that the family were wondering whether John Liddell should also come out to be by his son's bedside. It was unusual enough to have one parent allowed to travel out in this way, and special arrangements had been made warranted by the exceptional circumstances. Everyone was being immensely supportive, and doubtless arrangements would have been made if the family had asked for it. However, Emily was not convinced of the need and was concerned about the message that John's presence might give to Aidan.

Tell Daddy to go on with his shooting as usual. I will wire instantly for him if it be necessary, but as things are going I hope for the best, and he could do no good here and Aidan's nerves are in such a state that it might alarm him. The air here is simply splendid and the weather has been lovely. . .[279]

Monday 31 August was the feast day of St Aidan, the Bishop of Lindisfarne and Apostle of Northumberland, after whom Aidan had been named. It was also the day on which he died. After a long and brave fight the end came quite suddenly. As a Roman Catholic he had already received the sacrament of confession and taken Holy Communion a few days previously, but realising that his life was ebbing away Emily called for the Chaplain to return. He immediately came to the bedside and anointed Aidan with holy oil and administered the last rites. Then they prayed together for some time. Emily held Aidan's hand and said the prayers out loud, which he repeated after her. His mind was quite clear, and then he told her it was getting dark, and that he wanted to go home. She told him that he was going home and then felt him squeeze her hand gently before, very peacefully, he died.

Afterwards, in tidying Aidan's things, Emily found his rosary* tucked safely into his sporran, and as a devout Roman Catholic she would have derived some consolation from the manner of his dying. By strange coincidence, less than twenty-four hours earlier in the Dardanelles, Brigadier-General Paul Kenna VC, the hero of Omdurman, had been visiting forward elements of his Brigade on Chocolate Hill when he was sniped and died soon after at Suvla Bay. Thus, two Stonyhurst VC holders had died from enemy action within a few hours of one another.

73. *Aidan's rosary.*
Photo Peter Daybell.

* Aidan's rosary was taken from a dead French soldier and was subsequently carried with him throughout his campaigning. The beads were of a soft violet colour and the crucifix was silver. Later it was passed to his sister Monica Mary and became a cherished plaything of the later generations of the family. Now only the crucifix and a few beads remain.

It was then the usual practice for British soldiers to be buried where they fell, but as with the maternal visit, special arrangements were made for Aidan's body to be returned to England. The British Matron at the Red Cross Hospital at La Panne, Miss Rotely-Campbell, who had nursed Aidan and greatly admired his fortitude, was of great assistance in making the arrangements, and she accompanied the body home to England. His last journey began with a short service in the Hospital Chapel on 2 September, attended by Prince Alexander of Teck, the Colonel of the British Mission with the Belgian Army, and another of the many senior figures who had been so supportive of Aidan and his family. There were several officers from the RFC and the RNAS present and these included Lieutenant Benegough of No. 7 Sqn who was to accompany the coffin to England and would also attend the funeral.

After the body had been conveyed to England it lay in the Church of the Immaculate Conception, Farm Street, for the night of the 3 September. It was a fitting resting place, for this great London Jesuit church is of similar form and decoration to St Peter's at Stonyhurst. The following morning there was a solemn Requiem Mass celebrated by Fr Bodkin, the Rector of Stonyhurst, before the coffin was conveyed by road to Basingstoke for the funeral. Family and friends who attended the mass came down from London by train and then waited in South View Cemetery, adjacent to the Roman Catholic Church of the Holy Ghost, for the arrival of the cortege. F F Urquhart (Sligger), the History Don from Balliol, was in the congregation for the Requiem Mass, but government business prevented Sligger travelling to Basingstoke for the committal. It didn't matter, for the crowds were enormous as the town buried a local hero. In any case, J L Strachan Davidson, the Master of Balliol, attended to represent the College, and this time had no difficulty in remembering names.

The funeral procession formed at the entrance to the town on London Street and was led by representatives of the 3rd Battalion of the Argyll and Sutherland Highlanders who had travelled down from Edinburgh. The cortege was led by five pipers, and a bearer party of eight RFC men marched four and four on either side of the motorised hearse. Behind them paced two Warrant Officers from the 93rd, one carrying Aidan's broadsword and the other his feathered Highland bonnet. One of the men was Company Sergeant Major Conroy, whose life Aidan had saved at Le Maisnil. Aidan's close friend Major Maxwell Rouse led the Scottish contingent, and Lieutenant Benegough and 2nd Lieutenant Roland Peck* represented No. 7 Sqn and the RFC. The firing party of seventy-two men of the 57th Battery Royal Field Artillery also marched in the slow and solemn procession as it wound through London Street, Church Street and Chapel Street towards the cemetery, while massive

* See Appendix Two.

74. *Five Pipers of the 3rd Battalion the Argyll and Sutherland Highlanders lead the funeral procession. Photo Mark Liddell.*

75. *The motorised hearse. Photo Mark Liddell.*

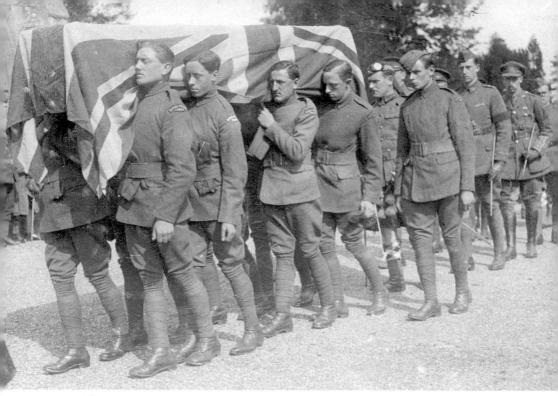

76. *The coffin was borne by bearers of the RFC. Photo Mark Liddell.*

77. *Company Sergeant Major Conroy pays tribute to the man who saved his life.*
Photo Mark Liddell.

78. (Top) Floral tributes at the grave.
Photo Mark Liddell.

79. (Left) Lt Benegough RFC, who
escorted the body from France and
attended the funeral.
Photo Mark Liddell.

crowds looked on. The flags on the town hall clock tower and on St Michael's church were floated at half mast, while the townsfolk witnessed the largest military funeral ever to have been held in Basingstoke.

At the cemetery gates the cortege was met by the Bishop of Portsmouth, the Rector of Stonyhurst and the Canon of Winchester. Then the enormous Belgian coffin, draped in the Union flag, was lifted from the hearse and carried to the graveside

on the shoulders of the eight RFC bearers. All the direct family were in attendance apart from Lance, who was at sea with the Royal Navy, and there was a vast array of friends, dignitaries and representatives. After the graveside service, conducted by the Canon with much use of incense and swinging of the thurifer, the coffin, adorned with a brass crucifix, was lowered into the grave. Three volleys of shots were fired each punctuated by a lament from the pipes. In the tower of the Church of the Holy Ghost the great bell 'John' tolled, a kilted bugler sounded the last post, and then Aidan was laid to rest among a sea of floral tributes. Among the banks of wreaths and ornate floral tributes were three from those who loved him most. They read 'To our Hero Son RIP', 'Peter from his sorrowing brothers and sisters' and 'Grief and love from Figs'. The simple inscription on the coffin plate below the crucifix read only:

80. (Top) Aidan's Observer, 2 Lt Roland Henry Peck 5 Service Battalion the Dorset Regiment and RFC. Peck was killed in air combat over the Tigris line on 5 Mar 1916. Photo Mark Liddell.

81. (Right) Peck, Benegough and Aidan's brother Cuthbert (15th Hussars) after the funeral. Photo Mark Liddell.

JOHN AIDAN LIDDELL
DIED 31st AUGUST 1915
AGED 27 YEARS
RIP

OUR FATHER ....
MAY THY WILL BE DONE ON EARTH AS IN HEAVEN.

82. Aidan's Remembrance Card - Picture. Photo Mark Liddell.

The extraordinary media attention that had marked first his courageous deed and then his Victoria Cross was replayed again with his illness and death, and finally with the funeral. Lengthy articles had become almost daily occurrences in newspapers large and small for over a month. The funeral was the final dramatic flourish that graced many pages. Afterwards the Liddell family were left alone with their grief, although letters of condolence continued to arrive for many months.*

The loss of Aidan inevitably had a dramatic effect on them all, but life had to go on. Towards the end of 1915 Sherfield Manor Military Hospital closed, to the obvious regret of the family, the dedicated staff and the two Liddell sisters that had worked there. Dorothy, the last Commandant, was particularly keen to continue with her nursing duties, and remembered the postscript in Aidan's final letter home. He had jestingly suggested that the Toad should nurse in Belgium, but it was Dorothy that went to La Panne and completed her wartime nursing career in the Red Cross Hospital that had tried so hard to save her brother's life. Her service was eventually recognised when she was appointed a Member of the Most Excellent Order of the British Empire.

For John Liddell, one of his proudest moments must have been his attendance at Buckingham Palace on 17 November 1916, when he received the Victoria Cross from the King on Aidan's behalf. The invitation was by telegram, and sent by Royal command with only three days' notice. It must at first have provoked some consternation at Sherfield Manor, with both Bertie and Lance still away at the war, for as the family knew, telegrams did not always herald good news!

In the fact, the boys both saw out the war without serious mishap.

---

* A selection of these letters are reproduced at Appendix One.

✝

Of your Charity

Pray for the Repose of the Soul of

CAPTAIN

John Aidan Liddell, V.C.,

*(3rd Argyll & Sutherland Highlanders
and R.F.C.),*

Who died of wounds at La Panne,
August 31st, 1915,

Fortified by all the Rites of Holy Church,

AGED 27 YEARS.

R. I. P.

— ✠ —

PRAYER BEFORE A CRUCIFIX.

BEHOLD, O kind and most sweet JESUS, I
cast myself upon my knees in Thy sight:
and with the most fervent desire of my soul
I pray and beseech Thee, to vouchsafe to impress upon my heart lively sentiments of faith,
hope and charity, with true repentance for my
sins and a most firm desire of amendment;
whilst with deep affection and grief of soul
I consider within myself and mentally contemplate Thy five most precious wounds, having
before my eyes that which the prophet David
said of Thee, O good JESUS: "They have
pierced my hands and my feet, they have
numbered all my bones."

R. & T. Washbourne, Ltd., London.

83. Aidan's Remembrance Card - Prayers. Photo Mark Liddell.

84. *(Left) Dorothy Liddell (left), who later nursed at La Panne, at the Sherfield Manor Military Hospital.*
Photo Mark Liddell.

85. *(Bottom Left) Cuthbert Liddell 15th Hussars. Photo Mark Liddell.*

86. *(Bottom Right) Lancelot Liddell (later in the war). In August 1915 he was a Midshipman at sea in the battleship* HMS Monarch, *and could not return home for the funeral.*
Photo Mark Liddell.

Bertie was wounded in the spring of 1918, but not dangerously, although there had been an alarming telegram informing the family that he had been wounded in the eye. It was quickly corrected by a second communication that substituted the rather less worrying word 'arm' for 'eye'. Bertie soon returned to active service to finish the war, as he began it, with the 15th Hussars. He was in action right up to the very end, and on the morning of 11 November his Squadron was preparing to lead yet another mounted attack when at 1115 the word came in the nick of time that hostilities had ceased at 1100. He wrote home in an excited and ecstatic letter 'The cheers, the noise that went up, I have never heard anything like it'. There were many sore heads among the troopers that night as Bertie explained. 'You can't imagine what it feels like out here, it's like being in a new world with something to look forward to instead of war and discomfort.'[280]

Lance also had an active war and moved from battleships to destroyers, and was on the fringes of the action at Jutland. 'That rather fearsome battle was rather a black affair. . .There were 37 people I knew quite well (lost) and a few of them were among my best friends.'[281] At the end of the war with Germany he witnessed the surrender of elements of the German fleet and reported that in some ships the officers had been thrown over the side by the ratings! His war was longer than for most because thereafter he served in Arctic waters in support of the White Russians against the Bolsheviks.

The energetic Emily Liddell was always busy and after the demise of the hospital took an interest in the local German PoW camp, and arranged for Roman Catholic prisoners to be ministered to by a priest. But in all of this activity Aidan was not forgotten by his family and friends.

Lengthy obituaries appeared in the *Stonyhurst Magazine* and Stonyhurst War Record, and a similar tribute was prepared by Balliol College. John Liddell made a substantial donation to Basingstoke Cottage Hospital and agreed to fund a modern low pressure heating and hot water system in Aidan's memory, complete with an engraved brass memorial plate. It was an unlikely monument, but Aidan would have approved of harnessing modern technology in the service of the sick.

In more traditional style, the family commissioned a magnificent portrait of Aidan from William Carter, a Royal Academician and distinguished portrait painter. It portrays him in the full dress uniform of the Argyll and Sutherland Highlanders with feather bonnet and broadsword, and his VC and MC pinned to his scarlet sash beneath golden RFC pilot's wings.* It was completed in 1917 and had been displayed in the Royal Academy before being hung at Sherfield Manor. John Liddell liked it so much that he asked William Carter to repaint the

---

* Full details of Aidan's medals are given at Appendix Three.

A portrait of Captain J. A. Liddell, V.C., M.C. by William Carter
(Courtesy of Stonyhurst College)

87. *Captain J A Liddell VC MC by William Carter. Photo Stonyhurst College.*

picture and so was able to present the second portrait to Stonyhurst College in July 1918. It still hangs there in the main Refectory alongside portraits of the other six Stonyhurst VCs. His name would also be inscribed on the Stonyhurst and Balliol memorials and on the Cross of Remembrance at Sherfield-on-Loddon.

The Argylls also remembered their fallen comrade. In 1926 the 3rd Battalion endowed seven beds for veterans in the Scottish Naval and Military Veterans Residence, then a sort of Scottish Chelsea Hospital. Each was named after a fallen comrade and marked by a small memorial tablet, and one was dedicated to Aidan. Maxwell Rouse wrote to Mrs Liddell:

> I like to think that the old fighters who will sleep in those cots will look up sometimes and remember the one who far from home gave his all for his country and King, and sleeps now with God. We who knew and loved him want no Brass, small or large, to recall him to us, for he will always be there – an inspiration.
>
> That as a Regiment we have been able to do this tiny thing is a Happiness. You will know, though, both of you, how we who still serve on in the old Corps are just proud that at any time and in any place we were with him as friends. [282]

In 1930 the Regiment paid its final tribute when the Duke of Montrose unveiled two more brass tablets in Holy Rood (West) church in Stirling. By his side walked Colonel Maxwell Rouse. Montrose began his speech with the following words: 'I had thought we had about finished in this country unveiling memorials to the fallen, but it is never too late to honour the brave.'[283] The first tablet was to the five officers and eighty-seven men of the 3rd Battalion who had fallen in the Great War, but the second was to Aidan alone and read:

> In loving memory of Captain J Aidan Liddell VC MC
> 3rd Battalion Argyll and Sutherland Highlanders
> Mortally wounded near Ostend, Belgium with the Royal Flying Corps bringing back his observer to safety behind our lines, August 1915.
> 'Greater love hath no man than this, that a man lay down his life for a friend.'

Much more recently, in September 2004, a memorial to the Royal Flying Corps was unveiled at St Omer and commemorates the 4700 members of the British Air Services who died on active service in France and Belgium during the Great War. Aidan and Major Mick Mannock, who also flew out of St Omer and was awarded the Victoria Cross, are the only two individuals named on the monument, and their portraits are etched into the zinc history panel.

After the war John Liddell's health declined. He had never fully recovered from a serious carriage accident in 1917 when his dog cart overturned on Chineham Hill on the road from Sherfield to Basingstoke. In the house Aidan's study was kept unchanged, with his gleaming brass microscope still in place on the desk. His glass slides were donated to Stonyhurst in 1916, with the hope that others might benefit from his industry. But the most memorable resident of the study remained the parrot, a large bird with a loud squawk and when Aidan's little niece visited in the mid-1920s the parrot was still in residence. She was allowed, under careful supervision, to feed the bird the top of her boiled egg, which it took from her hand with its claw. The parrot made a lasting impression and long outlived its master.

The Liddells sold the Manor in 1927 and moved to nearby Drayton House, where John died in 1930. Emily subsequently moved to nearby Sherfield Hall, but lived on only to 1934. Of the five remaining children, only Dorothy did not marry, and became a celebrated local archaeologist. Sadly, she died prematurely in 1938. John, Emily and Dorothy are buried together near the Church of the Holy Ghost, beneath a white marble crucifix, in a single grave that they share with Aidan.

Of the other siblings, only two had children. Monica, 'the Toad', had

88. *Aidan's grave at the RC Church of the Holy Ghost, Basingstoke. John, Emily and Dorothy Liddell are also buried beneath the memorial cross. Photo John Mulholland.*

a daughter, Gillian, the little girl who befriended the parrot. Lance had a son and called him Peter, the name by which he had always referred to Aidan. Peter Liddell followed in his father's footsteps and in the Second World War joined the Royal Navy, serving in Coastal Forces. He was a successful Motor Torpedo Boat commander and was awarded the Distinguished Service Cross. When Peter Liddell married, his first child was a boy. They named him John Aidan.

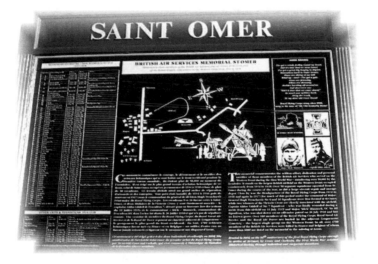

89. *The history panel, with its portraits of Aidan and Major Mick Mannock clearly visible. Photo: Peter Daybell.*

Appendix One

Letters to the Liddell Family 1915

(Taken from IWM documents IWM PP/MCR/281)

Aidan was a national hero, five times fêted in the national press, first as an unknown aviator, then by name and once again when his VC was announced. Finally the story was told yet again when his death was announced and his subsequent funeral was also reported widely. Not surprisingly the public reaction was immense and the Liddell family received over a thousand letters of condolence, from family and friends, from comrades in the army and RFC, and from members of the public. There were the usual official telegrams of regret from the King and Queen and from Lord Kitchener the Secretary of State for War. But there was much that was more personal. A small selection of those letters and the personal tributes they contained are included in this Appendix.

From the Queen of the Belgians

La Panne Sept 10th 1915

Dear Mrs Liddell,
I am so touched by the kind and generous thoughts of your husband and yourself, and I thank you in the name of the Belgian Red Cross and on behalf of our wounded soldiers. The King and I were very grieved at the death of your gallant son, who maintained to the end that calm and self control which enabled him only one month before to save his comrade. We all admired his heroic act, and we feel deeply with you the loss of your dear brave son.
I remain
Yours sincerely
Elizabeth

From Princess Louise – the Royal Colonel of the Argyll and Sutherland Highlanders

Kensington Palace
2nd Sept, 1915

Dear Mr Liddell,
I hope you will let me write you these few lines, to say how very deeply I feel for you, and your wife, in the loss of your beloved son, and am very proud that he belonged to my Regiment.
The memory of his marvellous and heroic deeds will for ever be treasured in the Regiment, he has indeed made a great name for himself.

How doubly sad for his parents and sisters, that he has now been taken from them. I grieve for you, and pray accept my profound sympathy.

The fact of your son's wonderful heroism, his coolness and daring in his actions having proved of what great service he has been to his Country, must, in a way, help you to bear your great loss. May God help and comfort you.

Sir O Wright being in France, I sent to him thinking it would be quickest, as he frequents most Hospitals, to enquire how Lieut. Liddell was, and convey to him my sympathy and congratulations, but alas, he arrived just too late, I much regret to say. I wanted him to know that my thoughts were with him.

Believe me
Yours sincerely
Louise

From Col. Gordon

3rd ('R') Bn.
Argyll & Sutherland Highlanders,
Morton Hall Camp,
Edinburgh
10 September 1915

Dear Mrs Liddell,
Our representatives at your son's funeral most truly represented all ranks of this battalion, in which we have felt his loss most keenly.

We should all have wished to be present if it had been possible, feeling that we could not honour his memory too highly.

We were very proud of our VC, and he will always be affectionately remembered, not only for the honour he has gained for us, but also for his great abilities and delightful disposition.

There has certainly been no more splendid instance of 'Devotion to Duty' throughout this war, and no brighter example of all a soldier could wish to be or to do.

Yours sincerely
John Wolrige Gordon

From Major Maxwell Rouse

3rd (R) Bn
Argyll and Sutherland Highlanders
Morton Hall Camp
Edinburgh
Sunday 12 Sept.

Dear Mrs Liddell,
I thank you from my heart for your kindness in writing to me at this sad time. We of the 3rd Battalion wanted so much to know all the details of his

illness. It seems only, though, the harder now to read – for poor Aidan – he must have suffered so, and he was utterly brave about it. Looking back it will be such a happiness to you to know how devoted he, too, was to you all at home. Among his interests I always noticed that. Some are different in that way. He loved home, and his ideals were all wrapped up there. Somehow I think that being so, his splendid sacrifice, for that it was, was finer than the world will ever guess. I can't write much, for we all feel as if the light had gone out – the light of our battalion. You see he was always bright. In snow, in muddy trench, or ante-room, he kept us laughing, and his influence will last. Soldiering had little to teach or give to him. His, by instinct, was the greatest gift a soldier can possess. And he gave it, freely, together with his life. . .to Soldiering. Ours is not vengeance to inflict but from the smallest drummer boy to the Colonel, this battalion asks only to be given the chance to avenge Aidan's death. We realized that his nature would triumph over the loss of his leg. We prayed only, here, and as a battalion in Church, that he might be spared to us a cripple for life – but spared. God has taken him. But Mrs Liddell,

> There is no death; the leaves may fall
> And flowers may fade and pass away;
> They only wait, through wintry hours
> The coming of the May.
> Someone wrote those lines. They comfort one.
> Goodbye.

From Jas C Thornton

Redhouse Park
Ipswich
Sep 3rd 1915

Dear Mrs Liddell,
I am very sorry to hear about Aidan. I can't say 'sad news', because the thing he did was so utterly magnificent that one must be very, very proud and glad of it, and no price could be too great to pay for the memory of such a thing, which is easily the finest achievement of the war, and beside which Warneford's VC is almost fraudulently earned.

I have heard from several of the RFC overseas of Aidan's deed, and in all modesty may I say no one who has not flown can understand and fully appreciate the wonder and marvel of what Aidan did, and the courage, determination, and absolute, unbelievable 'grit' which alone could have done it. When I heard of it first, I was proud to be able to claim acquaintanceship and connection with him. It cannot be any consolation to know that so many have died as he did for his country, but it must be to know his is the noblest deed and memory of them all, and apart from that, he was liked and popular with everyone whom he met.

Please forgive my badly written letter, but I do want to add my tributes of the admiration felt for him by those who can appreciate most fully the heroism and difficulty of what he did, and yet may not be able to tell you.

Yours sincerely

Jas C Thornton

From Prince Alexander of Teck

British Military Mission

With the Belgian Army

August 31st 1915

Dear Mrs Liddell,

I am so grieved for you, those in charge of him, and for the country in whose interests he died.

It is very, very sad, and we are all miserable that after his gallant fight lasting so long, his strength should at last have failed him. You may well be proud of having been the Mother of one who not only gained the VC, but kept on playing the game to the end. I understand you wish the funeral to take place in England. There is no difficulty about this, only the family must make the arrangements, and communicate with the General Lines of communication.

Believe me

Yours sincerely

Alexander of Teck

From FF 'Sligger' Urquhart

Dec 13th

Balliol College

Oxford

Dear Mr Liddell,

I wonder if you could let us have a photograph of Aidan for our Common Room. We should be very grateful if you would. We have never before put up photographs of the young men, but there is something so unique about Aidan's distinction that I should like very much to see him kept in our remembrance and that of our successors, in this little way.

I was very sorry not to be able to come to the funeral at Basingstoke. But I was working in a government office at the time, and had to content myself with the Requiem at Farm Street. Almost immediately after the funeral I was unexpectedly sent off at a moment's notice to Russia with despatches, and when I got back so much time had passed that I felt quite ashamed of writing to you. I was of course extraordinarily interested in the letters etc to the Stonyhurst Magazine. There is something so extraordinarily complete about his death. First a magnificent expression of the power of action that was in him, then a month of suffering, I hope it was not continuous, I believe it was not – to bring him out the other side of a complete man. Suffering which must have been terribly painful to you, but which does so much to make a man fit for heaven! How proud you must be of him: but the loss must be terribly hard for you and his mother.

Believe me
Yours very sincerely
F F Urquhart

From Harold Hartley

3 Army HQ
BEF
8. 9. 15.

Dear Mrs Liddell,
The news of Aidan's death was a great grief to me, and I can only tell you how deeply I sympathise with you and your husband. I heard so much of Aidan's coolness and bravery that his last gallant exploit was just what I should have been expected from him. All his skill and courage was focussed in it, and I wish you could have heard what people said of him here when his VC was gazetted. They all felt that his actions would always be remembered as one of the very finest in the war – and never before has a war called forth such personal courage. I am going round the trenches most days in different parts of our line, and it is wonderful to see all our young officers, some of them only 18 – their good spirits, coolness and skill are magnificent.

Aidan always interested me, he had unusual gifts, and I felt that he ought to do something big, while he was at Oxford he was never really fit, and I hoped that afterwards he would get stronger. I remember how anxious you used to be when he was ill.

I just wanted you to know how proud I am that he was my friend, and how much I regret his loss.

Yours sincerely
Harold Hartley

(of Balliol College, Oxford)

From Private Smith – Aidan's soldier servant.

2nd Argyll and Sutherland Highlanders
Northern France
Dec. 16th 1915

Dear Madam,
In a recent letter which I have received from my wife, she mentions that at her request you have very kindly presented her with some photographs of your son, the late Capt. Liddell VC as a memento of him. I acted in the

capacity of servant to Mr Liddell from the time of his first arriving in this country on active service, until he was admitted into hospital in Jan of this year, therefore we were thrown very much together during operations in the field in the earlier parts of the war, and in the trenches in the last few months that he was here. We who served under him here, whilst he was in charge of the Machine Guns, were not surprised when we read of the exploit by which he won that coveted honour, the Victoria Cross, as we knew from experience that he was a splendid officer and an exceedingly brave man. I regret to tell you that most of the men who served under him here have also had their names enrolled on the Roll of Fame, which indicates that they also have laid down their lives for King and Country.

Please accept my heartiest thanks for your kindness in sending my wife the photographs, also my sympathy for you in your great loss.

Yours sincerely

GA Smith 9095

Headquarters, 2nd Argyll and Sutherland Highlanders, BEF

From TA Powell RN

HMS ARROGANT

Sept. 14th

Dear Miss Liddell,

It was very kind of you indeed to write to me, you know what a very dear friend your brother was to me. I am so sorry I have not replied before, but I have only just come back to the Arrogant. I was round at Portsmouth when I heard of your brother's last flight, and we continually received news at Dover that he was getting better. The end must have been terribly sudden. I hope it is some small alleviation to your sorrow to think that when your brother won his Victoria Cross, he was doing what probably no other man in the world would have done, and his deed has astounded the flying men of both services.

He was loved and respected by all with whom he came in contact, and you must realize how proud we are that we ever knew him.

Do let me know if there is anything, however small, which I can do for him down here, though I suppose his affairs have been squared up by this time.

Yours sincerely

TA Powell RN

From R Ramsbotham (RN)

H.M.S. HAZARD,

4th SUBMARINE FLOTILLA

5th September 1915

Dear Mrs Liddell,

I am writing to thank you for replying to my letter to your son, and also to express my deepest sympathy to you in your irreparable loss. I met your son when he was undergoing the flying course, and he dined with me on board several times, and I've never in my life met a finer fellow, and when I found in the *Daily Mail* about an airman who had been severely wounded and had managed to bring his machine back to our own lines, I felt that it must be him, and I enquired at once and found out that it was. I cannot sufficiently express to you my sympathy in your sad loss, and also in England's loss. Should it ever happen that you are near a place called Crowborough in Sussex, I hope you will come and see my people at Crowborough Warren. I would have written before, but I was unable to on account of being at sea. Please do not trouble to answer this letter.

Yours sincerely
R Ramsbotham (RN)

From MAJOR-GEN SIR W G KNOX KCB

HILL HOUSE, SHERBORNE ST JOHN, BASINGSTOKE
21st Oct 15

My dear Liddell,
I saw Gen. Sir David Henderson the Director of Aviation yesterday, an old comrade of mine. He was so eulogistic of your hero son. What he praised most was that in spite of his terrible wound, he kept his nerve so well as to steer his machine with one hand and one foot to safety on Belgian soil, and that when he landed her slowly at the Aerodrome, he roundly abused the Belgian officer in charge for not having his arrows marked on the ground, for safe landing, pointing in the regulation direction. What glorious nerve!

Yours very truly
W G Knox

From an Old Soldier

Chantry House
Shoreham
Sussex
June 11 16

Dear Sir,
As an old soldier I can simply say that your son was the most ideal specimen in a camp of 20,000.

Please accept my sincerest sympathy in your great loss.

Yours faithfully
F. Carden Brodie

From Captain Purves

Argyll and Sutherland Highlanders
BEF
23.10.15.
Dear Mrs Liddell,
It has been on my conscience terribly that I have never written to offer you my deepest sympathy for Aidan's death, but at the time I had so very much to do, and later I felt that it was too late, but I am doing it now, for I feel that you will forgive me for not having done it before.

I wrote to him when he got his VC and have often wondered if he got my letter. I was so awfully pleased that they had recognised what a brave chap he was.

He was a very great friend of mine, and had been from the first, when he came up to be attached to us at Fort George. I don't suppose you ever knew how awfully well he did with us, for he wasn't a person to talk of what he had done.

At Le Maisnil he and Corporal Campbell, by their pluck and clever way of handling their machine gun, practically saved most of the regiment, and it was the greatest shame that he never got a DSO for it . . .(The next line or so which elaborated on the reasons why Aidan did not receive the DSO that Captain Purves and others, felt he deserved was expunged by Mrs Liddell, who felt that it should not be published.)

Then again when he was with the Middlesex at La Boutillerie, he did awfully well, and many of them have spoken to me, saying how cheerful and good he was in all that trying weather and intense discomfort.

Poor Corporal Campbell was killed during our attack the other day, but I am glad to say he was given a Russian medal just before the action. It was that long spell in the trenches at Boutillerie that really broke down Aidan's health, although he hung on for a long time before giving in.

He was one of my greatest friends, and it was always the greatest pleasure to do anything with him, and at home we were all glad when he would come and stop, Then while at the Depot, and training with the 3rd Battalion we saw a great deal of one another.

No one could have died more nobly, although that is small compensation for such a loss, but I who have seen him under fire know he was perfectly fearless, and it was the kind of death he would have preferred to any other.

Words in a case like this are so useless, but I do offer you my most heartfelt sympathy in what I know is an irreparable loss.
Yours very sincerely
H. de B. Purves

From Major Wheatley

> 3rd (R) Bn.
> Argyll and Sutherland Highlanders
> Staff College
> Camberly
> 12. 11. 15.

Dear Mrs Liddell,
I never had any opportunity today at Heckfield, to tell you how proud we are as a Regiment of Aidan, and in what honour his name will always be held, not only by the Regiment, but by every Friend or Enemy who knows what he did and how he did it. I only met him once, when he had just come back from the 93rd, but I felt that he would make his name through thoroughness.

I ask for no better example to follow, and in asking you to accept my deep sympathy in your loss, I also ask you to allow me to share with you the pride of his daring feat, and the consciousness of the great loss that our country has sustained.

I go myself in the near future, and should have the greatest confidence if I felt I could do as he did.
Believe me
Yours very sincerely
Leonard Wheatley

Appendix Two

Notes on Persons Mentioned in the Text

Maurice Dease

Maurice Dease, Aidan's fellow student at Frognall Hall and fellow Aviary Boy, joined the Army after Stonyhurst. By 1914, he was a lieutenant in the 4th Royal Fusiliers and the Machine-Gun Officer. At the Battle of Mons the Battalion was deployed to the north of the town in a vulnerable salient bounded by the canal. The two machine-guns of Dease's section were a vital component of the defence and covered two bridges. The Royal Fusiliers faced overwhelming German infantry assaults and the Machine-Gun Section took heavy casualties. Dease stayed with his guns, and when all his men were killed or wounded operated a gun himself and continued to hold back the enemy. By this time he had already been wounded four times. However, he carried on regardless until he was finally hit again, this time fatally. A brother officer carried him to the rear where he died soon after. Maurice Dease was the first Stonyhurst boy to die in the Great War and was also awarded the first Victoria Cross of the War.

Gabriel Coury

Gabriel Coury had arrived at Stonyhurst in 1907, so he was at the bottom of the school while Aidan was a Gentleman Philosopher. They would not have known each other well, but their lives did follow similar paths. When Gabriel left school in 1913 he began training as a cotton broker, but the war changed all that. He enlisted as a private in the King's Liverpool Regiment, and was subsequently commissioned into the South Lancashire Regiment (Prince of Wales Volunteers). He joined the 1st/4th (Territorial) Battalion, which became a Pioneer Battalion, and in the summer of 1916 took part in the Battle of the Somme.

On 7 August he commanded a half company of Pioneers who were to move forward behind a two-battalion attack on enemy positions, and dig a communication trench between the British front line and the newly captured trench. They had dug 60 yards of trench before the attack collapsed, but despite heavy enemy fire they completed their task and consolidated their position. The ground to the front was now littered with dead and wounded from the failed attack. Coury, seeing that the CO of one of the battalions was lying badly wounded, went forward to bring him back. He was chased by snipers and machine-guns but reached his man and brought him back to safety. He then rallied the survivors of the two attacking battalions and organised the defence so that a German counter-attack was checked.

For his gallant action in rescuing a wounded officer under heavy fire and rallying the defence in the face of an attack, Gabriel Coury was awarded the Victoria Cross. He received his VC from King George V on 18 November 1916, just two days after John Liddell had received Aidan's Cross from the King. Like Aidan, Gabriel Coury also transferred from the infantry to the RFC. He was at first an observer, and later became a pilot, although he was subsequently badly injured in a flying accident. He died in 1956.

Joseph Plunkett

Aidan's fellow Philosopher, the Irishman Joseph Plunkett became a member of the Gaelic League after he left Stonyhurst and was greatly interested in the Irish language, arts and the theatre. He was a co-founder of the Irish Theatre in Hardwicke Street Dublin, and his poetry, including 'I see His Blood Upon the Rose' received increasing acclaim. However, it was as a leading member of the Irish Republican Brotherhood that he made his mark.

Joseph Plunkett's only military experience had been with the Stonyhurst OTC in the woods around the College and during summer camp on Salisbury Plain. Despite this he became the Director of Military Operations for the Irish Volunteers and was a key figure in developing plans for the Easter uprising of 1916. Although by now suffering from advanced tuberculosis, he visited Germany and the United States in 1915 to try and organise clandestine arms shipments for Ireland. He took part in the Easter uprising and was one of the seven signatories of the 'Proclamation of the Provisional Government of the Irish Republic to the People of Ireland', although he spent most of his time in the Central Post Office confined to a sick bed. His aide during this period was Michael Collins.

The rebellion collapsed after a week of fighting and the leaders were seized and imprisoned in Kilmainham Gaol. They were tried before a Field Court Martial; fifteen of the group, including Joseph Plunkett, were sentenced to death, and were shot by firing squad. He had married his fiancée Grace Clifford on the evening before his execution, and the following morning was allowed a few brief moments with her before the sentence was carried out. There was one last drama, for the officer commanding the firing party recognised Joseph as a boyhood friend and refused to carry out the order. The execution was only briefly delayed and the officer was himself court-martialled and cashiered. There was no obituary to Joseph Plunkett in the *Stonyhurst Magazine*.

Fr Aloysius Cortie SJ

Father Cortie remained at Stonyhurst and continued to pursue his interest in astronomy. Such was his overwhelming enthusiasm that, it was said he had no acquaintances, only friends. Following the success of the Cortie/Liddell Spanish expedition of 1905, he observed solar eclipses in Tonga in 1911 and in Hermosand, Sweden, in 1914. When the eminent Fr Sidgreaves died in 1919, Cortie succeeded him as Director of the Stonyhurst Observatory, which in 1922 was recognised as an international centre for the visual study of the solar surface. He continued to travel and lecture, and was a popular and entertaining advocate for his science. In 1925, still at the height of his powers, he suffered a stroke. When told by the doctor 'You know you are not getting any better' he responded 'Well that's not my fault. I have taken all your medicines'. Shortly before he died he told those gathered about his bedside 'Chaps, I'm going to peg out'.[284]

Harold Hartley

Harold Hartley, the tutor who had assessed Aidan's unsuccessful attempt to win a scholarship to Balliol college as being 'interesting and thoughtful', went on to become a distinguished scientist, industrialist and public servant. In 1914 he joined the Leicestershire Regiment, but when it was appreciated that the Army had acquired a brilliant chemist, he was quickly diverted into the specialist area of gas warfare. He finished the war as a Brigadier General in the Ministry of Munitions in the appointment of Controller of the Chemical Warfare Department. After the war he returned to Balliol and was involved in the compilation of the *Balliol College War Memorial Book*, writing to the Liddell family and to officers of the Argyll and Sutherland Highlanders to secure more information about Aidan's war. He was knighted in 1928 and left Oxford in 1930 to pursue a career in industry. As an expert on energy and power, during the Second World War he played a significant part in determining Allied bombing targets. Among his many later achievements were the Presidency of the Institution of Chemical Engineers and of the British Association. He died in 1972 at the age of ninety-six.

Captain, J L Jack 1st Cameronians and Staff Captain 16th Infantry Brigade.

Captain Jack's personal diary has provided invaluable information on the operations conducted by the 19th Brigade and the 93rd in the campaigning of 1914. James Jack was a compelling diarist and an outstanding soldier. He was also a frequent visitor to RHQ of 1st A&SH to which the Machine-Gun Section were attached. He and Aidan must have known one another, although neither has written of the other. He left the Brigade Staff after his period of sick leave in late 1914 and returned to his battalion, 1st Cameronians in 19th Brigade where he commanded C Company. Between August 1915 and August 1916 he was a company commander and the Second-in-Command of 2nd Cameronians. He was then given command of the 2nd West Yorkshire Regiment a position he held until July 1917. Finally, in September 1918 he took command of the 28th Infantry Brigade. He thus fought throughout the war and took part in many of the great battles on the Western Front. He was promoted from Captain to Temporary Brigadier General. He was awarded the DSO, first as a battalion CO, and then received a bar as a GOC 28th Infantry Brigade. Having served almost continuously on active service throughout the war, he was injured in a riding accident in 1919 that necessitated his retirement from the Army in 1921. He died in 1962. *General Jack's Diary*, brilliantly edited by John Terraine, is one of the most remarkable accounts of soldiering in the Great War.

Graham Seton Hutchison

Aidan's friend and fellow diarist Graham Hutchison succeeded him as the Machine-Gun Officer of the 93rd. In due course he transferred to the Machine-Gun Corps and survived the war as a lieutenant-colonel with a DSO and MC. Later, he became a prolific author, writing books of military memoirs such as *Footslogger, Warrior,* and *Machine Gunner.* He also wrote a number of thrillers, including *The W Plan* and *Blood Money,* which were written under the name Graham Seton. Like a number of former military officers he developed an interest in right wing politics and founded the National Workers Party of Great Britain that was subsequently subsumed into Sir Oswald Mosley's British Union of Fascists. He died in 1946.

2nd Lieutenant Roland Peck, 5th Service Battalion the Dorset Regiment and RFC

Roland Peck had joined No. 7 Sqn at St Omer on 20 February 1915. Immediately after the action on 31 July he was sent home for a week of leave by his CO, Major Hoare, with the understanding that he would visit Sherfield Manor and explain the circumstances of Aidan's gallant action to the Liddell family. Soon after his return to France he was told that he had been selected for pilot training and was posted to CFS on 28 August 1915. This explains how he was able to attend Aidan's funeral on 4 September.

Peck qualifed as a pilot on 15 Nov 1915 and his record shows that he was then posted briefly to No.23 Sqn. He was Mentioned in Despatches on 16 January 1916, almost certainly because of his valuable service with No. 7 Sqn at St Omer, but by this time he was already on his way to join No.30 Sqn in the Middle East. This unit had formed in Mesopotamia the previous summer and incorporated a number of Australian airmen. In December 1915 the Turks commenced the siege of Major-General Townsend's forces at Kut al-Amara, and were supported in this by a German flying unit *Flieger Abteilung* 2, which operated Pfalz Parosol scouts.

On 5 March 1916 RFC Voisin VS1541 of No. 30 Sqn was lost over the Tigris Line. The crew, 2nd Lieutenant Roland Peck and Captain WG Palmer, were posted as killed in action. The kill was claimed by both *Flieger Abteilung* 2 and by Turkish machine-gunners on the ground.[285] Roland Peck and his comrade Palmer now lie somewhere in modern Iraq, and are remembered on the Commonwealth War Graves Commission Basra Memorial.

RE5 2457

RE5 2457 stayed with No. 7 Sqn until 30 September, when it was transferred to No. 12 Sqn. As previously recounted, Roland Peck flew another reconnaissance mission in 2457 on 14 August. It flew another seven such missions, including one with the additional notation 'special mission' before the transfer. Lieutenant Benegough, who had accompanied Aidan's body home and represented No. 7 Sqn at the funeral, had also flown briefly in the front seat as a passenger.

This aircraft was once again in combat during two of the reconnaissance missions, the first being on 18 September when a Fokker seemed to dive out of the sun, shooting the RE5 through the radiator and necessitating a forced landing. Fortunately, the crew were unharmed. Then on 26 September there was a second combat for 2457 with a Fokker, in which the enemy veered away after making an attacking pass. On both occasions battle damage repairs had to be made to the fabric of 2457.

On 17 October 1915 the machine was dismantled and the following day it was handed over to the aircraft park together with the log book. It returned to England on 30 December and was later operated by No. 7 Reserve Sqn at Netheravon. A part of the propeller, together with an engraved memorial plate referring to Aidan's flight, is now held by the Imperial War Museum in London.

Appendix Three

Aidan Liddell's Medals.

Aidan Liddell never wore his medals, which were received by his family in the years following his death. The first was probably the Military Cross, although there is no date of receipt recorded. The MC was issued unnamed, but Aidan's was privately engraved 'Lieut. John Aidan Liddell, 93rd A. & S. H. 19th Feby. 1915'. The date refers to the announcement of the award in the *London Gazette*, but is actually incorrect. Aidan's MC was gazetted a day earlier on 18 February 1915. This sort of private engraving of MCs was not uncommon during the Great War and was probably carried out at that time by the family. Aidan's VC was received from King George V by John Liddell on 16 November 1916. Unlike the MC the VC is officially engraved and it reads 'Capt. J. A. Liddell, 3rd Bn. P. Louise's (Argyll & Suth. H.) & R.F.C.; 31 July 1915'.

Aidan was also awarded three other medals. The first was the 1914 Star, which was approved in 1917 for those who had served in France and Belgium between 5 August and 22 November 1914. The medal was officially impressed with the name of the recipient and read 'Lieut. J.A. Liddell, A. & S. Highs.' In many cases the 1914 Star was not issued until 1919, and later in that year King George V agreed the award of a bar to the medal for those who had been under fire in France or Belgium during the qualifying period. Aidan had earned that bar, which would have been sewn onto the medal ribbon, although on his ribbon none was fitted. The bar also entitled the recipient to a silver rosette that was worn on the undress ribbon when the star itself was not worn. The delay between the issue of the medal and the bar meant that many recipients who were entitled never put up the bar, and so Aidan's example is not uncommon. The final two medals were the British War Medal and the Victory Medal, the latter with an oak leaf denoting Mentioned in Despatches. These medals were still being issued to recipients in 1924, and Aidan's were officially impressed 'Capt. J. A. Liddell'.

Aidan's medals were held in a special place of honour within the family for many years. They were displayed in a glass case with a matching set of miniatures and several mementoes, including his battle-damaged Glengarry, piccolo and golden RFC Pilot's Wings. There were Argyll and Sutherland Highlanders collar dogs and badges, and the brooch for pinning the dress plaid at the shoulder, as well as woven RFC badges. But in the early 1980s the medal group and memorabilia passed into the hands of an overseas collector after a private sale. Then in 1997 the medals returned to the UK and were auctioned at Spinks on 17 July for £85,000. The name of the purchaser was not disclosed but is believed to be a British collector of VCs. The miniatures were auctioned separately and acquired by the family.

The photograph of the medals was taken prior to the 1997 sale, and shows the original ribbons, which were replaced by Spinks before the auction. It should be noted that the oak leaf has been attached to the Victory Medal ribbon incorrectly and is facing the wrong way.

89. *The Liddell Medal Group with the original ribbons. Photo John Mulholland.*

Select Bibliography

Unpublished

Aidan Liddell Letters and Diaries Imperial War Museum
Unit War Diaries and other Miscellaneous Papers, Public Record Office/National
    Archive
Sir Harold Hartley's Papers, Churchill College Archives
Miscellaneous Papers and Records, Stonyhurst College - Arundel Library
Regimental Records, Argyll and Sutherland Highlanders Regimental Museum
Miscellaneous Papers, Balliol College Library, Oxford
Liddell Family Papers
Clayton Family Papers
Ailleen Elwes of Warwick Hall, Cumbria by Maurice French (1995) (privately
    circulated booklet)
The Liddell Family and Richard Granger and his Descendants by Molly Liddell
    (privately circulated manuscript)

Printed

Official Documents and Manuals
Infantry Training Manual (1914)
The London Gazette

Journals and Newspapers
The Aeroplane
The Campbelltown Courier
The Daily Mirror
Flight
The Hants and Berks Gazette
Letters and Notices (Jesuit Publication)
Stonyhurst Magazine
The Times

Published Books
Adam, Adela Marian, *Arthur Innes Adam*, Cambridge, Bowes and Bowers (1920)
Bailey, Cyril, *Francis Fortesque Urquhart*, London, Macmillan and Co. Ltd (1936)
Balliol College, *Balliol College War Memorial Book*, printed for private circulation
    (1924)
Baring, Maurice, *RFC HQ 1914–1918*, London, Bell and Sons (1920)
Barker, Ralph, *Royal Flying Corps in France – From Mons to the Somme*, London,
    Constable (1995)
Bruce, J M, *RE5/7, Windsock Datafile 62, Berkhamsted*, Albatros Productions Ltd
    (1997)
Brown, Malcolm and Seaton, Shirley, *Christmas Truce*, London, Pan Books
    (1999)

Buchan, John, *Memory Hold the Door*, London, Hodder and Stoughton (1940)

Carnock, Lord, *The History of the 15th The King's Hussars, 1914–1922*, Gloucester, Crypt House Press (1922)

Cassar, George H, *The Tragedy of Sir John French*, London, Associated University Presses (1985)

Cavendish, A E J, *An Reisimeid Chataich, The 93rd Sutherland Highlanders*, published privately (1928)

Cooksley, Peter, *The Air VCs*, Gloucester, Sutton Publishing (1996)

Dallas Brett, R, *History of British Aviation 1908–1914*, London, John Hamilton Ltd (1934)

Dunn, J C, *The War the Infantry Knew*. London, Abacus (1994)

French, Field Marshal Viscount, *The Despatches of Lord French*, London, Chapman and Hall (1917)

Gilbert, Martin, *First World War*, London, Harper Collins (1995)

Goodhall, G S *Flying Start, Flying Schools and Clubs at Brooklands 1910–1939*, Brooklands Museum Trust (1995)

Henshaw, Trevor, *The Sky Their Battlefield*, Grub Street, London (1995)

Hutchison, Graham Seton, *Warrior*, Hutchinson, London (1932)

Hutchison, G S, *Machine Guns, Their History and Tactical Employment*, London, Macmillan and Co (1938)

Irwin, Francis, *Stonyhurst War Record*, privately published, Stonyhurst (1927)

Jones, H A, *The War in the Air, Vols 2–6*, Oxford, Clarendon Press (series completed 1937)

Jones, John, *Balliol College, A History*, Oxford University Press (1997)

Keegan, John, *The First World War*, London, Hutchinson (1998)

Kirby, H and Walsh, R, *The Seven VCs of Stonyhurst College*, Blackburn, THCL Books (1987)

Lewis, Cecil, *Sagittarius Rising*, London, Warner Books (1993)

Lomas, D, *First Ypres 1914 - The Graveyard of the Old Contemptibles*, Oxford, Osprey Publishing (1999)

Lomas, D, *Mons 1914 - the BEF's Tactical Triumph*, Oxford, Osprey Publishing (1997)

Macdonald, Lyn, *1914 – The Days of Hope*, Penguin Books (1989)

Mileham, P J R, *Fighting Highlanders*, London, Arms and Armour (1993)

Muir, T E, *Stonyhurst College 1593-1993*, London, James and James (1992)

Norris, Geoffrey, *The Royal Flying Corps: A History*, London, Frederick Muller (1965)

Paris, Michael, *Winged Warfare*, Manchester, Manchester University Press (1992)

Raleigh, Walter, *The War in the Air Vol 1*, Oxford, Oxford University Press (1922)

Seton, Graham, *Footslogger*, London, Hutchison (1933)

Sire, Henry, *Gentlemen Philosophers: Catholic Higher Education at Liège and Stonyhurst 1774–1916*, Churchman Publishing (1988)

Terraine, John, *General Jack's Diary*, London, Cassell (2000)

Weintraub, Stanley, *Silent Night*, London, Simon & Schuster (2001)

Westlake, Ray, *British Battalions in France and Belgium 1914*, London, Leo Cooper (1997)

REFERENCES

Key to References
IWM   Imperial War Museum
PRO/NA   Public Record Office/National Archive

Key to Family References
JAL   John Aidan Liddell
JL   John Liddell (father)
EL   Emily Liddell (mother)
DL   Dorothy Liddell (eldest sister)
ML   Monica Liddell (middle sister)
VML   Veronica Mary Liddell (youngest sister)
CL   Cuthbert Liddell (brother)
LL   Lancelot Liddell (younger brother)

Introduction – Reuiescat in Pace
1   IWM PP/MCR/281 Letter from Major Hoare to JAL dated 2 Aug 1915.
2   Vol 13 Pt2 of the *Stonyhurst Magazine* contains a number of references to the Memorial Service. There is also an entry in the First Prefect's log in the Stonyhurst Archive in the Arundel Library. Phrases in quotations are taken from these sources.

Chapter One – From Benwell to Basingstoke
3   Liddell Family Papers, VML nursery notebook.
4   From a personal reminiscence by Gillian Clayton, dated 30 Mar 1999.
5   Liddell Family Papers, VML nursery notebook.
6   From a personal reminiscence by Gillian Clayton to the author, dated 30 Mar 1999.

Chapter Two – Stonyhurst College
7   Stonyhurst College, Prospectus of the 1890s.
8   *Stonyhurst Magazine* Vol 9 p.197.
9   *ibid* Vol 7 p.412.
10 *ibid* Vol 7 p.539.
11 Stonyhurst College, School Diary 16 Oct 1900.
12 *Stonyhurst Magazine*, Vol 8 p.3.
13 Stonyhurst College, School Diary 1 Jun 1901.
14 *ibid* 22 Jan 1901.
15 *Stonyhurst Magazine* Vol 9 p.61.

Chapter Three – Science and Spain
[16] *Stonyhurst Magazine* Vol 9 p.24.
[17] Clayton Family Papers, Letter JAL to CL undated but post marked 11 August 1905.
[18] Clayton Family Papers, JAL to JL and EL dated 11 Aug 1905.
[19] Clayton Family Papers, JAL to EL dated 21 Aug 1905.
[20] *ibid.*
[21] *ibid.*
[22] *ibid.*
[23] *Stonyhurst Magazine* Vol 9 p.410.
[24] Clayton Family Papers, JAL to JL dated 27 Aug 1905.
[25] *Stonyhurst Magazine* Vol 9 p.411.
[26] *ibid.*
[27] Clayton Family Papers, JAL to EL dated 3 Sep 1905.
[28] *ibid.*
[29] Clayton Family Papers, Fr Cortie to JAL 13 Sep 1905.
[30] Rev Francis Irwin SJ, *Stonyhurst War Record*, Stonyhurst 1927, p.160.

Chapter Four – Gentleman Philosopher
[31] *Stonyhurst Magazine* Vol 11 p.3.
[32] *Stonyhurst Magazine* Vol 10 p.419.
[33] Stonyhurst College, Philosophers' Diary, 25 Oct 1907.
[34] *Stonyhurst Magazine* Vol 10 p.174.
[35] *Stonyhurst Magazine* Vol 10 p.372.
[36] *Stonyhurst Magazine* Vol 10 p.418.
[37] *Stonyhurst Magazine* Vol 10 p.216.
[38] From Harold Hartley's notebook, the Churchill Archives.
[39] *ibid*

Chapter Five – Peter at Balliol
[40] *The Times*, 23 July 1908.
[41] John Buchan, *Memory Hold the Door*, 1940, p.52.
[42] Cyril Bailey, *Francis Fortesque Urquhart*, 1936, p.46.
[43] *ibid*, p.45.
[44] *ibid*, p.46.
[45] IWM PP/MCR/281. For full text see Appendix One page 278.
[46] *Stonyhurst Magazine* Vol 11 p.349.
[47] *ibid.* p.265.
[48] Bailey, *Urquhart*, 1936, p.62.
[49] *ibid.* p.183.
[50] *Balliol College War Memorial Book*. Printed for private circulation 1924. p.24.
[51] Balliol College Library. Letter from ETN Grove to Beryl Griffith dated 24 June 1912.
[52] *ibid.*

Chapter Six – The Young Squire

[53] Clayton Family Papers, JAL to DL and ML dated 2 Jan 1913.

[54] *ibid.*

[55] Liddell Family Papers, Letter from School of Musketry to JAL dated 15 Oct 1913.

[56] Clayton Family Papers, Letter from JAL to EL dated 2 Mar 1913.

[57] *The Aeroplane* 26 Mar 1914 p.351.

[58] *ibid*, 22 Jan 1914. p.78.

[59] R Dallas Brett, *History of British Aviation 1908–1914*, 1934, p.352.

[60] *ibid* pp.236/238.

[61] *ibid*

Chapter Seven – War

[62] *The Hants and Berks Gazette*, dated 4 July 1914.

[63] IWM PP/MCR/281 JAL Diary 7 Aug 1914.

[64] IWM PP/MCR/281 Letter from JAL to EL dated Aug 1914 only.

[65] *ibid.*

[66] IWM PP/MCR/281 Letter JAL to EL dated 30 Aug 1914.

Chapter Eight – France and the 93rd

[67] IWM PP/MCR/281 Letter from JAL to JL dated 1 Sep 1914.

[68] Captain J C Dunn, *The War the Infantry Knew*. Abacus, London 1994, p.14.

[69] IWM Sound Archives, Charles Harry Ditcham, 000374/07.

[70] John Terraine, *General Jack's Diary*, Cassell, London, 2000, p.32.

[71] *ibid* pp.34/35.

[72] *ibid* p.35.

[73] Brig-Gen J E Edmonds, Official History, August to October 1914, pp.164/165.

[74] P J R Mileham, *Fighting Highlanders*. Arms and Armour, London 1993 p.81.

[75] Terraine, *Jack's Diary*, p.37.

[76] *ibid* p.38.

[77] French, John Denton Pinkstone, Earl of Ypres, *The Despatches of Lord French*, Chapman and Hall, London 1917, p.11.

[78] IWM Sound Archives, Charles Harry Ditcham, 000374/07.

[79] Terraine, *Jack's Diary* p.42.

[80] *ibid* p.48.

[81] IWM PP/MCR/281 JAL Diary 5 Sep 1914.

Chapter Nine – On the Marne and the Aisne

[82] IWM Sound Archives, Charles Harry Ditcham, 000374/07.

[83] IWM JAL Diary 8 Sep1914.

[84] IWM JAL Diary 9 Sep 1914.

[85] IWM JAL Diary 10 Sep 1914.

[86] IWM JAL Diary 11 Sep 1914.

[87] Brigadier-General A E J Cavendish CMG *An Reisimeid Chataich, The 93rd Sutherland Highlanders,* published privately 1928 p.247.
[88] IWM JAL Letter to JL and EL dated 19 Sep 1914
[89] IWM JAL Diary 15 Sep 1914.
[90] IWM JAL Diary 17 Sep 1914.
[91] PRO WO 95/1365 60300 93rd War Diary. Sir John French. Special Order of the Day, 17 Sep 1914.
[92] IWM JAL Diary 19 Sep 1914.
[93] IWM JAL Letter to JL and EL dated 19 Sep 1914.
[94] IWM JAL Diary 20/21 Sep 1914.
[95] *Infantry Training Manual* (1914) (RHQ Argylls) p.15.
[96] IWM JAL Diary 26 Sep 1914.
[97] IWM JAL Diary 29 Sep 1914.
[98] IWM JAL Diary 30 Sep 1914.
[99] IWM JAL Letter to JL and EL dated 3 Oct 1914.

Chapter Ten – To Flanders and Le Maisnil

[100] PRO 93rd War Diary 7 Oct 1914.
[101] IWM JAL Diary 10 Oct 1914.
[102] Terraine, *Jack's Diary,* p.61.
[103] IWM JAL Diary 15 Oct 1914.
[104] IWM JAL letter to JL dated 15 Oct 1914.
[105] IWM Diary 19 Oct 1914.
[106] PRO WO95/1364 60300 19th Brigade War Diary 20 Oct 1914.
[107] Terraine, *Jack's Diary,* pp.66/67.
[108] IWM JAL Diary 20 Oct 1914.
[109] Dunn, *War* p.75.
[110] IWM JAL letter to EL dated 25 Oct 1914.
[111] PRO Message 19th Brigade War Diary 21 Oct 1914.
[112] Terraine, *Jack's Diary,* pp.67/68.
[113] PRO Message 19th Brigade War Diary 21 Oct 1914.
[114] PRO Message 19th Brigade War Diary 21 Oct 1914.
[115] IWM JAL Diary 21 Oct 1914.
[116] *ibid.*
[117] *ibid.*
[110] Terraine, *Jack's Diary,* p.68.
[119] IWM JAL Diary 21 Oct 1914.
[120] Terraine, *Jack's Diary,* p.68.
[121] IWM JAL Letter to EL dated 4 Dec 1914.
[122] IWM, Brigadier J C Cunningham MC, Memoirs pp.2/3.
[123] PRO WO95/1366 19 Field Ambulance War Diary, 21 Oct 1914.

Chapter Eleven – First Ypres

[124] Dunn, *War*, p.76.
[125] IWM JAL Diary 22 Oct 1914.
[126] *ibid* 23 Oct 1914.
[127] Terraine, *Jack's Diary*, p.69.
[128] Dunn, *War*, p.77.
[129] IWM JAL Diary 22 Oct 1914.
[130] Dunn, *War*, p.81.
[131] IWM JAL Diary 24 Oct 1914.
[132] Terraine, *Jack's Diary*, p.71.
[133] IWM JAL Diary 25 Oct 1914.
[134] Dunn, *War*, p.82.
[135] *ibid*.
[136] IWM Letter JAL to EL dated 25 Oct 1914.
[137] IWM JAL Diary 26 Oct 1914.
[138] Dunn, *War*, p.84.
[139] IWM JAL Diary 27 Oct 1914.
[140] Dunn, *War*, p.85.
[141] *ibid* p.87.
[142] IWM JAL Diary 28 Oct 1914.
[143] Terraine, *Jack's Diary*, p.75.
[144] *ibid* p.75.
[145] Dunn, *War*, p.89.
[146] IWM JAL Diary 30 Oct.
[147] Terraine, *Jack's Diary* p.76.
[148] IWM JAL Letter to EL dated 6 Nov 1914.
[149] IWM JAL Letter to EL dated 4 Dec 1914.
[150] IWM JAL Diary 3 Nov 1914.
[151] *ibid* 4 Nov 1914.
[152] IWM JAL Letter to EL dated 6 Nov 1914.
[153] IWM JAL Letter to JL dated 8 Nov 1914.

Chapter Twelve – 'Plugstreet' and the Middlesex

[154] PRO 93rd War Diary dated 7 Nov 1914.
[155] IWM Sound Archives, Ditcham. 000374/07
[156] Brig-Gen J E Edmonds, Official History, October to November 1914, p.410.
[157] IWM, Cunningham Memoirs p.??????????
[158] IWM JAL Diary 10 Nov 1914.
[159] IWM JAL Diary 11 Nov 1914.
[160] IWM JAL Diary 12 Nov 1914.
[161] IWM JAL Diary 13 Nov 1914.
[162] IWM JAL Diary 15 Nov 1914.
[163] IWM JAL Letter to EL 16 Nov 1914.

[164] IWM Sound Archives, Ditcham 0003 74/07.

[165] IWM JAL Letter to EL dated 17 Nov 1914.

[166] Clayton Family Papers. Letter from JAL to ML dated 22 Nov 1914. This letter is previously unseen.

[167] Lieut Graham Seton Hutchison DSO MC, *Warrior*, Hutchinson, London, 1932, p.48.

[168] IWM JAL Letter to DL dated 23 Nov 1914.

[169] *ibid.*

[170] *ibid.*

[171] Hutchison, *Warrior*, p.49.

[172] IWM JAL Diary 25 Nov 1914.

Chapter Thirteen – Trench Warefare

[173] IWM JAL Diary 26 Nov 1914.

[174] IWM JAL letter to JL dated 26 Nov 1914.

[175] Hutchison, *Footslogger*, p.131.

[176] IWM JAL Diary 27 Nov 1914.

[177] IWM JAL Letter to EL dated 4 Dec 1914.

[178] IWM JAL Diary 29 Nov 1914.

[179] Hutchison, *Warrior*, p.51.

[180] Hutchison, *Warrior*, p.47.

[181] IWM JAL Letter to Miss Finnegan dated 1 Dec 1914.

[182] Dunn, *War*, p.97.

[183] PRO 93rd War Diary 2 Dec 1914.

[184] IWM JAL Diary 2 Dec 1914.

[185] IWM JAL Letter to EL dated 4 Dec 1914.

[186] *ibid.*

[187] PRO 19th Brigade War Diary omnibus entry 4–9 Dec 1914.

[188] Hutchison, Diary 4 Dec 1914, *Footslogger*, p.135.

[189] IWM JAL Letter to JL dated 5 Dec 1914.

[190] IWM JAL Diary 6 Dec 1914.

[191] IWM JAL Diary 8 Dec 1914.

[192] IWM JAL Diary 9 Dec 1914.

[193] PRO 19th Brigade War Diary 9 Dec 1914.

[194] IWM JAL Letter to EL dated 13 Dec 1914.

Chapter Fourteen – To Christmas and Beyond

[195] Hutchison, *Warrior*, p.57.

[196] *ibid.*

[197] IWM JAL Letter to EL dated 13 Dec 1914.

[198] *Campbeltown Courier* 5 Dec 1914.

[199] IWM JAL Diary 14 Dec 1914.

[200] PRO 93rd War Diary 15 Dec 1914.

[201] IWM JAL Letter to JL dated 18 Dec 1914.

[202] IWM JAL Letter to EL dated 21 Dec 1914.

[203] PRO Document G.507: WO95/1560

[204] Hutchison, *Warrior*, p.58.

[205] Hutchison, Diary 21 Dec 1914, *Footslogger*, p.137.

[206] J M Craster, *Fifteen Rounds a Minute*, London, Macmillan, 1976, p.164.

[207] *ibid* p.169.

[208] *ibid* p.170.

[209] IWM JAL Diary dated 25 Dec 1914.

[210] Hutchison, Diary, 25 Dec 1914, Footslogger p.238.

[211] Terraine, *Jack's Diary*, p.88.

[212] Dunn, *War*, p.101.

[213] Terraine, *Jack's Diary*, p.94.

[214] IWM JAL Diary 26 Dec 1914.

[215] IWM JAL Letter to an old school friend dated 29 Dec 1914.

[216] IWM JAL Diary 2 Jan 1915.

[217] Hutchison, Diary 2 Jan 1915, *Footslogge*r, p.138.

Chapter Fifteen – Floods and Salmon Fishing

[218] Hutchison,*Warrior*, p.58.

[219] IWM JAL Diary 4 Jan 1915.

[220] *ibid* 5 Jan 1915.

[221] 93rd War Diary 6 Jan 1915.

[222] Hutchison, Diary 6-9 Jan 1915, *Footslogger*, p.138.

[223] Terraine, *Jack's Diary*, p.95.

[224] Hutchison *Footslogger*, p.147.

[225] IWM JAL Diary 1915.

[226] IWM JAL Letter to EL undated but around 8 or 9 Jan 1915.

[227] *ibid.*

[228] IWM JAL Diary 9 Jan 1915.

[229] PRO 93rd War Diary 10 Jan 1915.

[230] Dunn, *War*, p.109.

[231] PRO 93rd War Diary 19 Jan 1915.

[232] IWM JAL Diary 19 Jan 1915.

[233] *ibid* 20 Jan 1915.

[234] *ibid* 24 Jan 1915.

[235] PRO 93rd War Diary 25 Jan 1915.

Chapter Sixteen – England Again

[236] IWM JAL Diary 26 Jan 1915.

[237] IWM JAL Letter to EL dated 27 Jan 1915.

[238] PRO WO 339/8812 JAL Medical Papers.

[239] *ibid.*

[240] PRO 93rd War Diary.

[241] PRO WO32/5388 Letter from FEG Ponsonby of the Privy Purse Office at Buckingham Palace, to Lord Kitchener dated 10 December 1914.

[242] PRO WO32/5388 Letter from FEG Ponsonby of the Privy Purse Office to Sir Douglas Dawson GCVO CMG dated 19 Dec 1914.

[243] *ibid.*

[244] Walter Raleigh, *War in the Air* p.411.

[245] Raleigh, *Air* p.412.

[246] Raleigh, *Air* p.433.

[247] Peter Cooksley, *The Air VCs*, p.11.

[248] IWM JAL Diary 21 July 1915.

[249] Raleigh, *Air* p.13.

Chapter Seventeen – Per Ardua Ad Astra

[250] Raleigh, *Air*, p.5.

[251] IWM JAL Diary 24 July 1915.

[252] Ralph Barker, *Royal Flying Corps in France – From Mons to the Somme*, Constable, London, 1995 p.97.

[253] J M Bruce, *RE5/7, Windsock Datafile 62*, Albatros Productions Ltd, Berkhamsted, 1997, p.14.

[254] IWM JAL Diary 29 July 1915.

[255] Cecil Lewis, *Sagittarius Rising*, Warner Books, London,1994, p.55.

[256] Liddell Family Papers, Combat Report by 2/Lt R E Peck dated 31 July 1915.

[257] *ibid.*

[258] Liddell Family Papers JAL Letter to EL dated 3 Aug 1915.

[259] *ibid.*

[260] Lewis, *Sagittarius*, p.55.

[261] Liddell Family Papers JAL Letter to EL dated 3 Aug 1915.

[262] IWM Condolence Letters, from Maxwell Rouse dated 12 Sep 1915.

[263] *ibid.*

[264] Liddell Family Papers, Major Hoare's Report to RFC HQ dated 31 July 1915.

[265] Liddell Family Papers, Letter from Lt Dhanis commanding No. 3 Sqn Belgian Air force to Major Hoare dated 1 Aug 1915.

[266] PRO AIR1/2071/204/412/2457 RE5 2457 Engineering Log.

[267] Liddell Family Papers, Letter from Major Hoare to JAL dated 2 Aug 1915.

[268] IWM JAL Letter to EL dated 3 Aug 1915.

[269] *ibid.*

[270] Liddell Family Papers, Letter from Lieutenant L de Burlett to EL dated 13 Aug 1915.

[271] Liddell Family Paper, Telegram dated 18 Aug 1915 to Liddell, Sherfield Manor, Sherfield-on-Loddon, Basingstoke.

Chapter Eighteen – The Journey Home

[272] Liddell Family Papers, Letter from Major Hoare to JL dated 18 Aug 1915.

[273] Liddell Family Papers, Telegram from General Bridges to JL dated 21 Aug 1915.

[274] VC Citation, *The London Gazette*, 20 Aug 1915.

[275] Clayton Family Papers, EL letter to DL dated 23 Aug 1915.

[276] Clayton Family Papers, EL letter to DL dated 26 Aug 1915.

[277] *ibid.*

[278] Clayton Family Papers, EL letter to DL dated 28 Aug 1915.

[279] *ibid.*

[280] Clayton Family Papers, Letter from CL to EL dated 13 Nov 1918.

[281] Clayton Family Papers, Letter from LL to EL undated.

[282] Liddell Family Papers, Letter from Maxwell Rouse to EL dated 28 Jan 1925.

[283] *The Stirling Observer*, 15 April 1930.

Appendix Two

[284] The Jesuit Publication *Letters and Notices* (Vol XL), p.212. Stonyhurst College.

[285] Trevor Henshaw, *The Sky Their Battlefield*, Grub Street, London, 1995 p.528.

Index